Village Gone Viral

Anthropology of Policy

Cris Shore and Susan Wright, editors

Village Gone Viral

Understanding the Spread of
Policy Models in a Digital Age

Marit Tolo Østebø

Stanford University Press
Stanford, California

Stanford University Press
Stanford, California

Printed in the United States of America on acid-free, archival-quality paper

Library of Congress Cataloging-in-Publication Data

Names: Østebø, Marit Tolo, author.
Title: Village gone viral : understanding the spread of policy models in a digital age / Marit Tolo Østebø.
Other titles: Anthropology of policy (Stanford, Calif.)
Description: Stanford, California : Stanford University Press, 2021. | Series: Anthropology of policy | Includes bibliographical references and index.
Identifiers: LCCN 2020020351 (print) | LCCN 2020020352 (ebook) | ISBN 9781503614512 (cloth) | ISBN 9781503614529 (paperback) | ISBN 9781503614536 (epub)
Subjects: LCSH: Policy sciences—Computer simulation. | Community development—Ethiopia— Case studies.
Classification: LCC H97 .O84 2021 (print) | LCC H97 (ebook) | DDC 320.6—dc23
LC record available at https://lccn.loc.gov/2020020351
LC ebook record available at https://lccn.loc.gov/2020020352

Typeset by Motto Publishing Services in 10.5/15 Brill
Cover design by Kevin Barrett Kane
Cover photograph: Robert Joumard | Wikimedia Commons

To Julia, Victoria, and Terje

Contents

Acknowledgments

First of all, I would like to thank all the people who in different ways, both unknowingly and knowingly, have crossed my path as I have explored how Awra Amba, a small village in Northern Ethiopia became a global model for gender equality and sustainable development. Some have openly shared their thoughts and experiences. Others have been more reluctant and even afraid to talk. It is my hope that the story I have weaved together does justice to the multiplicity of voices and stories—actual and virtual, told and untold—that are part of the larger Awra Amba assemblage.

Funding from multiple resources has enabled me to do the research for this book. I conducted the initial fieldwork in 2015 as part of the larger project Protection of Women's Rights in the Justice Systems of Ethiopia. Funded by the Royal Norwegian Embassy in Ethiopia, the project was carried out by the International Law and Policy Institute (ILPI) in collaboration with six Ethiopian universities. I thank Kjetil Tronvoll for asking me to do the research in Awra Amba and for reading and providing valuable feedback on an initial report I wrote. I also thank Girmachew Alemu Aneme and Alebachew Birhanu for facilitating my first fieldwork in Awra Amba. Since 2017, I have been part of the project Developmentality and the Anthropology of Partnership, funded by the Research Council of Norway (project number 262524). I thank Jon Harald Sande Lie at the Norwegian Institute of International Affairs who invited me into the project, and for reading and providing valuable input on parts of the manuscript. At the University of Florida, a Global Fellows Award (2015), an International Scholars Program Award (2015) from the International Center, and a Teaching Award from the College of Liberal Arts and Sciences have provided crucial support that allowed me to conduct research and develop this book manuscript.

I could not have written this book without the inspiration and support of my students. More than anyone, they are the ones who have pushed my thinking and writing. I workshopped an earlier draft of this book in the following courses: Anthropology of Religion (Spring 2019), Feminist Anthropology (Spring 2019), and Human Rights and Culture (Fall 2019). Many of the students provided valuable feedback that helped me rethink how to frame the book in a way that would make it accessible for a broader audience. Additionally, I benefited greatly from facilitating a graduate seminar in Dissertation Writing (Spring 2018). I thank Karen Jones and Christopher McCarthy, who suggested that teaching the course would help my own writing, and the students for their willingness to offer honest and specific feedback on shorter sections of the text. I have also had the privilege of working more closely with and learning from a handful of brilliant, dedicated graduate students. My heartfelt thanks to Rebecca Henderson, Cady Gonzalez, Megan Cogburn, and Laurin Baumgardt, who in addition to reading either parts of, or the full manuscript, generously have given me invaluable, thoughtful input.

In my work with this book I have enjoyed the support and friendship of many outstanding scholars in Ethiopia. I thank Getaneh Mehari, Getnet Tadele, Fekadu Adugna Tufa, Meron Zeleke, and Hassen Kaw for inspiring, intellectual conversations. I also thank Belay Worku, Anchinesh Shiferaw, and an anonymous young woman for serving as my research assistants in Ethiopia. I have benefited much from engaging with other scholars and friends of Ethiopia, including Lovise Aalen, Alula Pankhurst, Lahra Smith, Kenneth Maes, Anita Hannig, René Lefort, Martha Camilla Wright, Frida Bjørneseth, Teferi Abate, Amanda Poole, Jennifer Riggan, Wallelign Shemsedin, and Terje Østebø.

I would also like to thank Victoria Bernal, Sandra Russo, Nancy Rose Hunt, and Alix Johnson who all read the full manuscript and provided substantial and critical feedback during a book workshop I organized at the University of Florida's Center for African Studies in January 2020. Thanks also to Kyle Fahey for taking detailed notes during the workshop. Other friends and colleagues who at different phases of this project have read all or parts of this manuscript include Dorothy Hodgson, Daniel Mains, Luise White, Yekatit Getachew, Susan Gillespie, Dereje Feyissa, and Manuel Vasquez. I am extremely thankful for their thoughtful and substantive feedback. I am also thankful to Richard Rottenburg, Jean-Pierre Olivier de Sardan, Claire Wendland, and Susan

Erikson for engaging with me in intellectual conversations, shaping the way I think about models and modeling practices. In addition I would like to thank Koen Engelen for helping me track down Arnold Merkies, who, in addition to giving me permission to reproduce the illustrations I use to explain model making (Chapter 4), went the extra mile in order to digitalize the images and provide me with a hard copy of his retirement lecture, "Zo."

In developing this book, I have been inspired and encouraged by many colleagues and friends. Special thanks go to Peter Collings, Brenda Chalfin, Adrienne Strong, Richard Kernaghan, Renata Serra, Alioune Sow, Leonardo A. Villalón, Fiona Mc Laughlin, Barbara Mennel, Benjamin Soares, Bergljot Olsen, Barb Ellmore, Elizabeth Outlaw Crawford, Veronika Thiebach, Michael Gorham, Andrea Berteit, and Zenthold Asseng. Many of the ideas developed in this book were inspired by research I conducted as a graduate student at the University of Bergen. I am deeply grateful to Astrid Blystad and Haldis Haukanes who, through their enthusiasm and relentless support, taught me to think and work as an anthropologist. I would also like to thank the people at Stanford: the editors of the Anthropology of Policy series, Cris Shore and Susan Wright, who have enthusiastically supported and encouraged this project; Stanford's anonymous reviewers; and Michelle Lipinski, Kate Wahl, Cindy Lim, and Jessica Ling, who made the publishing process so smooth.

My deepest gratitude goes to my family. To my parents Bjørg and Arne Tolo, who brought me to Ethiopia—a land I call home—in the first place, and to the rest of the Tolo clan. Special thanks to my sister Anne Kari Tolo Heggestad, who has been a valuable conversation partner when I have struggled with questions related to research ethics. To Terje, my husband and best friend, for being my most critical reader, and for encouraging me and keeping me going on the days when I have doubted my own capacities and abilities to complete this project. After all these years, you still make me laugh. Finally, to Julia and Victoria, who have grown up to become two beautiful, strong, and loving young women. You bring me so much inspiration and joy. I can't imagine what life would have been without you. This story is for you.

Abbreviations

AAU	Addis Ababa University
ADA	Amhara Development Association
ADLI	Agricultural Development Led Industrialization
AI	artificial intelligence
ANRS	Amhara National Regional State
CADU	Chilalo Agricultural Development Unit
EdTech	educational technology
EECMY	Ethiopian Evangelical Church Mekane Yesus
EiABC	Ethiopian Institute of Architecture, Building Construction, and City Development
EPRDF	Ethiopian People's Revolutionary Democratic Front
ETB	Ethiopian Birr
ETV	Ethiopian Television
FGM/C	female genital mutilation/cutting
GESA	Global EdTech Startups Awards
GTP	Growth and Transformation Plan
HIV	human immunodeficiency virus
ILPI	International Law and Policy Institute
LFA	Logical Framework Approach
MDGs	Millennium Development Goals
MVP	Millennium Villages Project
NAP-GE	National Action Plan on Gender Equality

NGO   non-governmental organization

NORAD   Norwegian Agency for Development Cooperation

PA   Peasant Association

PRI   Public Radio International

REWA   Revolutionary Ethiopian Women's Association

SDGs   Sustainable Development Goals

SEWF   Social Enterprise World Forum

SIDA   Swedish International Development Cooperation Agency

STEM   Science, Technology, Engineering, and Mathematics

TBL   team-based learning

TPLF   Tigray People's Liberation Front

UN   United Nations

UNESCO   United Nations Educational, Scientific, and Cultural
           Organization

UNICEF   United Nations Children's Fund

WDA   Women's Development Army

WEGE   Women Empowerment and Gender Equality

WHO   World Health Organization

Village Gone Viral

Introduction

I AM STANDING IN a clean and sparsely furnished kitchen in a rural village in Ethiopia. The room is crammed with local and expatriate development experts who all have come to see the fruits of a gender-focused development project undertaken by a local, faith-based non-governmental organization (NGO). As I take in the aromatic, smoky blend of coffee and spices, I turn my attention to the kitchen layout. A locally made, wooden, working table stands in the middle of the room. Its rough surface is a stark contrast to American shiny countertops. There are no fancy advanced electrical appliances in sight, but a relatively new invention—an energy efficient clay stove—has replaced the traditional three-stone fireplace commonly found in rural kitchens. The stove, which the Ethiopian government has singled out as a key indicator of a healthy home environment, is a testimony of a so-called model family: a household that has successfully implemented the comprehensive package of health interventions that are at the core of the country's highly acclaimed health extension program, and one from which other households are expected to learn.

As in many other places in the world, kitchens in Ethiopia are female-dominated spaces, places where men barely set foot. Yet, this morning and this kitchen are different. As our attention is drawn to the far-right corner of the room, to a tall, slim man in his forties, we are presented with a story that challenges the traditional gendered ordering of an Ethiopian kitchen. Dressed in his finest suit, slightly bent over an empty cutting board and with a knife in his right hand, the man proudly declares, "After my wife came back from a visit to the Awra Amba community where she witnessed how they practiced gender equality, things have changed. I now help her, and I work in the kitchen." To demonstrate the change in the intra-household division of labor, he starts moving the knife, explaining that he will assist his wife with chopping onions. But there are no onions on the cutting board, and there is no actual chopping. Only clumsy, pretend movements. "I also help my wife baking *injera*," he continues as he turns to the stove. Made from teff, a gluten-free grain indigenous to Ethiopia, *injera* is a large, sour, spongy pancake that is a staple food in many parts of the country. To bake it requires carefully crafted skills. The pouring of the fermented batter onto a big, clay plate positioned over open fire demands precise, controlled circular movements. Holding an empty jug over the cold plate, the man continues his performance. There are no circular movements. There is no fire burning.

I witnessed this episode while visiting a rural community in West Wellega Zone of the Oromia National Regional State (hereafter, Oromia) of Ethiopia in 2010. With the aim of exploring how Norwegian gender equality policies travel and intersect with different actors in the development field,[1] I had joined a delegation of international and national development experts involved in Women Empowerment and Gender Equality (WEGE), a multi-country program implemented by Digni, a Norwegian faith-based umbrella organization.[2] Representatives from Digni, two of their member organizations, and their respective African partners traveled together to visit one of the community development projects involved in the program. The four-day trip included an experience-sharing workshop[3] and a visit to one of the project's target communities. Built into the visit was a meeting with a local WEGE committee—formed as part of the project—and a home visit to one of its members. This is where the incident described above took place.

Awra Amba, a small, rural village located close to the city of Bahir Dar in the northern part of Ethiopia, was hundreds of miles away. Yet during our visit with the local WEGE committee, Awra Amba emerged as a central theme; an inspiration for the radical changes the project allegedly had brought to this rural community. In the meeting that followed the demonstration in the kitchen, members of the WEGE committee who, as part of the project's activities, had been given the chance to visit Awra Amba described it as "a place where there is no gender division of labor." As a researcher interested in exploring gender relations and conceptions of gender equality, this depiction surely caught my attention. In fact, after hearing about Awra Amba, I considered including that village in the research I was conducting at the time. But as I struggled to manage a rather complex research project where, in addition to following the organizational chain of command of two Norwegian development organizations, I was also conducting research in two rural communities in Oromia, I quickly dropped the idea. To add yet another research site, in a region located more than three days' travel from the areas where I already was working, did not make sense then.

As I researched how different actors who were involved in or impacted by Norwegian-funded gender-focused projects in Ethiopia conceptually and practically translated the concept of gender equality, references to Awra Amba occasionally emerged. Yet, it was not until five years later that I had the opportunity to visit Awra Amba and conduct research as part of a larger project on women's rights and plural legal systems.[4] When I finally arrived in the village in 2015, I quickly realized the preeminent position the community has gained as a model for gender equality and sustainable development in Ethiopia.

Awra Amba became publicly known when Ethiopian Television (ETV) aired a documentary about the village in 2001. The program told the story of a self-sustaining and gender-equal community, where women plowed, men worked in the kitchen, and so-called harmful traditional practices did not exist. The narrative radically challenged prevailing images of Ethiopia as a gender-conservative and aid-dependent place, capturing the attention of numerous governmental officials, gender and development experts, human rights activists, tourists, and educators. Within a short time, Awra Amba became a national model village. Known as the place "where gender equality is real,"[5] it attracted policy makers and development experts from NGOs and the Ethiopian government. With an interest in identifying best practices that could be replicated and scaled up in other places, they flocked to the village, eager to learn from its success.

While part of the story I tell in this book takes place in Awra Amba, this is not an ethnography of life in an African village. Reflecting the increasingly globalized and digitalized world we live in, this is a story about how a small, rural village, founded and led by an illiterate man, has become a policy model and *gone viral*. After ETV reported on Awra Amba and the community then became an official tourist destination, its story has been retold countless times. The main narrators are a few select members of the community who, on a daily basis, share the community's history and way of life with visitors to the village. But a wide range of national and international actors has also contributed to the spread of the Awra Amba story. In Ethiopia, Awra

Amba is ever present in the national media, even giving name to a newspaper, *Awramba Times*, and inspiring Ethiopian popular music (Ahmed Teshome, 2006).[6] When I tell people I meet that I do research in Awra Amba, whether taxi drivers in the capital of Addis Ababa or camel herders in the eastern lowlands of the country, I seldom have to explain what kind of place it is. Everyone has heard about the village where women plow and men make *injera*.

But Awra Amba is also well known far beyond Ethiopia's borders. The community has been featured on international news channels such as BBC World News and France 24, in various European magazines, on travel blogs, and on websites of feminist activists, NGOs, and human rights organizations. Several documentaries about the community are available on YouTube and Vimeo, and Awra Amba features in a photo essay in an African studies textbook (Salem Mekuria 2017). The Awra Amba story is, moreover, the flagship of Lyfta, an award-winning educational technology (EdTech) company with offices in Finland and the UK. Lyfta is a commercial learning platform that contains 360-degree interactive digital stories and short documentary films aimed at students in elementary and secondary schools in the United States and Europe.

In this book, I use the Awra Amba case as a point of departure to engage in a broader empirical and theoretical exploration of the role and politics of models and model making in an increasingly digital and transnational policy world. While models in various forms and throughout history have been used to explain or predict "real-world" phenomena and to inform policy and govern human behavior, the bourgeoning of models and modeling practices in our contemporary world suggests that we live in a *modeloscene*.[7] With an empirical and theoretical focus on *traveling models*—policy models that become "viral" and spread widely across different localities through various vectors, or carriers, ranging from NGOs and multilateral organizations to the internet—*Village Gone Viral* addresses three sets of questions. First, I am interested in exploring policy models from an ontological perspective. What constitutes models within the policy world and how do they come into being? The second set of questions pertains to the traveling nature of policy models. What characterizes the models that go viral? Why do some models gain followers while others do not? In other words, what facilitates and fuels a model's virality? Third, I explore ethnographically the hidden dimensions of policy circulation and the effects of the models' status on the models themselves. What happens to the original policy model—ideological or place-based—once it becomes a traveling model? Who benefits from the model's popularity? To what extent do models and modeling practices rely on, produce, and exacerbate unequal power relations?

Some of the questions I ask have been discussed by other scholars. There are ontological discussions about models in anthropology (Geertz 1973, 2007; Handelman 1998; Clarke 1972), philosophy of science (Toon 2010; Arnon 2012), and economics (Morgan 2012; Morgan and Morrison 1999). These theoretical conversations have, however, entered the field of policy and development studies to a limited extent. Anthropologists and scholars within the interdisciplinary field of critical policy studies have also sought to make sense of the increased transnational circulation of policy models and ideas by introducing analytical concepts such as policy mobility (Peck and Theodore 2010; Temenos and McCann 2012) and traveling models (Olivier de Sardan, Diarra, and Moha 2017; Rottenburg 2009). The effects of the models' status on the models themselves—a topic I explore in-depth in Chapter 8—have received limited scholarly attention.

The empirical material I present and the theoretical approach I adopt provide new and valuable insights that are crucial to an understanding of why certain policies, ideas, or innovations spread, while others do not. Inspired by assemblage thinking derived from the works of Gilles Deleuze and Félix Guattari (1987), Tony D. Sampson's (2012) resuscitation of Gabriel Tarde's social epidemiology,[8] and lessons from virology, my overarching argument is as follows: A traveling model can best be understood as a *viral assemblage*—here, dually defined as a messy, fluid, socio-technical process *and* a constellation of actors, things, unpredictable events, and relations that have *contagious and affective qualities*. I approach the traveling model and policy mobility through the theoretical lens of viral assemblage to highlight three important lessons that can be learned from the Awra Amba case. First, as an assemblage consisting of heterogeneous elements, a model is a unique, historic entity. A model is, in other words, not a neutral, universal, or static self-contained entity that exists independently of its historical, political, and economic context. Nor is it, as often assumed in the policy world, an example of success that can be scaled up and implemented in new contexts. A model is always in process of becoming, constantly being deterritorialized and reterritorialized in time and space. Since a model is the result of a chaotic process where heterogeneous elements come together—a cultural construction—it demands contextualization.

Second, just as for a virus, the model's travel and its contagious capacity are conditioned on vectors, hospitable environments, and receptive host cells. This means that the model does not spread unconditionally, but that the model's virality, to a certain extent, is restricted. For a model to spread, it has to find the right vector. It needs to "click" with a cell that has the right receptor. There needs to be an association or element of recognition and interaction between the model and the entities that may connect with it. These associations tend to be affective in character.

Third, similar to viruses, models have both destructive and constructive capacities. While many viruses are bad and generate much fear, others may be beneficial and even essential for the survival of their hosts. The designation of the assemblage as viral allows for a greater recognition of the model's affective qualities—of its ability to produce affect and be affected; to hold promises and threats; to set into motion fear and joy; to be emancipatory and oppressive. Looking at models through the lens of viral assemblage implies attention to how affect is both constitutive of the model and derived from it. The affective dimensions of model making and circulation are a crucial aspect that the existing literature on policy mobility and traveling models has overlooked.

In the next section, I give a brief synopsis of how models, in various forms, are increasingly used as policy instruments and in efforts aimed at generating social and behavioral change. I then detail my overall theoretical framework. Finally, I move to a methodological section where, in addition to situating myself in the field, I discuss how the concept of viral assemblage can also help us make sense of the methods, processes, and products that we, as anthropologists, engage in and create.

Models in a Transnational Policy World

Within an increasingly transnational policy world, much energy is devoted to the production and circulation of "the right policy models" (Mosse 2004, 640). A wide range of models exists: models for microfinance, disease prevention, health care delivery, maternal health, disaster management, and participatory development, just to mention a few. Many of these are pen-and-paper models that are rather methodological and prescriptive in nature. As programmatic schemes, they serve as road maps for a desired process or behavior, offering an explanation or procedure for how to implement a particular intervention successfully. While pen-and-paper models appear to be most prevalent within the policy world, other forms of models also attract considerable attention, such as epidemiological models, human role models, scale models, model cities, or, as in the Awra Amba case—model villages.

The increased use and circulation of models within the policy world and, more generally, as a tool for social and behavioral change, can be explained with reference to both technology and ideology. New computing technologies and access to big data have, for example, led to an upsurge in mathematical models used to predict, explain, and influence human behavior and social systems.[9] The COVID-19 pandemic has clearly and dramatically revealed this *model reality*. Models are no longer confined to policy experts or scientists but have become unprecedentedly public and popularized. Graphic models depicting and comparing the spread and consequences of COVID-19 in one geographical area versus another are on the front page of major news outlets, and numerous newspaper articles and op-eds have been written about predictive models. Models increasingly govern our lives, informing us of what the future may look like if we fail to wash our hands or comply with physical distancing rules.

Inspired by economic psychology, behavioral economics, and business studies, many of these models assume that human behavior is a matter of rational choice; that a rational person will make decisions based on calculations of cost-effectiveness (Kleinman 2012). The quest for models, particularly those commonly referred to as best practices, can also be linked to the rise of new public management and the business-oriented, results-driven, and evidence-based ethos that have come to influence contemporary politics and policy making (Biehl and Petryna 2013; Storeng and Behague 2014; Shore 2008). Within the global policy world, this has perhaps most clearly been crystalized in the establishment of the United Nations (UN) Millennium Development Goals (MDGs) in 2000, which now has transitioned into the Sustainable Development Goals (SDGs). Underpinned by a "linear cause-effect model of aid practice" (Eyben 2010, 2), the MDGs implied a strong focus on reaching preset measurable goals or benchmarks and was followed by the adaptation of results-based management by a number of major policy actors, including the UN (Bester 2012).

A widely held assumption about models in the policy field is that they are examples of success or best practices that can be transported, emulated, scaled up, and implemented to bring about a desired change across global spaces. A growing body of literature in anthropology, geography, and policy studies has challenged these presumptions (Behrends, Park, and Rottenburg 2014b; Gonzalez 2010; McCann 2011; Olivier de Sardan, Diarra, and Moha 2017; Rottenburg 2009). Emphasizing models as dynamic and context-dependent entities, this recent scholarship sheds light on how a wide range of actors— who are differently situated in power structures and whose social, cultural, political, and economic interests often diverge—negotiates, contests, appropriates, translates, and changes the models they encounter. In his book *Far-Fetched Facts: A Parable of Development Aid*, the German anthropologist and Africanist Richard Rottenburg (2009) introduced the concept of traveling models to analyze these processes. The concept has been further developed and applied by Jean-Pierre Olivier de Sardan, Aïssa Diarra, and Mahaman Moha (2017, 74). They define a traveling model as

> any standardized institutional intervention, whatever the scale or field (a public policy, a programme, a reform, a project, a protocol), with a view to producing any social change, through changes in the behavior of one or more categories of actors, and based on a 'mechanism' and 'devices' supposed to have intrinsic properties allowing this change to be induced in various implementation contexts.

The way these scholars apply the concept of the model is, however, skewed toward intentionally constructed prescriptive models—what we could term "models *for*" (Geertz 1973, 93ff.). This is reflected in Olivier de Sardan's, Diarra's, and Moha's focus on models as standardized, institutionalized interventions, exemplified in their analysis of widely used health models such as the partogram, focused antenatal care, and performance-based financing. Behrends, Park, and Rottenburg (2014b, 1) reflect a similar focus, defining a traveling model as

> an analytical representation of particular aspects of reality created as an apparatus or protocol for interventions in order to shape this reality for certain purposes. Models—and the ideas about reality inscribed into them—always come objectified and combined with material technologies to put them into practice and to transfer them as blueprints to new sites.

While I am inspired by and partly draw on the works of Rottenburg and Olivier de Sardan, Aïssa, and Moha, they neglect two important aspects. First, many models within the policy world circulate because they are perceived to be ideal examples of a particular phenomenon, policy, or desired behavior. While these models also have a prescriptive purpose, they tend to serve, to a much larger degree, as representative models, that is, as "models *of*" (Geertz 1973, 93 ff.). In addition to the human role model, I am thinking of projects, villages, districts, or cities that have become anointed, sanctioned, or promoted as models. Second, a one-sided focus on traveling models as standardized interventions, such as protocols and pen-and-paper models, fails to take into account that many models exist in or are closely associated with a particular place, or that they are constituted of and embodied in human actors. These models are much more than things or symbolic representations of the lived-in world. They are part of a living social world, made up of human actors who, as sentient beings, have the capacity to feel and experience, to be affected, and to produce affect. This has both empirical and theoretical implications. The effects that *becoming* and *being* a model have on these models are quite different from those of standardized interventions.

Viral Assemblage

My approach to exploring how models and policy ideas travel is best captured in the term *going viral*. While this expression is commonly associated with the rapid, global circulation of a story, image, or video via social media or the internet, my use of and reference to going viral moves beyond this narrow application. I have here found it useful to go back to the virus as a biological phenomenon. To think with virology can help us understand how social theorists such as Deleuze and Guattari use the term *assemblage*.

To use epidemiological metaphors and biological analogies to analyze social phenomena is a "delicate and ambiguous position" (Serres 2007, 43). As Sampson (2012) has argued, such an approach is potentially limiting and can block our conceptual flexibility. This is why Sampson (3) has developed an approach to social contagion "intended to probe outside the generality of metaphors and analogies." I contend however, that he too quickly dismisses epidemiological metaphors and analogies as analytical tools, and that his dismissiveness reflects unfounded bias toward and assumptions of viruses as solely pathological, destructive, lethal, and memetic entities. As I hope to show, perspectives from epidemiology and virology can be used fruitfully to make sense of social phenomena. Such an approach does not imply that

I "valorize(s) scientific practice as the source of rationality," as Steven Brown (2002, 9) has argued. I do not treat the virus as a blueprint or model for social processes, nor do I suggest that virality in the social world can be reduced to what happens in the biological world.[10] Inspired by Michel Serres (2007), who emphasizes the importance of not favoring one form of knowledge over another and insists on the middle position as a space for transformation, innovation, and meaning creation, I see the value of crossing disciplinary boundaries. In this case, this means that I draw, eclectically but reflexively, on epidemiological analogies from virology to make sense of the social.

It is chiefly the destructive capacity of a virus and its potential to spread rapidly and uncontrollably that have been used to describe the flow of information and ideas in our digital media age. This reflects a simplified and reductionist adoption of the virus metaphor. First, a biological virus is not a self-contained, evolutionary, imitating unit that spreads unconditionally. A virus is typically quite simple, with a single strand of ribonucleic acid, a protein coat that protects this genetic material, and a fatty envelope that enables it to bind to its host. It does not have a capacity to replicate on its own, with just its own components. In order for a virion—the non-living phase of the virus—to become an infectious virus, it must establish a set of relations with a susceptible and permissive cell. It has to find the right cell—a cell that has a functional and matching receptor that allows the virus to enter. Once the virus has entered the cell, it has to assemble using preformed, heterogeneous components from the cell and its interior, in effect hijacking the host's more complex and abundant cellular machinery and materials. It is a virus's ability to establish relations that allows it to reproduce, making it into a living entity. The fact that the virus is dependent on a living host has led biologists to conclude that it is the "ultimate parasite" (Claverie and Abergel 2012, 187).

Second, a virus's ability to proliferate and replicate is dependent on a variety of social, political, and biological factors. Some environments are, for example, more welcoming than others; some hosts are more susceptible to a particular virus than others. Let us take the human immunodeficiency virus (HIV) as an example. The World Health Organization (WHO) estimates that since the start of the HIV pandemic in the 1980s, more than 70 million people have been infected with the virus, and more than 35 million people have died. The burden of the epidemic varies substantially, however. Some regions of the world, such as Sub-Saharan Africa, have much higher infection rates than others. There are numerous social, political, biological, and behavioral explanations for these variations. The presence of another untreated sexually transmitted disease increases the likelihood of HIV infection, for example, as does high-risk sexual behavior such as having unprotected sex with multiple sexual partners. More importantly, structural violence—such as extreme poverty and poorly functioning health systems—impacts the spread of the disease. The spread of the virus is moreover conditioned on the mobility and on the networks of actors and vectors that serve as vehicles for its transmission.[11] The role mobility plays in terms of fueling and facilitating virus transmission explains why quarantine, isolation, and restriction on movement are extremely important measures during epidemics that are caused by lethal viruses. The spread of a virus is, in other words, a highly social, material, and relational process.

Finally, while viruses, due to their association with illness and deadly epidemics, often have a bad reputation and generate fear, it is important to keep in mind that some viruses are beneficial and mutualistic. For example, some viruses "are essential for the survival of their hosts, others give their hosts a fighting edge in the competitive world of nature and some have been associated with their hosts for so long that the line between host and virus has become blurred" (Roossinck 2011, 99). Infection with one type of virus may also reduce the mortality associated with another type of virus (Tillmann et al. 2001). In other words, not all viruses are bad.

While I have found it useful to draw lessons from virology in my analysis of Awra Amba as a traveling model, my theoretical approach is, as already indicated, best captured through the notion of viral assemblage. This notion offers a flexible, critical, and reflexive way of understanding the virus-like behavior of the Awra Amba model, addressing some of the potential dangers of using a biological metaphor. To avoid these dangers, Deleuze and Guattari use the concept of assemblage in multiple ways, making it— perhaps on purpose— a "traveling" concept, difficult to grasp once and for all. Manuel DeLanda (2006, 2016) has made an effort to bring together, in a cogent theoretical framework, the many ideas and definitions that Deleuze and Guattari introduce. His work provides the most comprehensive account of assemblage theory. In what follows, I draw on DeLanda's work to clarify Deleuze's and Guattari's assemblage thinking, especially as it applies to Awra Amba.

First, since an assemblage is a historic, unique, individual entity—"an individual person, an individual community, an individual organization, an individual city" (DeLanda 2016, 19)—it always has a signifying, proper name. For example, while *a* model—which is a general category, a noun that can be applied to a range of entities—is not an assemblage, *the* Awra Amba model village is one.[12] By approaching Awra Amba as an assemblage, I make it clear that I do not treat models as purely abstract, disembodied constructs. Instead, my approach implies a recognition of models as embodied and material entities and an analytical emphasis on the importance of contextualizing policy models in the particular political, economic, and cultural context in which they are situated.

Second, because "assemblages are always composed of heterogonous components" (DeLanda 2016, 20), they are not uniform in origin or in nature. They can include persons, material and symbolic artifacts, architecture, norms, natural resources, infrastructure such as roads and electricity, and tools and machines. This heterogeneity calls for careful analysis of the various components—covert and overt—that emerge in the Awra Amba assemblage.

Third, assemblages are often components of larger assemblages. For example, we can think of Awra Amba—the village—as an assemblage. However, there are additional assemblages within Awra Amba, such as the Awra Amba High School or the energy efficient stove used and promoted by the village as the Awra Amba Stove. This complexity requires that we carefully explore the interconnectivity between the different scales, or levels, in larger assemblages.

Fourth, the interactions between the different parts are what give rise to a particular assemblage. These relations are the emergent capacities of the assemblage. As with a virus, an assemblage is not a given, static whole; it changes and mutates. It is a multiplicity, where "what counts are not the terms or the elements, but what is 'between' them, the in-between, a set of relations that are inseparable from each other" (Deleuze and Parnet 2002, viii). In other words, adopting a Deleuzian-Guattarian approach to the study of models going viral implies a focus on relationality and mobility and on how models as assemblages are always becoming. It requires that we carefully examine the nature of the lines and flows that makes up the multiplicity, and how they "become entangled, connect, bifurcate, avoid or fail to avoid the foci" (viii).

By combining the concept of virality with assemblage thinking, I underscore the fruitful connection between Tarde's way of making sense of the social and Deleuze's and Guattari's philosophy.[13] Tarde's approach is rightly called social epidemiology because he drew inspiration from medicine and psychology, borrowing the notion of contagion to characterize the microdynamics of diffusion and relationality through which the social is constituted. Influencing not only Deleuze and Guattari but also Bruno Latour's actor-network theory, Tarde challenges, on the one hand, the idea of the "self-contained individual" (Sampson 2012, 9) whose agency is determined by conscious reasoning. On the other hand, Tarde rejects Émile Durkheim's idea that social institutions are fixed, autonomous entities that produce "powerful downward pressures" (18) and determine the actions of the individual. For Tarde, biological, psychosocial, and social phenomena are inseparable and mutually constitutive. Characterized by a clear break with the nature-culture divide, his account of the social is "not concerned with the individual person or its collective representation, but rather with the networks or relational flows that spread out and connect everything to everything else" (7).

My use of viral assemblage as an analytical term does more than acknowledge lines and connections between theories, however. First, while the concept of assemblage often is used to describe the *coming together* of heterogeneous elements into a unique historical and individual entity, the designation of the assemblage as viral implies a simultaneous emphasis on outward mobility—on spread, dispersion, and contagion. This is not an alternative or new interpretation of assemblage. Rather, it is a way of recognizing and making clear that the instability, fluidity, and complex interplay of multiple variables that characterize epidemiological and viral transmission processes are integral to the assemblage. While viral assemblage may be particularly applicable and useful for analyzing and understanding entities or phenomena that are traveling in nature, the concept is not meant to denote particular kinds of assemblages. Rather, viral assemblage allows for a more precise description of the fluid, unpredictable, and traveling character of all assemblages. As DeLanda (2016, 7) concludes, "Assemblages are everywhere, multiplying in every direction, some more viscous and changing at slower speeds, some more fluid and impermanent, coming into being almost as fast as they disappear." The simultaneous intrinsic and extrinsic nature of assemblage that the term viral assemblage denotes is also evident in one of the first definitions that Deleuze (Deleuze and Parnet 2002, 69) proffers in *Dialogues II*.

[An assemblage is] a multiplicity which is made up of many heterogeneous terms and which establishes liaisons, relations between them across ages, sexes and reigns—different natures. Thus, the assemblage's only unity is that of co-functioning: it is a symbiosis, a 'sympathy'. It is never filiations which are important but alliances, alloys: these are not successions, lines of descent, but contagions, epidemics, the wind.

There is a clear play with epidemiological language in this definition. As Martin Müller and Carolin Schurr (2016) have argued, Deleuze's use of the terms "contagions, epidemics, the wind" indicates the transient, unstable, and unpredictable nature of the assemblage. To approach Awra Amba as a traveling model through the lens of viral assemblage thus reminds us that models and model-making processes are as much about coming together—being territorialized, as they are about being pulled or drifting apart—being deterritorialized (McCann and Ward 2012). As Anna Tsing (2015, 23) has suggested, we may even think of them as "open-ended gatherings"—assemblages that "don't just gather lifeways; they make them." In other words, models are not totalized, given entities that spread in the way policy experts assume or plan.

Second, and most importantly, my designation of the assemblage as viral allows for a greater recognition of the role emotions and desire play in circulating ideas, models, and policies. As Deleuze and Guattari (1987, 399) attest, "Assemblages are passional, they are compositions of desire. . . . The rationality, the efficiency, of an assemblage does not exist without the passions the assemblage brings into play, without the desires that constitute it as much as it constitutes them." A reading of the traveling model as a viral assemblage—defined as a fluid, socio-technical process *and* a constellation of human and non-human actors, things, unpredictable moments, and relations that have contagious and affective qualities[14]—allows us to recognize the messy, material, discursive, *and* emotional relationships that have facilitated and fueled Awra Amba's virality.

By paying attention to the role that emotions and desire play in fueling a model's virality, my theoretical approach speaks to the affective turn in anthropology. While affect theorists often draw a clear distinction between affect and emotions—defining affect as the largely unconscious and unintentional forces and intensities that activate and deactivate human bodies and emotions as the subjective responses—my approach is inspired by scholars who have problematized this distinction. More specifically, I am influenced by Sara Ahmed (2004a, 117), who challenges the idea of emotions as coming from within a located, bound subject and which "then move outward towards others." Emotions are not "a private matter, that [. . .] simply belong to individuals" but "a way of being directed towards particular things" (Schmitz and Ahmed 2014, 99). As a form of capital, emotions circulate between bodies, "affecting bodily surfaces or even how bodies surface" (Ahmed 2004a, 120). Emotions do, in other words, have affective capacities—the power to move things. This is partly why the distinction between affect and emotions is problematic and the reason I use these terms interchangeably.

Thinking of Anthropology as a Viral Assemblage

In addition to serving as a theoretical and analytical concept, helping us make sense of how ideas and models travel in an increasingly transnational and digital world, viral assemblage is useful for thinking about the methods, processes, and products we, as anthropologists, engage in and create. While it may be fruitful to also think of viral assemblage as a method, I suggest it is first and foremost an analytical and therapeutic concept that allows us to recognize and make sense of the affective and largely unpredictable nature of anthropological practice. By looking at anthropology through the lens of viral assemblage, we acknowledge that our work as anthropologists—just as life itself—is a disordered endeavor: a result of unpredictable and affective moments where human and non-human actors, things, ideas, and memories are brought together in shifting relational arrangements. I would like to illustrate this by recounting a microevent from my fieldwork.

One of my key interlocutors in Ethiopia works as an expert in the Ethiopian Ministry of Culture and Tourism. Our very first encounter was not at all planned. I had just finished a meeting with my new research assistant at one of the many recently established hotels in the Casainches neighborhood in Addis Ababa. As I walked out of the hotel and into the parking lot, I realized I was hungry. Craving yet another chance to enjoy a spicy, delicious Ethiopian meal, I asked the guard if he could recommend a local restaurant. After reiterating that I was not interested in anything fancy, just good, local food, he pointed me in the direction of a restaurant, conveniently located on the way to my guesthouse and with a pleasant outdoor seating area. After placing my order, I went to wash my hands. Given that Ethiopian food is eaten with the hands by tearing off a piece of *injera* that is used to scoop up the sauces, every restaurant has a hand-washing installation conveniently located close to the dining area. I arrived at the sink, only to realize that there was no running water. So, I picked up the blue, plastic jug that opportunely had been placed next to the faucet, and I bent down to fetch water from a bucket. As I rose up, ready to pour water over my own hands, a young man arrived, so I offered to pour water for him first. This small, random encounter, the kind of unplanned contact through which one also might catch a cold, put us in conversation with each other. It turned out that he, through his former work as a lecturer in tourism studies at one of Ethiopia's oldest universities and later as an employee in an international NGO, had been involved in promoting Awra Amba as a tourist destination and as a model for sustainable development. We exchanged business cards, and a few e-mails, phone calls, and days later, we met in a nearby restaurant for our first interview. He became an important informant, helping me to identify and follow some of the components of the Awra Amba assemblage. If it were not for my hunger, my passion for Ethiopian food, and the fact that the water had been shut off that day, it is very unlikely we would have exchanged ideas and established a relationship. A biological and psychological state (my hunger and desire for Ethiopian food), an organic matter (water), the breakdown of infrastructure (no water in the faucet), and a thing (the jug), brought us together in a new relational arrangement.[15]

The detailed analysis of microevents illustrated here exemplifies the kind of sociology Tarde envisioned. In addition to demanding "an extraordinary attention both to detail, and to the singularity of the example," Tarde saw himself as a sociologist of the "inter-spiritual" or "inter-psychological" (Barry and Thrift 2007, 511). My role as a subject in this particular microevent facilitates a detailed analysis—of the affective forces that pushed me to take certain actions—which is far more difficult to make when analyzing stories or events in which I myself do not participate. Yet, the story reminds us of how important it is to be attentive to how every social encounter is produced through the partly accidental coming together of heterogeneous elements: persons, material things, organic matters, infrastructure, and desires.

Viral assemblage hence challenges the assumptions of linearity and rationality that tend to underpin common approaches to research method and design. Exploratory in nature, cultural anthropology is certainly less methodologically rigid than other disciplines. Yet, it would be naïve to think that we as anthropologists, regardless of our methodological flexibility, are unaffected by the hegemony of linear research design models. We follow and use these models when we write our armchair research proposals, and our ability to secure funding and succeed in the academic world rests on them. It is certainly not my intention to disavow these processes. I do see the value in research design and planning, carefully crafted research questions, and creative methodological approaches. Yet, on the other hand, it is important to acknowledge that what we do as anthropologists is to participate in largely unpredictable social processes. Hence, what we do can never be contained in or reflective of our prescriptive models.

I am not the first to approach anthropology and its methods through the lens of assemblage thinking. Jarrett Zigon (2015, 502 ff.) has, for example, suggested "assemblic ethnography" as a method of chasing and tracing "situations"[16] across different global scales and in a diversity of locations. He particularly highlights the method's unpredictability: "Just as one never knows if, when, and where they will get caught up in a situation, so too the anthropologist doing assemblic ethnography can never know beforehand where the research will lead and when it will do so" (515).[17] As I hope to show throughout this book, following and working with the Awra Amba model has, indeed, been an unpredictable journey. In addition to conducting participant observation on the ground in Awra Amba and in other rural communities in Ethiopia, I have followed the networks, things, and actors that have facilitated the model's travel. I have conducted interviews with journalists, feminist activists, government officials, and representatives from international and transnational organizations in Ethiopia; spent considerable time watching YouTube videos and researching the many blog posts and news articles that have been written about the community; and followed Facebook and Twitter accounts of people who are connected to and who, in different ways, have been caught up in the Awra Amba assemblage. My interest in exploring the Awra Amba model's virality also took me to the headquarters of Lyfta and to their virtual version of Awra Amba, an EdTech conference in Helsinki, and to a research university and primary schools in the United States. Just as the incident at the restaurant, my engagements in these multiple online and offline spaces have, to a considerable extent, been fleeting and accidental in nature. This does not mean that I did not make strategic and deliberate decisions. But many times, what I thought was a smart thing to do ended up being useless. Other times, what I initially may have considered to be a waste of time, such as accepting a dinner invitation or even hanging out on my cellphone, became important ethnographic moments.

While one could argue that the increased mobility and new digital realities that characterize life in the twenty-first century have created an unpredictable world that requires more flexibility and innovative methodological approaches, one should not forget that life has always been in motion, constantly changing and becoming. Viral assemblage is therefore not meant to denote a new method for a new era, nor is it—as is Zigon's assemblic ethnography—a methodological approach particularly suitable for those of us who study global, traveling phenomena or who are interested in assemblage theory and thinking. Viral assemblage is first and foremost a concept that can help us make sense of our anthropological engagements. By illuminating how our work as anthropologists is a messy constellation of heterogeneous elements and shifting relationships, viral assemblage can foreground our failure to comply with or follow our original plans and self-expectations, helping us cope with the uncertainty and complexity that follows from working in an unpredictable lived-in world. To approach our work as a viral assemblage encourages us to stop thinking we are wasting our time when we do something that we did not include in our initial plans, or that we are taking a break when we are invited to social events or decide to go on a hike. It allows us to recognize the value and productive possibilities in the unexpected or even the broken—such as a non-functional water faucet, a rejected manuscript, or a cancelled interview.

Most importantly, viewing anthropology through the lens of viral assemblage implies a recognition of emotions as integral to our work: as a "subject of ethnographic attention" (Biehl 2017, 263); a source of inspiration; and reflective of the uncertainties, anxieties, and dangers that doing anthropology and writing ethnography pose to ourselves and to those we study and write about. Viral assemblage is a concept that is meant to open up a space for discussing the various "WTF am I doing moments" (Reese 2019) that we all go through in our work as anthropologists, but about which we rarely speak. Hence, it has therapeutic potential, allowing us to acknowledge the unpredictable and emotionally laden processes that characterize our field work and providing room for talking about the emotional swings that follow as we "exit into ethnographic writing" (Mosse 2011, 52): when we dedicate our time to analysis and attempt to make sense of the many bits, pieces, and images from our field notes and headnotes[18] and when we are stuck with a messy draft and struggle to make clear the connections between our work and other academic texts and theories. And when our carefully crafted products finally drift off—to reviewers and publishers first, and later to a larger audience—the concept of viral assemblage can remind us that the ethnographies we produce are an affective force. Just like a virus, our work moves in ways we cannot control—inspiring new constructive connections; provoking and destroying; being accepted and giving us feelings of accomplishment; or being rejected and coming back to us like a boomerang. Once our work is finally published, it is a new journey into the unknown, since we do not know how our stories will be received. Will they benefit the vulnerable and oppressed? Or will they be used in a negative way by actors who are in powerful positions? These are ethical and moral questions that were on my mind as I wrote this book.

Shifting Engagements with Development

As I have become more attuned to seeing anthropology as a way of being with and in the world rather than as a mere professional task (Ingold 2008), it has become increasingly clear to me that I cannot separate my work from my personal background and life. My experiences in the field and the way I interpret and write about them do not exist in a vacuum. They cannot be disconnected from my personal history, memories, and emotions. I remember vividly the moment this first dawned on me; when it *really* struck me that who we are—our background and multiple identities—impacts the questions we ask and do not ask, what we see and what we do not see, and the stories we tell and do not tell.

It happened on a warm Sunday in 2006. Together with my husband and our two daughters—who at the time were six and three years old—I was visiting Dirre Sheikh Hussein. Located in the northeastern corner of Bale Zone, close to the Wabe Shebelle river and on the border of the Somali Region, it is one of the most important Muslim shrines in Ethiopia. This sacred site, where the tomb of Sheikh Hussein, one of the region's most revered Muslim saints, is found, has for centuries attracted thousands of pilgrims from all over the Horn of Africa who come several times a year to offer their sacrifice.

It was not the first time we visited the shrine. Having worked and lived in the eastern parts of Bale for more than five years, we had been there multiple times. Our visit this day fell outside the pilgrimage season, so the village was peaceful, almost deserted, making it a perfect place for a Sunday outing. After a slow walk through the village, which had allowed our daughters to run around, chase goats, and climb and slide down termite mounds, we were invited into the home of one of the guardians of the shrine. It gave my husband, who at the time was conducting research on the history of Islam in Bale, an opportunity to ask questions. I do not remember the questions he asked—he might have inquired about the history of the shrine or about a particular ritual, or perhaps he was collecting the genealogy of the shrine's guardians—what I remember is that an issue came up during the conversation that prompted me to get involved and ask questions about the role of women at the shrine. These questions opened up a new world of information and revealed aspects and perspectives that my husband had not considered. While we both had been trained in traditions that acknowledge the importance of self-reflexivity, this was an eye-opening moment, and the conversation we had in the car on our way home that evening revolved around issues of positionality. We discussed how our background and who we are, such as our education and our gender, inform our research; how our personal story and who we are matter. This revelation, which has informed my research and way of writing, has convinced me of how important it is to reflect on and make clear my multiple and shifting positions vis-à-vis the field I have studied, what commonly is labeled *international development*.

The term *development* is ambiguous and contested. Within mainstream development discourse it is often used normatively, as synonymous with modernization, and opposed to underdevelopment, which often is associated with primitiveness and backwardness. Within such an evolutionary framework, development is perceived as a "relatively easy process" (Gardner and Lewis 2015, 21) and as a product of preplanned, orchestrated, often technical solutions and activities that are expected to generate specific, measurable outcomes. Models are assumed to be key instruments in this process, and those working within the development field put forth much effort into crafting, identifying, and promoting successful and effective policy models. Anthropologists have both embraced and rejected this rather instrumental and technical approach to development.

Olivier de Sardan (2005) has grouped anthropology's engagement with development into three major orientations: *ideological populism*, *ideological deconstructivism*, and *methodological deconstructivism*. The first, ideological populism, is associated with the work of Robert Chambers (1994, 2013). It refers to various participatory approaches that celebrate local and indigenous knowledge, often in an unqualified and romantic manner. When my husband and I arrived in Ethiopia in 1999, my approach to development and my engagement with culture had all the ingredients that Olivier de Sardan attribute to this mode of engagement. I had been introduced to the ideas of participatory development when I, as a young student at a Norwegian nursing college, was given an opportunity to study abroad. Having spent most of my childhood in Ethiopia where my parents worked as missionaries, I chose to intern at an international NGO in Addis Ababa. This spurred my interest in participatory, bottom-up approaches to development. A few years later, when I returned to Ethiopia to work for the Ethiopian Evangelical Church Mekane Yesus (EECMY), which, in addition to being one of the largest Protestant churches in Ethiopia, is a major development and social service organization, I was deeply committed to community participation as key to successful implementation of health and development interventions.

Investment in local language and culture learning was a vital prerequisite for my engagement in community development and was also highly valued by the EECMY. While I had learned some Amharic, the lingua franca in Ethiopia, during my childhood, leaders in the EECMY insisted that my husband and I study Afaan Oromoo, the language spoken by the majority of the population in the area we were assigned to work. We attended a few months of formal language study in Addis Ababa, where we were introduced to the basics of the language before we moved to Robe, the capital of Bale Zone, in the southeastern part of Oromia. In Robe, we hired a high school teacher as our language instructor. As he was a Muslim and a native to the area, our daily lessons with him were invaluable in terms of language learning and important as an introduction to local history, culture, politics, and religious life. During the three years we lived in Robe, we rented a house in the middle of a densely settled neighborhood. We made new friends and spent most of our time the way anthropologists typically do, drinking coffee, hanging out, and doing "all the everyday things that everyone else does" (Bernhard 2006, 345). I cannot but conclude that these were, in many ways, and from an anthropological point of view, years of privilege. In addition to giving me the opportunity to learn a second Ethiopian language, it gave me, to some extent, insight into Arsi Oromo culture, religious practices, and political discourse. I was a rather unconscious participant observer, however. I did not pay much attention to systematic observation, exploration, or continuous analysis of particular phenomena, nor did I process my experiences through the use of field notes or a diary. But by participating in people's daily lives, observing a wide range of activities, and attending weddings and funerals, I developed a tacit knowledge of social norms and cultural practices.

In addition to being involved in an HIV/AIDS prevention and care program, from 2000 to 2003 my husband and I were responsible for conducting preliminary assessments for new development interventions in the area. Eventually, we decided to start up a small literacy program in a peripheral lowland district on the border of the Somali Region. We rented two rooms in the administrative center of the district, where we stayed for short periods of time. While we spent most of the days traveling to rural villages where we talked to people and conducted participatory rural appraisals and surveys, we spent the evenings socializing with people in town. The assessments we conducted during this period taught me how to navigate the political and administrative terrain of various governmental and non-governmental institutions and eventually led to the establishment of a larger community development project implemented by the EECMY but funded by the Norwegian Agency for Development Cooperation (NORAD) through the Norwegian Lutheran Mission.

During my years as a development practitioner, I was involved in many of the processes and practices I discuss and critically analyze in this book. I spent considerable time identifying and implementing best practices, organizing trips to projects that had a reputation of being particularly successful, and facilitating workshops that introduced particular programs and approaches to project staff and government workers. And when donors and external evaluators visited, I orchestrated tours to carefully selected project sites and activities that showed off the project's successful implementation. I was, in other words, actively, and partly unconsciously, involved in what David Mosse (2005, 157) has termed and discussed in-depth as "the social production of development success."

Through the years, particularly from 2005 to 2007, when I worked as a development practitioner and adviser and conducted field research for my MPhil degree in international health, my approach to development became less normative and more critically oriented. Being the one who, a few years earlier, had carefully crafted a project proposal that emphasized community participation and emancipatory pedagogical approaches, securing funding for the establishment of a brand new project, I became increasingly frustrated by both the donors' and the Ethiopian government's use of the Logical Framework Approach (LFA),[19] a linear model that assumes that development is produced by a "causal link of events" (Aune 2000, 688). This approach resulted in an increasing focus on measurable activities and the production of results in the form of the expected numbers that had been stipulated in the project's annual plans. I struggled to conform with this thinking—the prescribed model. I was committed to development as a slow process—time-consuming activities that implied hanging out with people and learning from them. These activities could not easily be counted and ticked off as results.

After I left the project and returned to Norway in 2007, I went through a longer period of self-scrutiny. I became aware and critical of the privileged position that I, as a white Norwegian, had held as an adviser for the project. I had, for example, much better access to the donors than what the Ethiopian project manager and my other coworkers had. This allowed me to bypass the organizational chain of commands and to negotiate and influence decisions at higher levels in the organizations.

When I started my PhD research in 2009, I was critical of international development efforts, which I viewed as a predominantly top-down Western enterprise. My position was close to ideological deconstructivism, a term Olivier de Sardan uses to describe theoretical approaches within anthropology of development that highlight the discursive power the West has over the global south. Olivier de Sardan (2005, 5) argues that such perspectives "tend to produce a caricature" and "a diabolic image" of a development world that is heavily controlled from the top. During the course of my PhD project and in the years that have followed, I have become more critical of the one-sided power-over perspective reflected in this positioning. It overlooks the complexities and the negotiations that are played out among the different actors within the field and "the collaborative complicity (or duplicity) of marginal actors/institutions in development" (Mosse and Lewis 2006, 4). This led me to a gradual shift toward methodological deconstructivism (Olivier de Sardan 2005). Scholars within this school of thought see development as a set of multidimensional social practices and share a commitment to investigate development empirically as a complex social phenomenon. The relationship between policy and practice is approached "not as an instrumental and scripted translation of ideas into reality, but as a messy free-for-all in which processes are often uncontrollable and results uncertain" (Mosse and Lewis 2006, 9). While methodological deconstructivism preserves the notion that policy making is a process thoroughly mediated by power, the approach offers a more nuanced understanding of power relations, recognizing the myriad asymmetric relationships that come together to stabilize salient social phenomena.

In this book, I strive to approach policy models and development practice in a descriptive and non-normative manner. This does not mean that I claim this study to be value-free or that I do not problematize the model as a phenomenon. Rather, my point is that it is not my objective to evaluate whether Awra Amba—as a model—has been successful. Nor do I propose changes or better alternative development models. Instead, *Village Gone Viral* is an effort to develop a more critical and context-sensitive anthropology of policy and model making. As such, it is a meta-normative, critical reflection on the unintended and intended—positive and negative—effects that models have on the lived-in world and the dangers and contradictions that surface in a world where the use and making of models is widespread and typically associated with success.

Chapter Outlines

In Chapter 1, I first outline key characteristics of the Awra Amba community and its history, *as commonly conveyed and globally known*. I then transition to an ethnographic vignette that draws on one of one my first visits to the community. In addition to introducing some of the ambivalences, paradoxes, and silences that spurred me to explore beyond and behind the official narrative, this account illustrates some of the methodological and ethical dilemmas I have faced while researching Awra Amba.

In Chapter 2, I stay true to the notion of the assemblage as a unique, historic entity, situating Awra Amba in a broader historical and political context. As I detail how development and gender-related policies have evolved and been implemented in Ethiopia, I pay particular attention to the prominent role that models, in various forms (both as ideologies and specific tools), have played in shaping the political ideologies and policies of the various Ethiopian regimes. The current government has positioned itself as an independent developmental state, setting conditions for donor involvement. Nevertheless, I show how Ethiopia's development policies have been, and continue to be, influenced by global currents and policies. This is clearly reflected in the way that gender and women's rights issues are framed in the Ethiopian context.

In Chapter 3 and Chapter 4, I explore the model as a theoretical and empirical category and phenomenon. By situating Awra Amba within the broader model village paradigm and in relation to a nearby expert-initiated model village, Chapter 3 deconstructs the different parts that constitute the Awra Amba model and the various ways models come into being. I draw on Geertz's (1973) distinction between "models *for*" and "models *of*" and Rottenburg's (2009) concept of traveling models to show how multiple models emerge in the Awra Amba case. I suggest that the power of the traveling model—its capacity to go viral—is conditioned on the existence of a representative model (model *of*), which is produced and performed at a specific place or location and reflects the ideologies and emotional sentiments (model *for*) of its interacting audience, who then picks it up—as one might pick up a virus—and facilitates its circulation. In other words, the *model for* and a corresponding *model of* enable and produce the traveling model.

With a particular focus on Awra Amba's contested history and ideology, Chapter 4 further explores the dynamics of model making. I argue that model making within the global policy world, similar to that in fields such as science and economics, can best be understood as a process of idealization—of ordering a complex assemblage. This is a process in which actors who benefit from the model and its status as an ideal type or utopia accentuate certain desirable elements of a perceived reality, while erasing or silencing elements that may disturb or create unwanted complexity. In the Awra Amba case, the disruptive elements are most clearly captured in its partly hidden past—more specifically, in the community's historical and ideological links to a Sufi community known as Alayhim. Here, I show how religion, and particularly Islam, is disruptive to a policy regime that has adopted a modernist, secularist bias. I end the chapter with an analysis of why Alayhim, just like a virus, represents a threatening and potentially disruptive element for the Awra Amba community, the Ethiopian state, and the mainstream gender and development discourse.

Dedicated to questions related to the model's traveling nature, Chapter 5 and Chapter 6 offer fresh perspectives on policy mobility and the traveling model. In Chapter 5, I discuss the vehicles and infrastructure—the multiple pathways and the networks of actors and vectors—that have facilitated the spread of Awra Amba as a transnational model for gender equality and sustainable development. To use an epidemiological term, we can think of this as the traveling model's *modes of transmission*. While the Awra Amba case illustrates that the exchange of ideas between conventional policy actors during "policy tours" (Temenos and McCann 2013; Gonzalez 2010; Baker and Mc-Guirk 2019) and at conferences, workshops, and seminars remains important in terms of facilitating a model's virality, it also points to the importance of looking beyond conventional policy actors and infrastructure. The constant emergence of new actors, partnerships, and technologies in our increasingly globalized and digitalized world has radically changed the ways policy ideas and models come into being and then travel.

Why do some models go viral, while others do not? What is it that has compelled the various vectors in the Awra Amba assemblage to pick up and spread the community's stories and values? These are the questions I explore in Chapter 6, where I expand current academic conversations on policy mobility and traveling models, examining stories told by people who have been "infected" by Awra Amba and as a result are transmitting and circulating the model. These stories reveal that affect, desire, and emotions play a key role in fueling a model's virality. This is an aspect that the existing literature on policy mobility and traveling models has overlooked.

In Chapter 7 and Chapter 8, I focus on the effects that emerge in the wake of models and modeling practices, paying particular attention to the some of the exclusionary practices and inequalities that the model creates and hides. While the policy literature to a very limited extent has recognized the role that emotions and affect play in fueling the virality of policy models and ideas, this is not at all the case for actors situated within the digital and creative industries. With an empirical focus on Lyfta and the company's flagship product, *The Awra Amba Experience*, Chapter 7 sheds light on how emotions and empathy both fuel and limit Awra Amba's virality. Driven by a passion to foster citizenship and empathy and to counter the negative and stereotypical images that dominate mainstream media through immersive storytelling, Lyfta's producers very consciously draw on the logics of affect in the creation and marketing of their product. Yet, the stories they have produced rely on and reinforce the very stereotypes they intend to challenge. In doing so, they exemplify what has been termed *The Postcolonial Exotic* (Huggan 2001), here understood as the increased global and digital commodification of cultural difference, ethnicity, and identity. While it is often assumed that empathy and immersion are key to greater social justice, the commercialization and commodification of *The Awra Amba Experience* that has followed Lyfta's entry into the EdTech market, along with the *othering*[20] that underpin their documentaries, produce exclusionary practices. This shows that empathy not only is insufficient for understanding power structures but it can also create and sustain them.

How authentic are the official Awra Amba narratives? Is Awra Amba a place where gender equality is real? By examining the Awra Amba community as an embodied and place-based model, Chapter 8 introduces critical and new perspectives that shed light on the effects that being chosen or identified as a model have on the model itself. I show how becoming a model has led to increased recognition, benefits, and preferential treatment for the community, contributing to infrastructural and economic improvements. Yet, it is also clear that the model status comes at a price: obligations, responsibilities, and pressures to engage in representational and performative strategies aimed at maintaining, controlling, and stabilizing the Awra Amba narrative. While the pressure to perform and conform applies to all members of the Awra Amba community, it poses particular challenges for the most vulnerable of the community's members—many of whom are women— and who have less access to the model's social, economic, and political capitals. The community's status as a model limits the possibility of questioning and challenging inequalities and injustices, shaping a community that only partly reflects the idealized model for a just, gender-equal, and peaceful society depicted in common representations of Awra Amba.

The Conclusion opens with an ethnographic, self-reflective vignette that describes how I myself, eventually, became "infected" with the Awra Amba virus. By linking my fascination with Lyfta's products—particularly *The Awra Amba Experience*—to a pedagogical model I use in the classroom, I show how this infection was conditioned on and linked to my own identity and desires as an educator. Finally, I return to the meta-normative concerns that animate my work, drawing out the lessons to be learned from this case study and the relevance of viral assemblage for a context-sensitive, critical anthropology of traveling models.

Chapter 1
The Village

AWRA AMBA IS strategically situated at the center of what is commonly known as the Historic Route within Ethiopia's tourist industry. It is located in Fogera district, east of Lake Tana, approximately halfway between the burgeoning cities of Bahir Dar and Gondar, the former capital of the Abyssinian Empire, and only two kilometers from the main road that leads to the medieval rock-hewn churches of Lalibela. The village, is, without doubt, outshined by the magnificent architecture and historical legacy of these well-established tourist destinations. Yet, it has in recent years attracted an increasing number of visitors. This is partly due to the promotional activities of the Amhara National Regional State (ANRS) Bureau of Culture and Tourism, whose efforts to mark the site with large road signs make it hard to miss the gravel road that leads up to the village. The most recent sign features a headshot of Zumra Nuru, the community's founder and charismatic leader, wearing his characteristic green hat. With matching green, bold text in Amharic and English on a bright, white background, it overshadows the wear, tear, and rust of the older signs originally put up to welcome visitors to Awra Amba.

Situated at the end of a dead-end road, on the slope of a small hill overlooking a green, lush valley and rolling hills, Awra Amba is an oasis for the many visitors who arrive in the village every day. "This is a perfect place to celebrate Shabbat," a young Israeli backpacker concludes as we sit to eat dinner under one of the grass thatched gazebos the community has constructed. She has spent the whole day on a blanket on the grass outside the guesthouse, reading, relaxing, and preparing herself for additional days on the road. None of the intrusive, pushy tour guides who typically hang around at the more famous tourist destinations have demanded her attention. No vendors have tried to sell her mass-produced Ethiopian icons, jewelry, or baskets. No children have shouted *ferenji,* the term used for white people in Ethiopia. And no one—except me—seems to be bothered by her careless and culturally inappropriate attire. "Too much leg," I thought to myself when I first saw her in short shorts and Chaco sandals passing by the guesthouse on her way to the bathroom.

But Awra Amba emerges not only as a peaceful sanctuary for foreign tourists and exhausted backpackers on low budgets. For Ethiopian visitors, particularly those arriving from larger urban centers such as Gondar and Bahir Dar or the busy, polluted, traffic jammed, never-ending construction site that Addis Ababa has become, Awra Amba's relaxed atmosphere produces feelings of serenity. Except for a couple of tourist cars, a minibus, and an Isuzu truck owned by the community, there is hardly any traffic in the village, and there are few signs of the typical street life that characterize even the smallest, rural, Ethiopian town. There is no *bunna bet* (coffee house) or *tej bet* (honey wine house)—terms used for places that serve alcohol—and no drunk men raving around in the street. The use of any substances is forbidden in Awra Amba, which explains the total absence of groups of young men hanging out chewing khat, the light stimulant leaves commonly found all over Ethiopia. Even the traditional coffee ceremony, which in recent years has become a national street phenomenon, is nowhere to be seen.

This does not mean that there are few activities in Awra Amba or that it is a sleepy village. The members of the Awra Amba community are hardworking people who have, over the past decade, managed to transform the community into one of the most important trade hubs in the area. There are a number of shops in the village, including one where tourists and visitors can buy Awra Amba's weaving products. The community also runs four mills and has a large grain store where people from neighboring communities come to sell their agricultural products. Still, compared to other semiurban centers in Ethiopia, Awra Amba appears to be an unusual, quiet, and peaceful place. The clacking sound of the shuttles from the community's weaving workshop—pulsing through the air from eight o'clock in the morning to five o'clock in the afternoon—quickly turns into an ambient, relaxing background noise. Awra Amba is moreover one of relatively few places in Ethiopia where one can enjoy an undisturbed, quiet night. There is no nightly chanting from Christian orthodox churches nor is there a call for prayer from mosques.

It is perhaps no wonder that Ethiopian intellectuals, based in Addis Ababa and abroad, dream of spending more time in and even settling down in the village. As friends of Awra Amba, they have been captivated by Zumra's values and what they see as the community's way of life. When I met with a senior official at the headquarters of one of the many transnational organizations in Addis Ababa, whose involvement with the community stretches over two decades, she told me she plans to write her memoir in Awra Amba when she retires. And when a few days later, I sat down with a young journalist—host of a popular TV program—at one of Addis Ababa's many new and posh hotels, he passionately said, "I love Awra Amba. I wish I could live there. I plan to visit at least once a year."

Yet, apart from being a popular tourist destination and a place many visitors associate with peace and tranquility, what is this place called Awra Amba? With an official population of 480, Awra Amba is a rather small, rural community. The number of people living in the village exceeds this number, however, since the schools located in the village attract a relatively high number of teachers and students from neighboring communities. Rather than reflecting the actual size of the population, the number 480 refers to those who are members of the Awra Amba Community New Chapter for Behavior Building and Development Multipurpose Association. This represents the least restrictive of the two levels of possible membership. In fact, any person who adheres to the principles and values developed by Zumra Nuru can become a member. Hence, some members reside outside Ethiopia, and at one point the community even offered an Awra Amba ID card for visitors who would like to become members.

The Awra Amba Community Farmers and Handicraft Multipurpose Cooperative, which in 2015 counted 156 members, comprises a much more exclusive membership.[1] In order to qualify, one must be eighteen years of age, devote one's time to work for the cooperative, and live according to the community's principles and rules. In order to remain a member of the cooperative, one must live a life in accordance with these principles. While young people who grew up in Awra Amba can easily become members, outsiders interested in joining the community must undergo a trial period, which may last from one to seven years, depending on their behavior. In the documentary "Awra Amba–Utopia in Ethiopia" (Tervo, 2009), a potential new member describes the process: "To join you have to be free from evil things. No conflict, no immoral behavior. No stealing. No cursing. If I fulfill these criteria, I can become a member. You must get rid of all bad habits like getting drunk. You must only

Table 1.1   Committees in Awra Amba.

Name of Committee	Male	Female	Total
Development committee	6	3	9
Weekly development committee	2	3	5
Work assignment committee	1	2	3
Sanitation committee	2	1	3
Elder care committee	2	3	5
Safety/security committee	3	0	3
Education committee	3	2	5
Welcoming committee	1	2	3
Found property handling committee	2	1	3
Grievance hearing committee	2	1	3
Community code of conduct drafting committee	11	4	15
Research/problem identifying committee	1	2	3
Committee for assignment of members to take care of elders and mothers who gave birth	1	2	3

SOURCE: Data from Awra Amba's welcoming center. Created by the author.

pursue good things." While the Awra Amba community is part of the Wojia-ramba *kebele*,[2] and government institutions such as a health post and primary, secondary, and high schools are present, the community has developed a separate system of self-governance that seems to have set aside the regular bureaucratic mechanisms and structures that are in place elsewhere in Ethiopia. The general assembly is the community's highest decision-making body; it is where decisions about annual share, investment, and matters related to membership in the Awra Amba cooperative are supposed to be made. The community is furthermore structured into thirteen committees. The development committee is "the central committee of the community" (Awra Amba Community 2012, 12), responsible for overseeing and supervising the remaining committees. Table 1.1 lists the committees and the gendered distribution of committee members as displayed in the welcoming center in August 2015.

In addition, all members of the cooperative are expected to participate in bi-weekly family meetings. These gatherings are presented as "a key tool to bring peace and development by discussing and solving problems" (Awra Amba Community 2012, 28). The meetings can consist of a single family or of three to four neighbors who decide to hold discussions together. During these meetings, the participants will discuss planned activities, achievements, and "the occurrence of bad speech and bad deeds" (28), and the members will give each other advice on how to improve their behavior and their contribution to the community.

Commonly known, as already mentioned, as the place where women plow and men bake *injera*, Awra Amba is first and foremost celebrated for being a community where the gendered division of labor has ceased to exist. But the community is also known for its strict work ethics. Hard work is a key value in the Awra Amba community, and each member of the cooperative is assigned jobs according to his or her abilities. The majority of the members work in the weaving workshop, handling manual weaving machines, spinning, or sewing bedclothes and scarfs sold in the community's shops in Awra Amba, in neighboring towns, and in Addis Ababa. A member of the cooperative is obliged to work according to the Awra Amba working schedule, which runs from Monday to Saturday from eight o'clock in the morning until five o'clock in the afternoon, with a one-hour lunch break. The cooperative's regulations prohibit members from engaging in work that generates private income during these hours. Members are moreover not allowed to participate during working days in funerals or weddings of family members who may live outside the community. On Sundays, each member is free to spend the day according to his or her individual needs. This is, for many of the members, the day when, in addition to doing chores related to maintaining their individual households, such as going to the market, doing the laundry, and cleaning the house, they work in order to generate private income. Many of the households in Awra Amba have private weaving looms.

Awra Amba is, in other words, not a place with abundant leisure time. The community does not celebrate weddings, and if a member passes away, there is no time set aside for mourning, as described in the official Awra Amba document "Journey for Peace" (Awra Amba Community 2012, 35):

> The funeral ceremony consists of a few community members accomplishing the burial procedure. Some members of the community will stay with the family of the deceased to help them forget their grief. After the burial

ceremony has been completed, the family of the deceased will go with other people to work. This is to make them forget their grief. With this the mourning ceremony is finished.

The near absence of funerary practices and death rituals in Awra Amba stands in sharp contrast to how death is dealt with elsewhere in Ethiopia. For Awra Amba's predominantly Orthodox Christian neighbors, funerals function as an important social marker of belonging, and having an unattended funeral is, according to Tom Boylston, "to live a life unrecognized and unsocialized. It means you have established no meaningful connections nor any of the status or respect that would compel people to attend and commemorate you" (Boylston 2015, 294).

Awra Amba is also known for rejecting institutionalized religion. The community only recognizes and celebrates one annual holiday—the Ethiopian New Year. The lack of institutionalized religion and religious infrastructure, and the relegation of marriage and death rituals, do not, however, mean that the community is areligious. The community believes in the existence of one creator and claims that they practice the golden rule: "Do unto others as you would do unto yourself" (Awra Amba Community 2012, 5). They have formalized this principle by dedicating one weekday to fundraising aimed at social redistribution. Every Tuesday, members of the cooperative, the majority of them women but also a few men, will gather under one of the big trees in the village square where visitors can observe them spinning cotton. Together with the entrance fee collected from the visitors, the income generated through this work makes up a fund called *lewegen derash* that is used to run the home for the elderly and to support the sick, the needy, and students.

An observant tourist, who would have likely visited and observed the people and life around one of the many orthodox churches in Lalibela or around Gondar or Lake Tana before arriving in Awra Amba, may notice a clear difference in the way people, particularly the women, dress. The majority of the women who gather in the village square on Tuesdays do not wear the traditional, white cotton dresses and the huge, silver cross necklaces commonly worn by rural, predominantly Christian women in this part of the country. This does not mean that their attire is areligious. In a country where dress is an important religious marker, their way of dressing can tell us something about their religious identity and affiliation. While it is rather common for both Christian and Muslim women in rural Ethiopia to wear ankle-long or full-length dresses or skirts and to cover their heads, there is a marked difference between Christian and Muslim women when it comes to the style and the wearing of headscarves. The majority of women in the northern parts of Ethiopia will often wear a white scarf known as *netela*. It is made of a very thin and delicate, soft fabric, with a colorful border called *tibeb* at each end. The *netela* can be worn in different ways, but it is commonly cast loosely around the head, allowing parts of the woman's hair to be visible, and at times it is only used to cover the shoulders. It is associated with the Ethiopian Orthodox Church, where it is typically used during religious services. While Muslim women also may wear the *netela,* they tend to wear headscarves that are more colorful and are made of other kinds of fabrics. They wear their headscarves tight around their faces to prevent hair from being visible. Many women in Awra Amba wear scarfs like Muslim women in Ethiopia typically do, in a way Christian women never will. This explains the reaction of a friend of mine, a Christian man who grew up in one of Ethiopia's larger cities, after watching one of the documentaries about Awra Amba: "They dress as if they are Muslims."

The influence of Muslim clothing tradition is only visible among some of the married and the majority of elderly women in Awra Amba. The men in the village do not wear any of the identifying pieces common among Muslim men in Ethiopia, such as the headscarf typically worn by Muslim men. A few of the elderly men wear the characteristic green hat that commonly is associated with the community's leader. The young generation's clothing is strongly influenced by urban fashion trends, partly reflecting the community's investment in higher education: a surprisingly high number of Awra Amba's younger generation have completed their degrees at one of the many universities in Ethiopia.

The Welcoming Center

Since Awra Amba was recognized as a tourist destination in 2001, more than 67,000 people have visited the community. The majority of the visitors are from within Ethiopia, and they often arrive for educational purposes. As illustrated in the Introduction, Awra Amba has become a popular site for policy tourism, actively used by various non-governmental, state, and private actors. During the past four to five years there has, however, been a significant increase in the number of foreign visitors. Most people who visit Awra Amba stay for a couple of hours, but there are groups, particularly backpackers, who may decide to spend the night in the guesthouse. Visitors to Awra Amba go through a well-prepared introductory information session conducted by members of the welcoming committee, which, in addition to Zumra and his wife Enaney, consists of three individuals. One of the guides is fluent in English and thus responsible for guiding foreign tourists. Before visitors are taken on a tour through the village, they receive an introduction to the community's history and philosophy at the welcoming center.

Located a few steps from the village square, the welcoming center is the first and natural stop on the guided tour offered to all Awra Amba visitors. It is furnished with several rows of small, unique, locally crafted wooden chairs and clay-plastered benches along the perimeter of the room. The center easily accommodates the occasional busloads of large tour groups that arrive in the village. Handwritten posters displaying ideological slogans and quotes by Zumra and statistics outlining the community's demographics and achievements cover two of the walls in the room. A huge, inbuilt, almost-empty bookshelf fills up the third wall. It has shelves so big that even the largest coffee table book would appear small.

There is only a small, single window in the welcoming center, and the walls and much of the furniture are painted in a coal-bluish-black color. With electricity available 24/7, foreign visitors who walk into the room for the first time would perhaps wonder why the guide does not flip on the light switch. But in a country that boasts thirteen months of sunshine, it makes little sense to waste electricity during the day, something a minute or two of eye adjustment confirms. The rays of sun that seep through the open door and the partly shuttered window brighten up the room in an almost magical way, revealing the community's artistic and inventive handicraft skills. Blue-and-black woven cushions cover the chairs and the benches, threads of red, green, and pink make up part of the chairs' backrests, and a colorful, striped tablecloth covers the only table in the room. The room does appear welcoming.

It is a warm, sunny afternoon in May 2016. Joined by Megan, one of my graduate students, I walk around in the welcoming center and study the posters as if I am a first-time visitor. But I am not. I have been here before. I have surveyed the room and listened to the story that, during the peak tourist season, is often told several times a day. I have paid visits to the museum where artifacts and pictures that highlight the Awra Amba story are on display. I have taken the official tour through select parts of the village: a relatively well-equipped kindergarten, a fully stocked library, the cafeteria and the guesthouse area, the weaving workshop, a demonstration site for the ecological stove used and promoted by the Awra Amba community, a private home, and finally, the home for the elderly. If I had kept my feet on these narrow paths and not moved astray from the official narrative and the guided tour when, a year earlier, I first came to Awra Amba, I would perhaps have been warmly welcomed as a returning visitor. But my efforts to research the community's history, including its role as a model for gender equality and its relationship to neighboring communities, and my attempts to engage in the deep hanging out that is seen as vital for anthropological research, have created suspicion. I have asked questions; too many questions, and the wrong kind of questions to the wrong kind of people.

So, when a member of the community's welcoming committee enters the room and sees me this afternoon, he does not seem too excited, nor do I feel particularly welcomed. After a brief introductory exchange, he uses his head to point at Megan—a first-time visitor—and says: "I assume she already knows the story." It is as if he hopes for a chance to take a short cut—to not tell the story he has told a thousand times. I confirm that she perhaps is more informed than other visitors but that she nevertheless wants to hear him tell the story. A little hesitant and with limited enthusiasm, he begins:

> Awra Amba has a total of 480 members, but only 157 are members of the Awra Amba cooperative. Zumra Nuru is our leader. Since the Jimma University has given him recognition as an honorable doctor, we will also call him honorable doctor. We know about Zumra's childhood activities and how he was as a child, because his mother lived with us until 1996. She told us that when Zumra was only six months old, he could walk and move around on his own. When he was two years old, he started asking critical questions, particularly about religion. He observed how his family was living and what they practiced. His father was a Muslim and his mother a Christian. Muslims and Christians lived together side by side, but they would not eat each other's meat. "Why is this so?" Zumra asked; "We are all humans, we use the same materials when we slaughter, so why can we not eat each other's meat?"

The guide pauses as two newly arrived tourists—a couple from Spain—step into the room. He welcomes them to Awra Amba and informs them about the entrance fee—20 Ethiopian Birr (ETB) per person (less than one USD)—and the guided tour. After quickly reiterating the introduction, he continues the story.

When Zumra was four years old, he formulated four of the five principles that are guiding our community today. First, there should be equality between men and women. There should be gender equality. Zumra had been observing how his mother was working together with his father all day in the field. When they came home, she would cook and take care of the children, while his dad would sit like a king, doing nothing. There was, in other words, no work equality in the family. The second principle he formulated was about the rights of children. He saw how adults would kick and beat the children if they did not do something properly. Zumra believed children should be treated with respect and given duties according to their abilities. Third, he claimed that bad speech and bad deeds should be totally abandoned. Zumra postulated that if we strive for peace, love, and unity, it is possible to create heaven on earth. In his fourth principle, he emphasized the importance of helping the sick, the needy, and the elderly. He saw how his community treated people who were aged or had health problems with disrespect. Zumra stressed the importance of respecting their dignity and providing them with support. Zumra formulated these principles when he was only four years old. Of course, it may seem unbelievable, but this is what he did.

Because of his principles, Zumra's family and people in his home community considered him to be mentally ill. So, when he was thirteen years old, Zumra left his home and started wandering around. He stayed in churches, mosques, in the forests, and on the road, often with no shelter and no food. He tried to share his vision and philosophy but was met with much resistance. After five years he came back to his community. His family then saw him and thought he had become normal. He started working in the fields, but at harvest time he began to give out foods to the elderly and to orphans. His community then said, "He is not normal. He is crazy. He cannot identify his relatives from his non-relatives." Zumra's idea is that we are all one family.

We often classify people based on geography, ethnicity, or color. The last and fifth principle Zumra formulated is that we should accept our human brothers, regardless of our differences. He started traveling again, and in 1972, he was able to convince people around what today is Awra Amba to accept his philosophy. They accepted his idea of creating peace and heaven on earth. Zumra's idea is that if you can avoid or remove bad speech and bad deeds, it is possible to build peace on earth. If there are problems, they should be solved during the bi-weekly family meetings. If a problem is not solved during these gatherings, it will go to the grievance hearing committee, and it can in some cases also go as far as the general assembly. If people do not change their behavior, they may be excluded from the community by the general assembly. But this never happens.

After Zumra established Awra Amba, people in the neighboring areas tried to eradicate our community. We were sixty-four households in the beginning, but we lost members—so only nineteen members remained. In 1988, we had to leave the area. We left to Bonga, which is a village close to Jimma in southwest Ethiopia. We stayed in the forest, and we used clay as an ingredient to make *injera*. We also ate cottonseeds to survive. After five years we came back here. In 2001, the government recognized us and gave us 17.5 hectares of land. We also made the news on the national media. The same year, we became an official tourist attraction and we started weaving activities.

The guide has come to the end of his story, and after responding to a few questions raised by the Spanish tourists and Megan, he says, "I assume you also would like to meet with Zumra?" I can feel my pulse rising when the guide, after completing the story, asks the question. Even though I had spent several weeks in Awra Amba and the surrounding areas the previous summer, I never had the chance to meet Zumra, the legendary man in the green hat. Asked to do commissioned research in Awra Amba, I was told at that time that Zumra had approved the research and knew I was coming. But when I arrived, he and his wife Enaney had left for Addis Ababa. Every time I asked members of the welcoming committee when he would return, they shrugged their shoulders. "They never tell you where he is and when he will return," a young teacher told me, when I had shared my frustration over the lack of information.

But today, Zumra is here. As I had climbed out of the car an hour or so earlier, I had seen the green hat from afar. Sitting in the shade of a tree, on a bench built of layers of stone located by the road that leads up to his house, he was overseeing members of the community who were digging, shuffling, and carrying soil and stones for the construction of what I was told would be a new toilet. I had sat at the same spot a year earlier, trying to engage in a conversation with one of the armed guards who often occupied the place. With a perfect view of the lower part of the village, the place was an ideal observation post. Not only did it allow one to oversee the traffic that passed through the village square, it also provided full view of the people from neighboring communities who would cross the river down in the valley and arrive in Awra Amba on foot.

"I would love to meet him," I nervously stutter. There is a strange kind of unease growing in my belly. Having heard so much about the man and having watched numerous YouTube videos of him as the community's unquestioned protagonist, I suddenly realize I am a bit starstruck. But there is something else that adds to my uneasiness: I suspect I will be met with suspicion. After having completed my first fieldwork in Awra Amba the previous summer, I had asked Belay, one of my research assistants, to return to Awra Amba to collect additional data that I felt was needed in order to complete the report I had been commissioned to write. "We have been blacklisted," he wrote in the field notes I received when he returned from the field. "There are rumors that we have published something that does not represent Awra Amba." He went on to detail how we had been closely monitored when we were conducting research earlier that summer: "They knew every person we talked to and interviewed outside the community, and where and when we met with them. They even have information about what we discussed in meetings with district government officials." At a point when I was still analyzing the data and my research was far from close to anything that looked like a publication, I was being accused of producing incorrect accounts and misrepresenting the community. Belay assured me that in a meeting with Zumra and his wife, he had spent considerable time mitigating the situation, convincing them that nothing yet had been published, and he had managed to restore both their trust in us and our access to the field. Nevertheless, my sense of unease remains this afternoon. I am worried things might become more complicated. And when Zumra walks into the room a few minutes later, my suspicion is confirmed. He is polite as we exchange greetings in Amharic, but his mouth is set in a hard line.

"I am happy I finally have a chance to meet you." I switch to English and ask Belay to translate. The conversation is too important to be carried out in my imperfect Amharic. Focusing my eyes and attention on Zumra, I dive straight into the hornet's nest, reiterating that I have not yet published anything. "I have come back because I want to understand the role Awra Amba plays as a model for gender equality. I don't think I can do that based on only one short visit." I look at Zumra, expecting him to respond. But the first reaction to my introductory speech comes from the other side of the room, from a woman who had arrived together with Zumra but whom I have totally overlooked. As I study the beautiful, rounded face, I realize who she is: Enaney, Zumra's wife. She is younger than I had expected—probably my age—and he could have been her father.

With authority, and with determination in her voice, she catches my attention. "We discussed this with your research assistant last time. We assumed, at that point, that the research was published, but he told us that it was still a work in progress. We value research conducted on Awra Amba. It is important. But sometimes, researchers obtain information from people who have left, or from people who live outside our community. If conclusions are made based on information from the outside, things can easily be distorted." I assure her that I am aware those who have left Awra Amba may speak badly about the community, and that it is therefore my duty as a researcher to critically assess and scrutinize every source. "Yes, it is important that you check your sources. You should make sure that the data collection is conducted in a proper way," Enaney chimes in before Zumra, in the rasping voice with which I—after watching hours of documentaries about Awra Amba—am already familiar, finally breaks his silence: "When you write, you should make a clear distinction between what are the insider and the outsider perspectives. What is most important, though, is that you tell our story, because the story we tell reflects our way of living."

To tell the story of Awra Amba from an insider perspective, what in introductory textbooks in cultural anthropology is called the emic perspective, may appear as good and reasonable advice. As argued by Jeppe Sinding Jensen (2011, 32), privileging the insider perspective is "an idea that appeals intuitively [. . .] to us all." Yet, the distinction between an insider and outsider perspective is highly problematic and has been much debated (Jensen 2011; Headland, Pike, and Harris 1990). First, this dichotomy assumes there is a clear demarcation between the inside and the outside. The traveling nature of the Awra Amba model makes the boundary between what and who is inside and outside both fuzzy and fluid. Second, the distinction between an insider and outsider perspective reflects an essentialist conceptualization of what constitutes a community or a culture. It assumes that all members of a given community—the insiders—share the same ideas, values, and experiences and hence constitute a homogenous whole. To tell the story about Awra Amba in the way Zumra suggests would, in other words, obscure relations of power and the multiplicity of voices and positions that exist within a community. The Awra Amba story is complex and full of contradictions. Hence, it cannot be reduced to a single story.

Much has already been written about Awra Amba. In addition to myriad journalistic and media accounts and a few scholarly publications (Joumard 2012; Ibrahima 2017; Mengesha, Meshelemiah, and Chuffa 2015; Gebeyehu Yihenew, Haileeyesus Adamu, and Beyene Petros 2014), many Ethiopian students have conducted research in Awra Amba and written their bachelor's and master's theses about the community (see for example Anteneh Tesfahun 2012; Mengesha, Meshelemiah, and Chuffa 2015; Eskinder Teferi 2012; Abebe Endale Assefa 2013). While these accounts, on one hand, provide valuable insights by shedding light on a specific feature of the community, such as gender equality, children's rights, or sustainable and cooperative development, they are, on the other hand, remarkably coherent and tend to rely on, convey, and confirm the official narrative. In fact, if we were to draw a conclusion based on the existing stories, including the various research narratives, it would be hard *not* to conclude, as many of the storytellers explicitly do, that Awra Amba is a "utopia in Ethiopia."

One of the few members of the community who finally let his guard down, openly telling me about some of the challenges the village is facing, explained this homogeneity: "They (researchers, journalists, etc.) all speak with the same people. And they only speak with those who have been approved to talk. Zumra and the people around him are the ones controlling the story." This also speaks to some of the methodological challenges associated with doing research, not only in Awra Amba, but in Ethiopia more generally. I have discussed this elsewhere (Østebø, Cogburn, and Mandani 2017), linking the control of information and the tendency informants have to reproduce official discourses and narratives, to the political context and Ethiopia's long history of authoritarianism. In this context, interviews with key informants and focus group discussions may have reduced value, particularly if they have been organized and orchestrated by and are controlled by people in power. The importance of participant observation and informal conversations, combined with in-depth knowledge of historical and political context, cannot be overestimated in such an environment. This implies careful attention to multiple and alternative voices—to voices that so far not have been heard, and to unspoken and hidden narratives.

Reflecting my commitment to viral assemblage, not only as a theoretical concept but also as a way of thinking and approaching what we do as anthropologists, I here tell a story in which my presence in the field, my experiences, and my emotions are visible. The story is, therefore, to some extent *my* Awra Amba story. This does not mean that I have set aside and overlooked methodological and epistemological questions related to reliability, truth, and representation. Nor does it mean that this is a fully subjective and relativistic account—that what is written on the next pages only is true for me. On the contrary, I consider my encounters with different publics and my emotions to be valuable sources of knowing that can serve as "openings to the deeper issues at play" (Biehl 2017, 263). *Village Gone Viral* hence illustrates how anthropology can offer alternative ways of comprehending social worlds.

Inspired by Didier Fassin's (2017, 9) approach to public anthropology, I am driven by a passion to "speak truth to power." My personal trajectory, emotions, and habitus as an anthropologist enable (and constrain) a disciplined contextualization, allowing me to foreground and critically explore certain saliences—what Bruno Latour (2004) calls *matters of concern*—regarding the various voices I heard and phenomena I witnessed as I researched Awra Amba as a traveling model. Latour distinguishes between *matters of fact*, which are predicated on an untenable positivism that assumes unmediated access to reality, and matters of concern, which are saliences that emerge and are stabilized within the networks of actants in which the critical scholar is embedded. I am convinced that my approach and analyses of the matters of concern I have encountered while researching the Awra Amba assemblage convey something important. By approaching Awra Amba as a complex assemblage, *Village Gone Viral* relativizes the story of a utopian, emancipatory model of equality, providing meaningful perspectives that can propel a broader and more critical discussion about what is at stake when certain policy models become hegemonic and are uncritically adopted as tools for social change and development. My objective is to communicate "a conception of truth grounded in [. . .] empirical and theoretical work against prejudices, interests [and] powers" (Fassin 2017, 9). This does not mean that the story I tell is the "the absolute and definitive truth" (9). It is a narrative that strives for positioned rigor; one that is meant to be discussed, challenged, and disputed.

Methodological and Ethical Ambiguities

To conduct anthropologically informed research on policy models is a thorny task. This is partly due to the political and ideological nature of the models that circulate within the transnational policy field. In a world where efficiency, quick results, and economic viability take precedence, an uncritical take on models dominates. It appears as if global actors, such as the World Bank and the Bill and Melinda Gates Foundation, and NGOs, governmental entities, and research communities are vying for scalable, innovative solutions and models that can contribute to solving the world's problem in a timely, efficient, and economically viable manner. As David Mosse (2011, 58) argues, "Never before has so much been made of the power of ideas, or right theory, or good policy in solving the problems of global poverty. Extraordinary power is invested in context-free "global" models and frameworks that travel and are expected to effect economic, social, and political transformation across the globe." In an increasingly transnational policy world, there is limited room for considering complexity and context. It is the highly standardized and simplified "miracle mechanisms" (Olivier de Sardan, Diarra, and Moha 2017, 71), often developed by expert communities in the global north, that count. These highly political models are rarely questioned; they appear to persist and uphold their status, even in the face of strong empirical evidence against them (Olivier de Sardan, Diarra, and Moha 2017; Roe 1991).

Here, I want to underscore that a model's status in the policy field is quite different from that in the sciences. While the incompleteness and uncertainty of models are acknowledged within fields such as science and economics, where they are continuously assessed and reevaluated (Bailer-Jones 2003; Morgan 2012), models used for social engineering and development are rarely questioned. They are typically associated with "success." Success here does not necessarily mean that the model has been fruitful or that it has been effectively implemented, but rather that it has been socially constructed or framed around a success story. This framing is not only foundational for the model (Olivier de Sardan, Diarra, and Moha 2017; Roe 1991); it also provides the model and its social and political apparatus with a powerful hegemonic status. The "culture of optimism" (Closser 2012, 385) that tends to surround these models is closely related to funding and resource allocation, making it very difficult for researchers, practitioners, or policy makers to question the models and their associated narratives.

Some of the challenges associated with doing research on models have been eloquently discussed by Mosse (2005, 2011). He describes how experts and bureaucrats in a prestigious development project in India worked hard to maintain coherent representations of the project activities so they aligned as much as possible with the project's preset goals and objectives. Mosse challenged the narrative of a successful development project by arguing that the scheme and its related processes were social constructions of success rather than successful reflections of a prescribed policy model. His insider accounts of the project created objections, complaints, and accusations, particularly from program managers and his international consultant colleagues who attempted to stop the publication of his book *Cultivating Development*. He was accused of being inaccurate and disrespectful, and some of his informants "appealed to codes of research ethics" and used "ethical rules and procedures [. . .] to evade social science scrutiny, resist critical analysis, gain control over research and protect reputations and public images of success" (Mosse 2011, 51). The reactions and actions his analysis created among key stakeholders, particularly among those in powerful positions, reflected a need for maintaining and controlling a particular narrative, illustrating that "success in development depends upon the stabilization of a particular interpretation, a policy model" (Mosse 2004, 646).

As I will show throughout this book, many of the methodological and ethical challenges that Mosse describes in his research with professional and powerful development experts also apply to my research. Yet, as a lived-in miniature model, Awra Amba presents additional challenges and ethical dilemmas for me as a researcher. Due to the community's model status and role as a tourist destination, the members of the Awra Amba community are under pressure to perform in accordance with the narrative that gave the community its status in the first place. This pressure influenced the encounters that I, as an anthropologist, had with members of the community and even led me to change my research strategy. For example, in the early phase of my fieldwork, I realized that my attempts to engage with community members who were not part of the community leader's inner circle could create suspicion and potentially harm them. I therefore decided to scale back my efforts to immerse myself in the daily life of the community. This decision, combined with the fact that Awra Amba is a small community, has moreover influenced the way I have crafted this ethnography. In order to protect vulnerable community members, I have limited my portraits and descriptions of ethnographic encounters to people who are part of or closely affiliated with Awra Amba's official apparatus and to former members of the community.[3] I have in some instances found it necessary to rewrite and slightly change details of ethnographic moments to prevent potential readers from recognizing or associating events I describe with individual members. My motivation for doing this is not only informed by the ethical principle of protecting informants' anonymity, but also by the fact that a community member who speaks out and challenges the official Awra Amba community could risk being shunned and even excluded. This does not mean that the stories I tell in this book are fictional. I have done what I can to be true to the main content and to the messages conveyed in a particular incident or interview.

I have, more than once, debated with myself and with others whether I should tell this story. I finally made up my mind to write this book and to convey "a conception of the truth" (Fassin 2017, 9) that challenges the official Awra Amba narrative and uncritical and blind belief in models as emancipatory tools and examples of success: First, I felt ethically obliged to convey the alternative and hidden stories that some of my interlocutors, in hopes of being heard, shared with me. Vulnerable not only to the persistent inequities of Ethiopia's political culture but also to the consequences of Awra Amba's status as a model, some of them expressed their disappointment with other researchers and journalists who had listened to their stories but failed to share them publicly. This realization strengthened my sense of obligation. Second, I was convinced that the ethnographic account I offer has the power to create a much-needed contextual understanding of the strengths and limitations inherent in the model paradigm.

To contest hegemonic narratives, to go against the grain and convey a different truth, is not unproblematic, however. This is perhaps even more so when one is studying and challenging something which is widely known and recognized. In addition to having a prominent place in the Ethiopian public mind, the official Awra Amba narrative holds considerable currency among various publics. This includes numerous entities within the Ethiopian government, NGOs, transnational organizations, the media, and more recently, actors within the digital industry. To communicate to these publics the kind of knowledge and analyses that we as anthropologists produce, is a difficult and unpredictable endeavor. It is a risky affair, which, in addition to implications for us as researchers, may also have an unpredictable impact on some of those we write about.

The potential harm this ethnography may pose for those I write about has been one of my primary concerns. Words and stories are not only powerful; just like a virus, they tend to have a life of their own, often independent of our intentions. It is hard to know in advance the reactions that our words and our stories might generate. While ethnographies can have an empowering potential, particularly if they shed light on inequalities and injustice, they can also be used to silence. This is partly because people in power, through their privileged positions, often are better situated to control and tell stories. They can potentially use our stories to cover up and change things in favor of themselves, ultimately leading them to make decisions that do more harm than good for those who are the most vulnerable. They can use the stories we tell to strengthen their own position and to silence others. Knowing that my writing can be instrumentalized in ways I never intended has made it challenging to write about Awra Amba.

Anthropologists have dealt with some of these challenges in different ways. Mosse (2011, 50) describes how he carefully crafted *Cultivating Development* "to avoid controversy." He "anonymized all individuals, reported only on actions taken in people's professional capacity, documented the genuine difficulties and dilemmas involved in addressing chronic poverty, and—while emphatically not an evaluation study—maintained that this was a worthwhile project with important benefits for thousands of very poor people." Still, his book generated strong reactions. Richard Rottenburg (2009) went even further. His book *Far-Fetched Facts* is a fictionalized account of a development project based on his long-term engagement in various development projects in Africa. Rottenburg, who also emphasizes his project as an experiment in ethnographic writing, provides sound arguments for his decision. For him, the fictionalization was a question of decency. He writes, "It seemed to be intrusive and offensive to publish a text in which real human beings were so ruthlessly exposed, even if they had previously given their approval for the study" (xix). Rottenburg's concern is real enough, and his attention to decency is a reminder of the responsibility we have as anthropologists to write mindful accounts. While I also have, to some extent, used fictionalization as a strategy to avoid harm, a complete fictionalization would, in the case of Awra Amba, be highly problematic, if not impossible. We could perhaps say that Awra Amba's uniqueness, both within Ethiopia and as a viral phenomenon, has made it "too public." But there are also other reasons why fictionalization would be problematic. Not only is careful consideration of political and historical context key to making sense of assemblages as unique phenomena embedded in time and place, it is also a defining feature of anthropology. It is, as Kelly Gillespie (2017, 70) argues, "what makes ethnography different from other kinds of writing." The story about how Awra Amba has gone viral cannot be written without due attention to the historical and political context in which it is situated.

While there certainly are risks and uncertainties associated with writing public ethnography—with speaking truth to power—my decision to write this book is informed by my commitment to and belief in the value of the kind of knowledge produced by anthropology. The strength of ethnography, and this is perhaps also what makes it controversial and threatening, is that it "draws attention to different points of view and does not involve, or require, a drive to consensus" (Mosse 2011, 55). Anthropology's commitment to complexity and to the importance of considering and understanding context is, in many ways, the opposite of the quasi-religious belief in quick fixes, magic bullets, and universal scalability that characterize the model paradigm. *Village Gone Viral* is therefore a call for a more informed and nuanced engagement with what a model is, what it does, and what it can and cannot do. In other words, my commitment lies in an urge to speak context-sensitive truth to the model as a universal, scalable fix.

Chapter 2

Ethiopia—The Real Wakanda?

THIS CHAPTER SITUATES Awra Amba in a broader political and historical context. Following a brief historical overview that highlights the shifting popular and academic images of Ethiopia, I provide a synopsis of how development and gender-related policies have evolved in Ethiopia. I pay particular attention to three themes. First, I outline the prominent role that various forms of models have played and continue to play in the Ethiopian context. Throughout the history of modern Ethiopia,[1] models have not only shaped the political ideologies of various Ethiopian regimes but also have been widely used as policy tools in efforts to induce social change. Second, I introduce the cooperative, first put forth as a key instrument for mass mobilization and economic production during the Marxist Derg regime (1974–91). During that period, cooperatives were much resented and far from a success. However, they have remained one of the main strategies—or models—for social and economic development in Ethiopia. Third, I show how development efforts in Ethiopia have been, and continue to be, influenced by global currents, priorities, and policies. While models and cooperatives as tools for social change reflect the political ideologies of the various Ethiopian regimes—and scholars have argued that the current government, by setting conditions for donor involvement, has positioned itself as an independent developmental state (Borchgrevink 2008)—national policies and projects including those that focus on gender and women's rights do not exist in a vacuum. In our increasingly globalized world, the boundaries between state and non-state entities are fluid, and projects and initiatives aimed at generating social change are situated within a larger framework "in which multiple states and suprastate organizations such as the United Nations intersect with particular national and local contexts" (Bernal and Grewal 2014, 3). Hence, norms and models, largely developed in the global north, have significantly influenced development initiatives and political processes in Ethiopia.

Shifting Images of Ethiopia

When the movie *Black Panther* was released in spring 2018, it attracted enormous attention and broke many box office records. In the US, headlines such as "Black Superheroes Matter: Why a 'Black Panther' Movie Is Revolutionary"[2] and "The Revolutionary Power of Black Panther"[3] emphasized the movie as groundbreaking in terms of addressing questions of race and identity and what it meant to be black in America. In Africa, the movie's positive reception was attributed to its success in challenging dominant, negative perceptions and stereotypical images of the continent. While the film was also very well-received in Ethiopia, the reactions among the Ethiopian audience stood out. Ethiopians did not treat the movie as pure fiction. They proudly claimed that Ethiopia is the real Wakanda.[4]

There are, indeed, parallels between Wakanda and Ethiopia. Ethiopia is commonly known as the only African nation never to be colonized by European powers. With its victory over the Italians in the Battle of Adwa in 1896, Ethiopia proved it could win warfare against European powers and established itself as a "beacon of independence and dignity" (Bahru Zewde 2002, 81). The similarities between Wakanda and Ethiopia do not stop with their successful resistance to European colonization, however. Parts of what today is Northern Ethiopia and Eritrea were once the land of the powerful, ancient Axumite Kingdom (c. 150 BC–AD 700), ranked by its contemporaries as "the third among the great powers of the world" (Levine 1974, 7). Axum's status as a leading world power and an independent and prosperous empire was expressed through architecture and technological innovations. Axum was the first state in Sub-Saharan Africa to introduce a coinage, and the Axumite kings erected huge monolithic stelas, or obelisks, and constructed royal palaces and churches. While these structures were influenced by architectural trends found in the Roman Empire, Southern Arabia, India, and Meroe, an ancient city in present-day Sudan, they also reflected "a striking originality" (Kobishanov 1981, 386).

The construction of churches or transformation of pre-Axumite temples into churches followed King Ezana's conversion to Christianity in the fourth century. With the help of a group of Syrian monks known as "the nine saints," the new faith spread through the northern highlands of Ethiopia, and by the sixth century, Axum achieved status "as a champion of Christianity in the whole Red-Sea area" (Tadesse Tamrat 1972, 25). Two centuries later, the Axumite kingdom had lost much of its control over the Red Sea trade to Muslim merchants. The center of government moved to Lalibela in present-day Wollo, marking the start of the Zagwe dynasty, again to be succeeded by the Solomonic dynasty in 1270. This dynasty, which claimed descendance from the biblical King Solomon and the Queen of Sheba, ended in 1974, when a military junta known as the Derg overthrew Emperor Haile Selassie as a reaction to a severe economic crisis, mismanagement, and famine.

Ethiopia's rich history is relatively unknown among contemporary Western audiences. Since the 1980s, Ethiopia has first and foremost been associated with famine, poverty, and war. A BBC News documentary that showed images of starving people shook the world in 1984, inspiring the first music-based fundraising event, the Live Aid concert, held simultaneously in London and Philadelphia in 1985. While Ethiopia's reputation as a destitute nation, in dire need of salvation, is still alive and may even dominate Western popular conceptions, the past decade has seen an increase in stories and reports that paint Ethiopia in a much more positive light. Headlines, such as "Ethiopia Hailed as 'African Lion' with Fastest Creation of Millionaires"[5] and "Ethiopia, Long Mired in Poverty, Rides an Economic Boom,"[6] have figured in international media outlets. In one of the many blog posts Bill Gates has written about his work in Ethiopia, he encourages readers who may think Ethiopia is the land of famines to "think again."[7] Ethiopia's success in achieving steady, two-digit economic growth, combined with reports of improvements in a number of human development indicators, have inspired these alternative and rather optimistic accounts. While the country continues to be a place of intervention, it is now also a place associated with success. In fact, scholars and policy makers increasingly highlight Ethiopia as a model for other countries to emulate.[8]

The images of Ethiopia as a magnificent, ancient kingdom, a starving nation, and an African rising star all hold some truth. Yet, these images are also highly problematic. In his book *Greater Ethiopia: The Evolution of a Multiethnic Society*, Donald Levine (1974) provides a detailed historical analysis of the shifting popular and scholarly images of Ethiopia.[9] He cautions against the simplicity that these images convey, and he points to the importance of recognizing complexity and of "developing a holistic conception of the Ethiopian experience" (23). While one may ask if the latter is at all possible—Levine himself has been accused of conveying a reductionist and centrist view of the

Ethiopian state, failing to recognize its colonial legacy—it can still be something we strive to achieve.

Social Engineering and Change in Ethiopia

While the famines in the 1980s established Ethiopia as a target for humanitarian and development intervention, efforts to modernize and "develop" the country through the emulation of models from other "more developed but ostensibly comparable states" (Clapham 2006, 137) started long before international NGOs began flocking to the country in the 1990s.[10] Acutely aware of "the backwardness of his country" (Bahru Zewde 2002, 37) and inspired by the Imperial Russian model (Clapham 2006), Emperor Tewodros II (1855–1868) was eager to restore "a conception of Ethiopia as a single state led by a powerful emperor" (Clapham 1988, 27) and to introduce European technology. However, it was not until the reign of Menelik II (1889–1913), who was considered the founder of the modern Ethiopian state, that we can see the first signs of state-initiated social engineering. Menelik was the "first Ethiopian ruler, perhaps the first Ethiopian, with a project of modernity, a conception [...] of Ethiopia as a developed state, along the lines of states in Europe" (Clapham 2006, 138). His victory over the Italians in the Battle of Adwa and his enlarging of Ethiopia's borders through brutal territorial expansions and enforced incorporation of a variety of ethnic groups served to bolster the country's position as an independent African power. In addition to his military achievements, Menelik established Addis Ababa as the capital and initiated the construction of a railway to Djibouti.

It is difficult to discern or associate "any broader concept of 'modern' Ethiopia" (Clapham 2006, 140) with Menelik, but in the two to three decades that followed his death in 1913, Japan emerged as the new model for the Ethiopian empire to emulate. "The 'lesson' of Japan" was, according to Christopher Clapham (2006, 142), "that a powerful emperor could create a united country and that this would in turn promote the blessings of development and preserve the country's independence." The influence of the Japanese model—as an ideal or role model to follow—materialized in the 1931 constitution, which drew heavily on the Meiji Constitution of 1889. When Haile Selassie returned from exile in 1941, after Ethiopia had been liberated from a five-year Italian occupation, the Japanese model was abandoned. During most of his reign (1930–1974), no particular model was adopted for the country's economic and

political development. Haile Selassie was pragmatic and rather than looking at a particular state as a blueprint, he "relied, instead on amalgamations
of models, the elements drawn very largely from Western experience" (142).
Haile Selassie "spread his contacts widely"; in addition to establishing a dip-
lomatic relationship with the United States, he had close connections with
Yugoslavia, Sweden, Norway, Holland, Denmark, Western Germany, France,
Britain, India, Czechoslovakia and Japan (Halldin Norberg 1977, 54).

Besides strengthening international relations and securing Ethiopia's
admission to the League of Nations in 1923, Haile Selassie established modern schools and hospitals, invested in developing an educated elite by sending Ethiopian students to European and American universities, initiated a
road-building program, recruited foreign advisers, developed a state apparatus, and strengthened the military. It was also during his reign that the Organization of African Union was established, with its headquarters in Addis Ababa and with Haile Selassie as the first chairman (Clapham 2015). The
modernizing efforts that took place during the reign of Haile Selassie were,
however, largely concentrated in and limited to urban areas. The first five-
year plan launched in 1957 reflected the interests of the major landowners
and paid little attention to the socioeconomic development of the rural peasant population (Abeje Berhanu and Ezana Amdework 2011). The third five-
year plan (1968–73) was the first to pay attention to the role of small-scale agriculture and was followed by the introduction of a "comprehensive package
approach" which, in addition to green technologies, implied a focus on im-
proving marketing infrastructures and access to and quality of social services
(Abeje Berhanu and Ezana Amdework 2011). First implemented in a Swedish-
funded development project known as the Chilalo Agricultural Development
Unit (CADU), the comprehensive package approach was modeled after the
Comilla project in Bangladesh. This was an experiment of "cooperative capitalism" that served as the showcase of the Integrated Rural Development Programs that emerged as the dominant model in international development in
the 1970s (Khan 1979; Ruttan 1984).

While Haile Selassie played a key role in the formation of modern Ethiopia, the most comprehensive and radical modernizing attempts were introduced during the Derg regime. According to Clapham (2006, 144), this is
the time when the "politics of emulation reaches its most intense form" and
when the Soviet Union emerges as a model for political and social processes

in Ethiopia. The groups behind the 1974 revolution—students, army officers, and civil servants—were mainly from urban centers of the country and had "little conception of conditions in the countryside" (Clapham 1988, 33). Yet, their opposition to the imperial government, which eventually led to the deposition of Haile Selassie and the end of the Solomonic dynasty, was framed within a Marxist paradigm and with clear reference to the need for transformation of the rural class. According to Donald Donham (1999, 27–28), the revolution, particularly its focus on redistribution and nationalization of land, owed much "to Ethiopian modernism—that is, to the intelligentsias' image of their society as 'feudal,' as a type of society that Europe and the developed West had left behind centuries ago."

Influenced by Marxist-Leninism, and eager to facilitate the journey from feudalism to socialism, the Derg regime introduced a one-party system and carried out a number of radical and economic social reforms. Reflecting the slogan "land to the tiller," a sweeping land reform was introduced in 1975, which entailed nationalization of land and the redistribution of feudal land. In order to ensure that reforms were successfully carried out and that socialist visions reached all corners of the country, the Derg regime established the Development through Cooperation, Enlightenment and Work Campaign—in Amharic known as the *zemecha*—in 1974. More than 50,000 secondary and university students were recruited as a "rural mobilising force" (Clapham 1988, 49) and sent to propagate the revolution, teach the people how to read and write, provide agricultural advice, and provide basic health education (Donham 1999; Paulos Milkias 1980). The use of the word *zemecha*—which is the Amharic word for "campaign"—had a clear military association. It was the word used in connection with the crusade Menelik undertook in Somali and adjacent lowlands in the late nineteenth century, where his forces brutally raided the pastoralists for their livestock. While the Derg regime emphasized community participation, and the "weapon" of the *zemecha* was knowledge and not military arms, the campaign and other reforms that followed—such as the villagization program from the early 1980s and the forced settlement of starving people from the northern part of the country to the south in the mid-1980s—were characterized by extensive use of control, coercion, and brutality, and remained, in many ways, military in nature.

The Derg regime also established new bureaucratic structures and institutions, with the *kebele*, or PA, as the lowest administrative unit. All households living within the territorial jurisdiction of the *kebele*—which typically encompassed 800 hectares or more—were obliged to be members (Ståhl 1989). The *kebele* was responsible for redistributing land, informing the peasants of government directives and proclamations, and mobilizing or forcing the peasants to participate in meetings and development schemes (Ståhl 1989; Pausewang 2009).With an emphasis on community participation and mobilization, the *kebele* was, in principle, "a very innovative institution," and the ultimate goal of the Derg regime was to transform the *kebeles* into agricultural cooperatives (Bellucci 2016, 6).

The large-scale villagization program forcefully moved large parts of the rural population into new settlements. Villages were constructed based on an "ideal model layout" specified in government issued guidelines (Cohen and Isakson 1987, 449). The official rationale behind the program, which was deeply unpopular throughout the country, was to promote social and economic development and facilitate social service delivery, such as health care provision and education. Forced movement of the population into villages was perceived as a precondition for the establishment of cooperatives, which the Derg regime introduced as a key tool to increase agricultural production and transform the peasant population "along socialist lines" (Ståhl 1989, 27). Membership in cooperatives was imposed, like most social engineering during the Derg period, and the cooperatives were not independent institutions but were heavily controlled by the party and the Ministry of Agriculture (Dessalegn Rahmato 2002). There were two types of cooperatives: service cooperatives and producer cooperatives. Perceived to be the driving force for socialist transformation, the producer cooperatives were to promote collective farming. Three stages of cooperation were envisaged for these cooperatives: *melba*, *welba*, and *weland*. These stages represented "increases in joint ownership of the means of production" (Pankhurst 1992, 35), with the last stage, *weland*—which implied that the means of production and natural resources were communally owned—considered the ideal one. This was, as one of my informants described it, "the final level of communism." The service cooperatives provided basic consumer goods such as salt, sugar, matches, soap, and coffee, and some also established grain banks, purchasing grain from its members and selling it to the state purchasing agent, the Agricultural Marketing Corporation. The accumulated profit was used to establish development projects or given as loans to members. The service cooperatives would eventually also start distributing agricultural inputs, such as fertilizer and certified seeds (Ståhl 1989).

While non-members and members alike were resentful toward both forms of cooperatives, the producer cooperatives were particularly unpopular (Dessalegn Rahmato 2002) and, in the end, only a small minority of the population was involved in them. Except for a few model cooperatives that were used to showcase the regime's policies, most of the producer cooperatives failed (Cohen and Isakson 1987). While they received preferential treatment—they had better access to agricultural inputs, extension services, and tax advantages, and they paid less for inputs and produce—the majority of the cooperatives struggled with internal feuds and produced less than individual farmers (Cohen and Isakson 1987; Pankhurst 1992). The Derg regime's experiment—including the cooperatives—was unpopular and unproductive and ended in May 1991, when several ethno-nationalist movements led by the Tigray People's Liberation Front (TPLF) overthrew the Derg regime.

The Developmental State Model

When the Ethiopian People's Revolutionary Democratic Front (EPRDF) came to power in 1991, it pledged to end the country's long history of authoritarian rule. The new constitution of 1995 aligned with international human rights instruments and secured Ethiopia's formal status as a democratic state. In addition to a commitment to political and economic liberalization, the new regime embarked on major decentralization reforms. Formalized through the system of ethnic federalism, this implied a restructuring of the country into nine autonomous, administrative regions according to assumed ethnolinguistic boundaries and a recognition of the rights of its many ethnic and religious groups. By ascribing "self-determination" to all groups, the new regime anticipated that ethnic federalism would provide the majority of Ethiopia's agricultural and pastoral producers with increased decision-making power and give them better control over resources. This would in turn "democratize relations between them, and release their potential for socio-economic development and competitive politics" (Vaughan 2015, 284).

Along with ethnic federalism, the political economy of EPRDF was influenced by the "twin commitments to revolutionary democracy and the developmental state" (Vaughan 2015, 306). Revolutionary democracy implied a strong focus on group rights and consensus, a rejection of the liberal democratic focus on the individual (Bach 2011; Gagliardone 2014), and an emphasis on the role of a class or developmental elite that "has both will and ability" to generate economic development (Meles Zenawi 2012, 166). The late Prime Minister Meles Zenawi described it as "a revolution from above" (166). In 2001, the EPRDF adapted the developmental state model as "part of the wider framework of revolutionary democracy" (Dereje Feyissa 2011, 791). Inspired by the experiences of East Asian countries such as China and Taiwan (Fantini 2013; Fourie 2014), the developmental state model that Meles Zenawi and the EPRDF promoted was framed as an alternative to "the neoliberal relegation of the state to a 'night watchman role'" (DiNunzio 2015, 1182). The EPRDF maintained that to build, rather than to deprive the state of its responsibility and capacities, would prevent "rent-seeking" behavior and facilitate economic growth. According to the EPRDF, successful economic and social development depended on a strong state playing a "key role in guiding and supervising the economic process" (Dereje Feyissa 2011, 799).

While cooperatives and the infrastructure of the *kebeles* weakened in the immediate period after the fall of the Derg regime, it did not take long before they reemerged as tools for social engineering. In the mid-1990s, the EPRDF launched the Agricultural Development Led Industrialization (ADLI) policy in order to accelerate economic transformation. In addition to a focus on agricultural extension packages, this plan entailed a new focus on cooperatives. The EPRDF's development strategy also meant a gradual move toward a market economy (Planel and Bridonneau 2015) and increased focus on the new urban and rural entrepreneurs, small-scale enterprises, and microcredit schemes (Di Nunzio 2015; Lefort 2012). In 2004, the government introduced Business Process Reengineering as a tool in the public sector (Tesfayie Debela and Atakilt Hagos 2011) and in 2010, the ADLI was replaced by the Growth and Transformation Plan (GTP) (2010–11 to 2014–15). The aim of the GTP was to achieve broad-based, accelerated, and sustained economic growth and to transform Ethiopia into a middle-income country by the mid-2020s. In addition to highlighting the role of the state in construction of large-scale infrastructure, education, and healthcare, the GTP "promoted an engagement with the market which had been inexistent in the country's past development policies" (Planel and Bridonneau 2015, 2).

The political strategies of the EPRDF appeared to be effective. The country repeatedly reported a staggering double-digit economic growth, and remarkable, although contested, achievements in terms of global development goals. However, the political developments in the country drew massive critique. The 2005 national elections, which revealed strong support for the opposition, led to a significant increase in legislative and administrative measures that were authoritative in nature and were meant to control political dissent (Aalen and Tronvoll 2009; Arriola and Lyons 2016). In 2008 and 2009 respectively, the regime ratified a new press law and an anti-terrorism law that severely impinged on the freedoms of speech and association and resulted in the imprisonment of a number of journalists and bloggers. Additionally, a new Civil Society Law was adopted in 2010, prohibiting international NGOs from engaging in work related to politics, good governance, and human rights. Local NGOs that received more than 10 percent of their income from abroad were subject to the same restrictions. The new law forced the civil society into a much closer relationship with government bodies. "Traditional" and religious leaders and civil society organizations, including international NGOs, were increasingly co-opted by the government (Hagmann and Abbink 2011).

The developmental state model, as it evolved in Ethiopia, drew heavily on and expanded the vertical, authoritative, and administrative structures that were established during the Derg regime. When EPRDF came to power in 1991, the country was restructured into nine independent regional states organized into zones, *worredas* (districts), and *kebeles*, the latter being the smallest administrative unit. Prior to the national election in 2010, the EPRDF started the process of dividing the *kebeles* into even smaller units known as *gott* and *garee* (Emmenegger 2016). Each household in a *gott* was later organized into what became known as the one-to-five networks, in which one model farmer was given the responsibility for leading and following up with five other households. The model farmers were all members of the ruling party or were required to become members. The establishment of this highly organized, detailed network was fueled by the regime's need for political control prior to the 2010 elections. However, the one-to-five networks were also intended to serve as a key tool in Ethiopia's quest for development and social change (Aalen 2014).

The adoption of the model farmer approach to development in Ethiopia is not a new phenomenon. We can trace the model farmer's phenomenon back to the late 1960s when the comprehensive package approach was introduced. The model farmer approach was "one of the building blocks" (Abeje Berhanu and Ezana Amdework 2011, 8) used by the CADU to scale up their activities. The project would identify farmers who appeared to be more responsive to the new technologies, provide them with training and support, and actively use them to demonstrate how new farming innovations could be applied. CADU's internal review of the approach concluded that "the model farmers were imminently suitable information disseminators . . . a relatively cheap method for reaching the grassroots level" (Cohen and Isakson 1987, 85). The approach, however, was also criticized for being "pro-rich farmers, with land-lords reaping almost all the extension services provided by the CADU project staff" (Abeje Berhanu and Ezana Amdework 2011, 9).

While the Derg regime more or less abandoned the model farmer approach, it continued to focus on the model as a tool for development; but with an increased emphasis on cooperatives and collective farming, the model approach moved from a focus on successful individuals to a focus on model cooperatives and model villages (Abeje Berhanu and Ezana Amdework 2011). A more comprehensive approach was introduced by EPRDF as models and model thinking became one of the building blocks of the developmental state model. This is well captured in a statement by Kesete Admasu, a former Minister of Health (2012–16), in an article on Bill and Melinda Gates's website The Stories Behind the Data: "Model families create model communities, which lead to model districts and eventually to a model country."[11] As reflected in Kesete's statement, EPRDF promoted a number of model categories in addition to model farmers: model students, model health workers, model cooperatives, model projects, model *kebeles,* model villages, model families, and model women.

The inclusion of women in this network of models deserves further elaboration, as it reflects an engagement with the private sphere that was close to non-existent during the Derg regime. In her study of gender and development in Ethiopia during the Derg regime, Helen Pankhurst argues that "there was little engagement between women and the state" (Pankhurst 1992, 47) and that the state was particularly absent in issues related to birth and reproduction. This has changed dramatically during the past decade. In close cooperation with various international and transnational organizations, EPRDF made significant efforts to intervene and change women's lives. This change, which has to be seen in relation to the increased global commitment to women- and gender-focused development interventions, was facilitated by the introduction of model families, model women, and the one-to-five networks.

The organization of women into one-to-five networks began in 2001 and was particularly fueled by an increased focus on the very issues that the Derg regime had neglected: reproduction and birth (Dynes et al. 2012; Maes et al. 2015; Koblinsky 2014). The promotion of model families and model women, and the organization of women into one-to-five networks, was integrated into Ethiopia's health extension program, launched in 2004 to increase the quality of and access to primary health care. The program, which was part of a general decentralization process initiated in 2002–3, entailed substantial infrastructure development, particularly in the rural and underserved areas. The rapid expansion of physical health infrastructure, most clearly reflected in a surge of new health centers and health posts, was followed by a simultaneous focus on the development of a national cadre of health extension workers. By 2010, more than 33,000 young women had received one-year training and had been dispersed all over the country to serve at the health posts, the lowest level of the primary health care system. They were given the responsibility of implementing a primary health care package consisting of basic preventive and curative health services.

The leaders of the women's one-to-five networks, which also has been termed the Women's Development Army (WDA), were expected to work in close cooperation with the health extension workers. They were responsible for following up with women in their communities, making sure that each woman complied with and practiced what the health extension workers and other public servants taught them. The women in the WDA, moreover, played an important role in implementing the government's zero policy for home-births, as they were given the task of identifying pregnant women and encouraging institutional deliveries (Koblinsky 2014). The health extension workers and WDA have been described as the backbone of a "women centered health system" (Ramundo 2012). However, many perceived the WDA to be a political and partly coercive tool created by the government "to solidify a countrywide, grassroots network of women who will conduct surveillance over their neighbors" (Maes et al. 2015, 473).

With the adoption of the developmental state model, Ethiopia positioned itself as a strong, independent state. This led researchers to conclude that Ethiopia, compared to other African states, has faced limited donor conditionality (Dereje Feyissa 2011). By adapting the developmental state model and voicing a strong antineoliberal rhetoric, EPRDF was able to frame its political agenda as homegrown and independent. Yet, the influence of global norms and policies on Ethiopia's development policies have been substantial. Since 1991, Ethiopia has been heavily funded by international donor organizations, including the World Bank, International Monetary Fund, and Bill and Melinda Gates Foundation—by "institutions commonly represented as embodying the very neoliberal dogma that the EPRDF is portrayed to be fighting against" (Di Nunzio 2015, 1182). EPRDF did not only implement the various poverty reduction strategies that have been pushed by the international community, it also "endorsed donor assumptions on the intrinsic link between delivering economic growth and 'ending poverty'" (1183).

While EPRDF and the increased authoritarianism that have characterized the various development interventions in Ethiopia were problematized and criticized by human rights organizations and scholars of Ethiopian studies, and the developmental state model was contested among international donors, these critiques had limited impact on the donors' involvement. In spite of many reports about human rights abuse, Ethiopia remained a donor darling and continued to be hailed as a model for other countries to emulate. The rather uncritical and naïve belief in Ethiopia's development progress was, however, challenged by major political demonstrations beginning in 2014. Fueled by a new master plan for Addis Ababa that would entail incorporation of land from Oromia into the capital—interpreted by many as land-grabbing—and by high unemployment rates and increasing inequality, the country experienced substantial unrest. The demonstrations were followed by violent crackdowns by the state, where thousands of demonstrators and activists were killed or detained. After a week of rage and attacks on foreign-owned businesses, the government declared a state of emergency in October 2016. This was lifted in 2017, but when Prime Minister Hailemariam Desalegn abruptly resigned in February 2018, a second state of emergency was imposed. Two months later, in April 2018, political developments in Ethiopia took an unexpected turn when Abiy Ahmed was confirmed as the country's new Prime Minister. Within a short time, he launched radical political reforms, transforming the country from one of the most authoritarian regimes to a beacon of hope for democracy in Africa. Following his bold actions, which included signing a peace agreement with neighboring Eritrea and releasing political prisoners, his popularity skyrocketed, albeit only for a brief period. In October 2019, Abiy Ahmed was announced as the winner of the Nobel Peace Prize, acknowledged for his reforms and his efforts to establish peace in the region.

A dramatic increase in ethnic conflicts—in 2018 more people were internally displaced in Ethiopia than in any other country[12]—and an attempted coup d'état by factions of Amhara Region security forces against the regional government in June 2019, have led to concerns about Abiy Ahmed's political reforms and his ability to lead the country into a new democratic era. A few weeks after he was honored with the Nobel Peace Prize, the country experienced a new wave of political unrest as protests erupted against the Prime Minister and his political and economic reforms. Fueled by what was perceived to be an attack by the Prime Minister on the prominent media activist Jawar Mohammed, the protests reflected increasing ethnic and religious conflicts and confirmed the concerns that political analysts raised following the Nobel Peace Prize committee's announcement: that the honor may have come too early. In December 2019, just a few days before he received the Nobel Peace Prize in Oslo, Abiy Ahmed managed to dissolve the EPRDF coalition and establish a unitary national party called the Prosperity Party. This fueled increased skepticism and outright opposition, even among his closest allies. Oppositional voices have continued to grow, particularly after the onset of the Covid-19 pandemic. The introduction of a five-month state of emergency and a decision to postpone the 2020 elections indefinitely are viewed by many both as a means to crack down on opposition activity in general and as a sign of a return to authoritarianism.

It is too early to assess the impact of recent political reforms on Ethiopia's development policies. It is, for example, unclear to what extent the one-to-five networks are still functioning. It would be naïve to think that a sudden change in political leadership will put an end to Ethiopia's long history of top-down, coercive interventions. As the historical overview of social engineering in Ethiopia illustrates, there is a clear continuity in terms of how the various Ethiopian governments have sought to foster social and political change. The continued promotion of cooperatives and models by the various governments shows that we cannot separate current policies from the past. This illustrates, as Clapham (1988, 13) has argued, how important it is to understand "history as something that continues with undiminished force into the present."

Gender Equality and Women's Empowerment in Ethiopia

While women in Ethiopia have always been engaged in various informal and traditional institutions, the first formal women's organizations, the Ethiopian

Women's Welfare Association and the Ethiopian Women's Volunteer Service Association, were established in 1935. These associations were established by elite women in Addis Ababa, including from the royal family, as a response to the threat of an Italian invasion (Emebet Mulumebet 2010). The activities of the two organizations, which merged into one when the Italian invasion ended in 1942, were abruptly halted when the Derg regime came to power in 1974. This does not mean that issues related to women and equality were not on the agenda of the new regime. Women's emancipation was part of the revolutionary ideas, and the Derg frequently expressed its commitment to address and change the gendered division of labor and "women's double oppression, based on class and gender" (Yeshi H. Mariam 1994, WS60). In fact, during the first years of the revolution, messages about the situation of women in Ethiopia—how they suffered from harmful traditional practices, had limited access to education, never participated in political decision-making, and had limited job opportunities and skills—were so frequently addressed in the state media that "it became a mocking subject" (WS60). Donham (1999, 43–44) also describes how a district official in south Ethiopia in 1975 addressed gender relations in his speech to the people: "There are other things that we must do if Ethiopia is to mature. In the past, women have had a disproportionate share of the work. Now men must help them."

To address the problems women faced, the Derg regime created the Revolutionary Ethiopian Women's Association (REWA) in 1980 and, in line with its socialist ideology, the 1987 constitution explicitly stated equality of men and women as an aim. While the women's organizations established during the imperial regime mainly had engaged elite women in the capital, REWA was a nationwide organization with branch offices at all levels of government administration, including at the *kebele* level. Nevertheless, according to Pankhurst (1992, 30), the REWA "only operated on the level of rhetoric" and lacked "real power." Rather than being a channel for women's issues, the organization's main aim was "to advance the interests of the ruling party" (Biseswar 2008, 135). It was hence associated with state oppression.

When the EPRDF came to power in 1991, gender equality and women's rights received renewed and amplified attention, with a Women's Affairs machinery gradually developing at a structural level. The Women's Affairs office was initially established under the Prime Minister's office but became independent in 2005 and renamed the Ministry of Women, Children, and Youth

Affairs. Women's Affairs Bureaus were also established in the regional governments, with branch offices at subregional levels. The promotion of gender equality and women's rights was also enshrined in legislation and policy documents. The first national policy on Ethiopian women from 1993 listed fourteen strategic areas where change should be sought, including raising awareness to "eliminate prejudices against women" (Sosena Demessie and Tsahai Yitbark 2008, 97). The first National Action Plan on Gender Equality (NAP-GE) was launched in the early 2000s, followed by a second NAP-GE (2006–10) in 2005. Measures to promote gender equality have also found their way into various laws: the constitution in 1995, the revised Family Law in 2000, and the revised Penal Code in 2004.

Since 1991, there have been a number of instances of what Lombardo, Meier, and Verloo (2009, 3) call "fixing" of gender equality in Ethiopia, or the temporary freezing of gender equality by its enshrinement in legal or political documents. This fixing is much in line with global authoritative texts such as the Convention on the Elimination of all Forms of Discrimination Against Women and the Beijing Declaration and Platform of Action.

Issues such as early marriage and, especially, FGM/C are high on the agenda of both state and non-state actors. While these issues undoubtedly are important to address, the one-sided images of Ethiopian women's life and experiences that often are conveyed in policy circles tend to reinforce colonial representations of rural African women as oppressed under patriarchy. As an increasing number of anthropological studies have shown, women's lives and gender relations in Ethiopia are complex and multifaceted (Bruzzi and Zeleke 2015; Hannig 2017; Østebø 2018). It is, for example, highly problematic to assume that all rural women in Ethiopia are powerless victims of violence and harmful traditional practices. In some of my earlier work (Østebø 2018), I have shown how women who belong to the Arsi Oromo ethnic group are highly respected. They have access to institutions that, in addition to securing them certain rights, have given them political, economic, and religious power.

Ethiopia gender policies have also been much influenced by the World Bank's (2006) "gender as smart economics" rhetoric. This is perhaps most clearly reflected in the government's GTP in which women's (and young people's) empowerment has been defined as one of seven pillar strategies. Women's participation in the economy is particularly emphasized, evident in statements such as this: "Unleashing the power of girls and women will have profound effect on the speed, equity and sustainability of Ethiopia's growth and development" (Federal Democratic Republic of Ethiopia 2010, 12). This "bending" (Lombardo, Meier, and Verloo 2009, 1) of gender equality toward economic growth and poverty reduction is an example of what Michelle Murphy (2017, 5–6) calls "the economization of life [. . .] a historically specific regime of valuation hinged to the macrological figure of national 'economy'."

Since Abiy Ahmed came to power, Ethiopia's gender politics have undergone a radical transformation. Among his new counselors, 50 percent of the ministers are women, making Ethiopia, along with Rwanda, one of the only African states that has equal gender representation in the cabinet. The new prime minister has also appointed the human rights lawyer Meaza Ashenafi, a prominent women's rights activist and the founder of the Ethiopian Women Lawyers Association, as the new president of Ethiopia's federal Supreme Court. In addition, Billene Aster Seyoum has been appointed as the prime minister's press secretary, while the former UN official Sahle-Work Zewde was elected the first female president in October 2018.

While women's increased political representation and participation in the formal economy can have a positive and transformative impact on women's lives and gendered power relations, it is important to keep in mind that an emphasis on these two issues reflects a particular ideology: liberal feminism. These issues are, as Murphy (2017, 121) has argued, "symptomatic of the affective bonds between Western liberal feminisms and financial logics." In other words, there is a confluence between liberal feminist understandings of the autonomous self and women's empowerment and the neoliberal capitalist development agenda of consumption and wealth production. Such a confluence requires us to proceed with a certain degree of caution when examining the conception and implementation of models such as those connected with the second NAP.

In what ways does Awra Amba fit in this landscape of models, cooperatives, and gender politics? In Chapter 3 and Chapter 4, I pay particular attention to what makes Awra Amba a model by introducing two of the village's neighboring communities. In addition to shedding light on what Awra Amba is, and what it is not, my encounters with these communities can contribute to our understanding of what constitutes models within the global policy field and the different ways they come into being.

Chapter 3
The Emergence of a Traveling Model

"DO YOU KNOW THAT the NESTown Group is planning to construct their second model village in Awra Amba?" asks a good friend and fellow anthropologist with long experience living and working in Ethiopia. We have just finished a meal at his family's home in Addis Ababa, where we have been catching up and discussing the recent and highly unexpected political developments in the country. "NEST . . . ? What did you call it?" Completely taken aback by the new information, my question reveals that I have absolutely no idea what he is talking about. "NESTown is a project initiated by a group of architects from the Swiss Federal Institute of Technology Zurich[1] and the Ethiopian Institute of Architecture, Building Construction, and City Development [EiABC]," my friend explains. "They have been working on developing and constructing a new model town in the Amhara region. By bringing the town to the people, they hope to prevent the rapid flow of rural people into the existing cities." Having just spent more than an hour in an almost standstill traffic jam to travel the few kilometers from my guesthouse to my friend's house, I have no problem understanding the novel idea behind the project. Estimated to have reached a total population of six to seven million, Addis Ababa has become disturbingly crowded. "Now that they have completed the works with the first model town, they are interested in moving on to Awra Amba," my friend continues. "They have already met with leaders of the community to discuss their plans."

Back at my guesthouse a few hours later, I open my laptop and start browsing the internet for information about the NESTown project. A year earlier, in the summer of 2017, online browsing would have been out of the question. For days, the government had closed down the internet in order to curb political dissent and prevent people from using social media to mobilize antigovernment demonstrations. While the reforms that have been advanced by Abiy

Ahmed, the new prime minister, have opened up the internet and lessened censorship, the infrastructure is still weak, and the speed this evening is too slow to properly open the graphically loaded NESTown Group's website.[2] An image of what looks like a digital drawing and map of the town, with an arrow indicating a video, finally appears at the top of the page. I click on the arrow, only to realize that the video requires that I download Adobe Flash Player. With the slow Wi-Fi connection, it is an unrealistic project.

In the following days before my scheduled departure to Awra Amba, I continue browsing for information about the NESTown project. I send emails to people whose names appear on various websites and in European online news articles. No response. I visit the EiABC to see if I can find some of the people who have been involved, only to find empty offices. I make phone calls. I leave messages. Still no response. "It is the beginning of September and the end of the summer break," I tell myself, apologizing on their behalf.

Despite the slow internet connection and my unsuccessful attempts to track down and get in touch with people who have been involved in the NESTown project, I manage to piece together the limited and scattered information available on the web. I learn that the new town, Buranest, is expected to accommodate up to 20,000 people. It has been constructed around a central square where a large fig tree provides an inviting shade for people to gather. The new town has a vocational training center, two-storied housing facilities with rainwater tanks, tree nurseries, an alley road, a bridge, and an irrigation system. I learn that the inhabitants of the new town have formed a cooperative and that construction of a school, a health center, and a church is underway. The people in the new town will no longer live scattered, far away from public service facilities. With the new water collection and irrigation system, their farmland will be in their backyards and women will no longer have to walk far distances to fetch water. The vocational training center will help the new town inhabitants develop new skills and serve as a place for children to take computer courses. This is not only a modern town; it is, according to a 2018 article from the German news website *Spiegel Online*, "the role model" for the Ethiopian Ministry of Urban Development and Housing's ambitious plan to turn 8,000 rural settlements into urban centers.[3] In other words, the model will spearhead a new internationally backed national policy of villagization. As I sift through all the information, I realize that Buranest is located in the Libo Kemkem district, less than a twenty minutes' drive north of Awra

Amba. Considering the potential new partnership between Awra Amba and the NESTown Group, I decide to include a visit to the new town in my field-work itinerary.

"This is a perfect example of a white elephant," I sigh and turn to Nuriya,[4] my research assistant, who stands next to me, her mouth wide open in sur-prise. We have just arrived in Buranest after having spent the morning going from office to office in the regional capital, Bahir Dar, attempting to get in-formation about the NESTown project. With the ANRS listed as a major col-laborative partner, we had started out optimistically, expecting to learn more about the new model town at the Urban Development Housing and Construc-tion Bureau. But the officials we had met with shook their heads, referring us to other offices. When we had finally met someone who seemed to know about the project, he had told us that it had been "phased out." In the world of development policy and practice, this means that the project no longer re-ceives funding. Eager to get on the road, we had left Bahir Dar with limited in-formation and with no idea of the specific location of the new town. "We will stop and ask along the road," the driver had promised.

Now, we are here, looking at what should have been a new town. Only three buildings stand at the site: the vocational training center and two two-story housing units, each meant to accommodate eight families. The eco-friendly architectural style of the houses and the rainwater collection sys-tem scream of innovation and creative design, but none of the houses are fully completed. What should have been a town looks more like a deserted construction site. Except for a handful of grazing cattle and their shepherds, there are no signs of inhabitants.

"Why are there no people living here?" I ask the guard, a farmer in his mid-fifties, a few minutes later. "People do not trust the design," he answered. "We were told that since the houses have been planned and designed abroad, they should be strong. But the people are not convinced. They are afraid the structures will not stand the rain and wind." His honest response is reflec-tive of the recent political changes, illustrating how people are no longer afraid to speak their minds. As we walk up the stairs to the second floor in the only housing unit that is close to completion, I understand the skepticism. The narrow stairs are dangerously steep. With no railings, they are unsafe for both children and adults. "This is very scary," Nuriya concludes, as we walk across the single-layered board floor which divides the first and the second stories. "I could never live here." Her upbringing in an upper-class family in Addis Ababa cannot fully explain her reaction. The house feels like a dilapidated barn.

I have introduced the NESTown project here for two reasons. First, in addition to exemplifying the model town or model village phenomenon, the NESTown project can shed light on what Awra Amba is and what it is not. Second, and perhaps more importantly, a comparative analysis of the two models can elucidate what constitutes models within the global policy world and how traveling models come into being. In the next section, I present a short summary of model theory, focusing particularly on Clifford Geertz's distinction between models *for* and models *of.* I then introduce the model village phenomenon and situate it in relation to theoretical literature that deals with "global forms" (Collier and Ong 2005, 4) and "pastoral power" (Foucault 1982, 782) before detailing and analyzing the multiple ways models are present in NESTown and Awra Amba. I pay particular attention to the differences between the two places in terms of their capacity to enact and perform an affective representative model—a model *of*—that reflects and serves as a prescriptive model, that is, a model *for* the implementation of particular policies. I suggest that the traveling model—its capacity to go viral—is predicated on the existence of a representative model that is produced and performed at a specific place or location and that reflects the prescriptive models—the normative visions and interests—of its interactive audience, who picks it up and facilitates its circulation. In other words, the convergence of model *for* and a corresponding model *of* enable and produce the traveling model.

Models *for* and Models *of*

Reflecting the central role that models play in fields such as physics, mathematics, chemistry, and economics, the most comprehensive theoretical discussions about models are found in philosophy of science (Bailer-Jones 2003; Hutten 1954), economics (Morgan and Morrison 1999; Morgan 2012), and science and technology studies (Godin 2017). While there is much contestation about what constitutes a model within the sciences, the model is commonly approached as a heuristic device—a method of enquiry—used to depict one aspect of reality in a "schematic, miniaturized, simplified way" (Morgan 2012, 3). Scientists therefore acknowledge the limitations of models. They emphasize that models only "offer a partially accurate predictive framework" (Clarke

1972, 2). Scientific and economic models are therefore not to be treated as true representations of reality, and the inaccuracy, incompleteness, and uncertainty of models are widely acknowledged (Bailer-Jones 2003).

The model also features as a tool and as a theoretical concept within anthropology (Clarke 1972; Geertz 1973, 2007; Handelman 1998; Behrends, Park, and Rottenburg 2014a). The British archaeologist David L. Clarke (1972, 1) concluded as early as 1972 that models are "undeniably fashionable." While he acknowledged that models, particularly if misused, can be "dangerous toys" (1), he made strong arguments for why it is important to be concerned with models. Introducing "controlling models" as a significant model category, Clarke argued that these were "mind models" consisting of a "partly conscious and partly subconscious system of beliefs, concepts, values, and principles, both realistic and metaphysical" (5). The models that control the way we think and see things are accumulated over time through "exposure to life in general, to educational processes and to the changing contemporary systems of beliefs" (3).[5]

The model is furthermore a central concept in Geertz's (1973) discussion of religion as a cultural system.[6] According to Geertz (93), models are systems of symbols "whose relations to one another 'model' relations among entities, processes or what-have-you in physical, organic, social or psychological systems by 'paralleling,' 'imitating' or 'simulating' them." They are "extrinsic sources of information [that] provide a blueprint or template in terms of which processes external to themselves can be given a definite form" (92). A distinction that Geertz and others (Hutten 1954) make is between models *for* and models *of.* A model *for* serves as a tool for the manipulation of non-symbolic systems—as a guide for physical, psychological, political, or social systems or processes. It provides "information in terms of which other processes can be patterned" (Geertz 1973, 94). We may say that models *for* are prescriptive, as they provide a protocol or an apparatus for particular interventions (Behrends, Park, and Rottenburg 2014b). They offer an instruction, a code, or a template for how to behave or for how to implement a specific process. The assumption behind implementing these "procedural cultural plans" (Reyna 2007, 78) is that if you do x, y will happen. As "technologies of social ordering" (Behrends, Park, and Rottenburg 2014b, 28), models *for* have a clear normative dimension, reflecting a need for control and order of the chaos that characterize much of our lived experience.

While models *for* serve as tools for the manipulation of non-symbolic systems, models *of* denote, according to Geertz (1973), manipulation and organization of symbolic systems or structures so that they correspond to or reflect a particular preestablished non-symbolic system as much as possible. Models *of* do not necessarily provide sources of information in terms of how a particular structure, process, or idea should be implemented, but they serve to illustrate them and help us understand or apprehend them in an alternative way. They are "axiomatic icons" of social realities (Handelman 1998, 94).

The distinction between models *for* and models *of* is useful from an analytical perspective, but it may appear abstract and hence difficult to comprehend. To tease out and illustrate the main difference between the two, let us return to the villagization program initiated by the Derg regime in 1985. The villages in this program were constructed based on an "ideal model layout" (Cohen and Isakson 1987, 449), specified by the government in a "strict template which local surveyors and administrators were ordered to follow" (Scott 1998, 284). These guidelines provided details on how to construct the villages—including maps (see fig. 3.1)—and served as a prescriptive model, or a model *for*. However, not all villages were constructed according to the prescribed model. Some stood out as more representative or exemplary of the original model than others. Villages that were perceived to represent a successful implementation of the original policy model were identified as more successful than others and were singled out as model villages. They were actively used to showcase the ideals and policies of the regime. We can say that they were models *of* the ideal village first prescribed in the guidelines.

While I have found Geertz's distinction helpful to analyze Awra Amba and compare and contrast it to NESTown, I need to emphasize that the distinction between models *for* and models *of* is not absolute. As Don Handelman (1998, 24) has pointed out, this binary is often collapsed in scientific model theories in which a model "at one and the same time" is seen as "a derivation of reality [model *of*] as well as one that should be informative of that reality [model *for*]." My analysis of Awra Amba and the NESTown project will show that this is similarly true when it comes to the models that circulate in the policy world. The categorization of prescriptive and representative models assumes that one is operating within a much more orderly and structured field than what de facto is the case. There is considerable fluidity between models *for* and models *of*; in fact, most models—if not all—can be classified

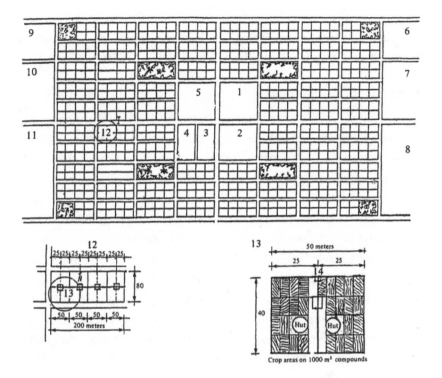

Figure 3.1 A government plan for an ideal village. The model shows (1) mass
organization office; (2) kindergarten; (3) health clinic; (4) government
cooperative shop; (5) *kebele* office; (6) reserve plots; (7) primary school;
(8) sports field; (9) seed-multiplication center; (10) handicrafts center;
(11) animal-breeding station; (12) enlargement of compound sites;
(13) two sites in greater detail; (14) neighborhood latrine. Reproduced
with permission.

as both models *for* and models *of.* Depending on the context, a model may
have, at one point, an ontological and epistemological function, representing
reality. At another point, the same model may have a normative and prescriptive function.

   If the distinction between models *for* and models *of* is as fluid as I here
have indicated, why dwell on this distinction? Is it useful at all? I will return to this question later in the chapter, but allow me to explain why this
is a fruitful heuristic distinction to make. The pair model *for* and model *of*
should not be used in an ontological sense, to categorize what a particular
model *is.* Rather, the distinction is useful because it can tell us about a model's

poly-functionality—about how a model works and the effects it has in various settings and for different actors. This distinction can help us explain how a model comes into being and begins to travel.

The Model Village Paradigm

While there are significant differences between the NESTown project and Awra Amba, they are, just as the villages constructed as part of the Derg's villagization program, both situated within what has been termed the "model village paradigm" (Wilson 2014, 107). The model village first emerged as a phenomenon in eighteenth century Europe and was largely a "creation of the landowning classes" (Darley 2007, 11). These model villages were, according to Gillian Darley (2007), not innovative in terms of architecture or improved building techniques. Reflecting the formalism of Dutch and French seventeenth-century gardens, it was the planning of the village—the systematic organization of houses and infrastructures along symmetrical lines—that made them groundbreaking. The rational concentration and distribution of previously scattered populations facilitated a new kind of administration—a new "way in which the conduct of individuals or of groups might be directed" (Foucault 1982, 790). The model village phenomenon soon spread to other parts of the world, influencing the construction of slave villages in European colonies (Chapman 1991) and new settlements in America (Murtagh 1967). This form of modeling—the planned and careful design of socially and physically coherent settlements—has been thoroughly discussed by James C. Scott (1998, 62) as a common feature of the modern state and its "authoritarian modernizing schemes." Along with a discussion of the villagization program implemented in Ethiopia during the Derg regime, Scott's historically informed account provides a thorough analysis of the construction of model villages and model cities in authoritarian and socialist states, such as in the Soviet Union and in Julius Nyerere's Tanzania. Characterized by an ambition to create order and a legible reality, these schemes were, according to Scott, informed by a "high-modernist ideology"; by a blind belief in scientific progress as the way to solve the world's problems, often to the neglect of existing resources and traditional knowledge, which were dismissed as primitive and parochial. Scott (1998, 4) argues that

> carriers of high modernism tended to see rational order in remarkably visual aesthetic terms. For them, an efficient, rationally organized city, village,

or farm was a city that looked regimented and orderly in a geometrical sense. The carriers of high modernism, once their plans miscarried or were thwarted, tended to retreat to what I call miniaturization: the creation of a more easily controlled micro-order in model cities, model villages, and model farms.

The model village phenomenon exemplifies what critical geographer Henri Lefebvre has called "colonization of everyday life," which intends to govern and produce everyday life "in accordance with reductive visions of social order" (Wilson 2014, 108). This form of governance is both singularizing, involving specific forms of subject-making, and collectivizing, in the sense that it attempts to form docile classes of people whose labor and resources can be used to advance particularly politico-economic projects (Foucault 1982).

While the model village phenomenon appears to have gained a strong foothold in authoritarian socialist states, it would be a mistake to restrict it to a particular political ideology. The ideological motives and the historical-geographical contexts in which the model village has emerged reflect great diversity (Wilson 2014). In her analysis of the rural reconstruction movement that began during the Cold War period, Nicole Sackley (2011, 481ff.) has, for example, shown how policy makers and experts—"from missionaries and colonial administrators to nationalist politicians and social reformers"—embraced the model village as a key instrument and a "category of development knowledge" across Asia, Africa, and Latin America. The model village, "imagined as a small, unified community of ordered living," appeared as the ultimate form "with which to contain unruly peasant politics, mobilize labour, and construct an ideal social order." Yet, it was also tied to Cold War anti-communism and counterinsurgency and many model villages became "instruments of war," most notably during the Vietnam War.

A more contemporary example of model villages can be found in the Millennium Villages Project (MVP). The MVP was launched in 2006 by Jeffrey Sachs, who had been given the mandate by the then-UN Secretary-General, Kofi Annan, to lead the Millennium Project—a task force responsible for producing a strategy that could lead to the achievement of the MDGs. The MVP selected fourteen cluster villages in remote, rural areas of Sub-Saharan Africa, investing between 101 USD and 127 USD per person per year for a period of ten years to implement a set of interventions that were assumed to lead to sustainable change and poverty eradication (Mitchell et al. 2018).[7] The villages were, particularly during the first phase of the project, framed as model villages and as examples of a holistic, socially engineered development program that could be scaled up and implemented in other places (Wilson 2014).

The wide circulation of the model village, across diverse political and ideological contexts and by a wide variety of actors, suggests that it is an example of a "global technology" or "global form" that can be "decontextualized and recontextualized, abstracted, transported, and reterritorialized, [. . .] designed to produce functionally comparable results in disparate domains" (Collier and Ong 2005, 11). As a global form in which panoptical techniques of "pastoral power" (Foucault 1982, 782ff.) are applied on a larger scale, the model village is a spatial technology of power that "transcends competing political ideologies" (Wilson 2014, 109). Hence, it can be capitalist, socialist, colonial, and even, as demonstrated below, religious in nature.

Intentional Design vs. Discovery

As a designed and planned settlement intended to create a new form of social order, the NESTown project bears a strong resemblance to the villages constructed through the Derg regime's villagization program. Both are examples of expert-initiated villages, planned and modeled with little—if any—grassroots involvement. Both initiatives relied on carefully crafted master plans and attempted "to redesign rural life and production from above" (Scott 1998, 184). In the NESTown case, the plans were visualized in town maps and virtual models partly developed in the Future Cities Laboratory in Singapore.

Awra Amba is, in contrast, not intentionally designed as a model village and may therefore, at first glance, appear as an anomaly. The establishment of the Awra Amba village was not the result of an externally initiated social engineering project. There were no policy makers, high-ranking architects, or engineers involved in its design or construction, and the physical layout and grid-like structures that are the defining features of intentionally planned model villages are not present in Awra Amba. Instead, as detailed in Chapter 1, Zumra established the community together with a group of people who believed in and were supportive of his ideas. Zumra and his followers certainly had visions and plans for the community they established. And as we shall see in Chapter 4, their visions did not emerge out of the blue. Yet, the founders of Awra Amba did not construct the village based on rigid pen-and-paper models, nor did they purposefully construct the village based on particular policy ideas or as a policy model in the first place. Awra Amba emerged as a global policy model because it was discovered rather than intentionally designed.[8]

It is not easy to determine who *first* discovered Awra Amba. According to a higher official in the Ethiopian Ministry of Culture and Tourism, the community was identified as a potential tourist destination in 1995: "We were assessing the resources in the Amhara region. What resources do we have that we can use for economic development? This is when we came across Awra Amba," the official told me in an interview. While the Ethiopian government's recognition has been crucial, not only in terms of establishing Awra Amba as a tourist destination but also in legitimizing the village's model status, the local media also played a key role. Rumors about the village were circulating locally through the 1990s, inspiring local radio stations to tell the community's story. However, it was not until the first documentary was aired in Amharic in the early 2000s that the village gained national recognition. "The timing of the documentary was very important," a young man who grew up in Awra Amba told me during a conversation we had in 2018. "It was a local production, but it was screened on national TV during the break of a national team football match. It was a big game and everyone was watching. That is why Awra Amba became known."

Emerging from something that already existed and independent of external interventions, Awra Amba rose to its status as a model because it exhibited certain qualities that attracted the attention of the Ethiopian government, the NGO community, and the media. I will return to an in-depth discussion of what has facilitated and fueled Awra Amba's virality in later chapters. For now, it suffices to say that the village was recognized as a model by these national and international actors because it corresponded with their controlling models—or their normative world view. These actors were, in other words, receptive to and could easily associate with the ideas and values displayed in Awra Amba. If they had not discovered Awra Amba and its potential as a policy instrument, it would not have become a model. To borrow a phrase from Hannah le Roux (2017, 479), we may therefore say that Awra Amba is an example of a "found model."

While Awra Amba as a found model in many ways deviates from the model villages intentionally constructed by policy makers and experts, the community is by no means a unique phenomenon. There are, for example, clear similarities between Awra Amba and some of the model villages that emerged in Europe in the eighteenth century. Gillian Darley traces the model village movement in Europe back to the Moravian Church (also known as the Bohemian Brethren), a Protestant pietistic denomination established in the mid-fifteenth century in Moravia.[9] In the early eighteenth century, a group of German-speaking Moravian refugees fled from the Counter-Reformation measures enacted by the Habsburg rulers and established the Herrnhut village in what today is Germany. Herrnhut provided a prototype for the physical as well as social organization of new settlements in both Britain (Darley 2007) and America (Murtagh 1967). Just as in the case of Awra Amba, it rose to its status as a model because it had certain desirable qualities. The fact that the first model village had religious roots, particularly in a pietistic movement that was concerned with the intimate care of the soul, gives new meaning to Foucault's thesis that modern biopower, and the spatial regulation and disciplining of populations described by Scott, emerged as an extension of pastoral power. Even the name of the first Herrnhut village, "The Lord's village," signaled a divine panoptical vision that eventually became secularized.

A Miniature World of Models

Being a found rather than a designed and planned model does not necessarily exclude the existence of deliberate model making processes. These processes are, however, more difficult to trace and make it challenging to identify what specifically constitutes the Awra Amba model. Given that Awra Amba—as a physical place consisting of a group of people and their everyday practices—is commonly cast as a model village, it is easy to assume that Awra Amba is a single, monolithic, and seamless model. Yet, if we apply assemblage thinking and Geertz's (1973) distinction between models *for* and models *of*—between prescriptive and representative models—it soon becomes clear that what constitutes the model is far from given. A careful analysis of Awra Amba reveals that there are assemblages within the assemblage; there are multiple models at play. Just as with a Russian *matryoshka* doll, once you open and start examining one model, another model appears, and the larger model, although not always easy to identify, often elucidates the smaller ones.[10] This suggests that rather than talking about models as separate and distinct entities, it makes more sense to talk about model worlds. In fact, it is fruitful to think of Awra Amba—or other model villages—as a place where various physical and ideological models coexist, overlap, and even co-construct new models. As such, it is an assemblage of models: an example of how heterogeneous sets and forms of models—ideas, things, technologies, and people, or models *for* and models *of*—come together in a miniature world. For example, a physical model that is associated with and promoted through Awra Amba is the community's improved cooking stove. According to the official narrative, Zumra originally designed the stove, which in addition to bringing the burning fire up off the floor, also has a chimney that prevents the room from being filled with smoke. It is an example of a "development device" (Redfield 2016, 168) that has been widely promoted by the Ethiopian government. During my first fieldwork in Awra Amba in 2015, the community hosted a workshop funded and organized by an international NGO. Over a period of three days, members of the Awra Amba community taught health extension workers from neighboring communities how to construct the stove. In addition to showcasing Awra Amba's innovative and entrepreneurial capacities, the stove that was used during the training served as an instructional device for the construction of new stoves. In other words, it functioned both as a model *for* and a model *of*.

Geertz (1973) suggested the distinction between models *for* and models *of* to stress the active dimension of culture as a system of symbols. In other words, culture is not just a passive reflection, a representation, or a map of the physical world, as excessively materialist views would have it, but it is also a blueprint or a template—a model *for* action upon that world. Extrapolating to the anthropology of policy, we can say that models *of* primarily have a symbolic function. Rather than providing information in terms of how a particular policy, structure, program, or idea should be implemented, they are "graphic examples" (Lane 1981, 19) of a social or cultural phenomenon, created in order to help us apprehend a particular aspect of the lived-in world. In contrast, models *for* have a clear prescriptive function. They serve as guidelines for how to order or transform the lived-in world (Handelman 1998, 23ff.).

In Awra Amba, the model *for* is perhaps most evident in Zumra's visions and his five principles for how to create heaven on earth: an emphasis on gender equality, children's rights, the abandonment of bad speech and deeds, care for the needy, sick, and elderly, and the importance of respect for all people, regardless of geographical background, ethnicity, or color. Just as for the NESTown masterplan, these principles form a prescriptive framework for action—for the things one should or should not do. This normative frame-work, what in Geertz's (1957) terms could also be described as the communi-ty's ethos, does not exist in a vacuum, nor is it static. While Awra Amba has, as already discussed, developed a separate system of self-governance that ap-pears to function independently of the Ethiopian government's bureaucratic mechanisms and structures, the community is not unaffected by national policies and global norms. The Awra Amba community relates to and nego-tiates the various packages and policies that the Ethiopian government puts in place. This is perhaps most visible in the community's commitment to gen-der justice, which to a considerable extent aligns with liberal feminist values. With its emphasis on equality as sameness, economic empowerment, and the community's rejection of harmful traditional practices such as early marriage and FGM/C, Zumra's values mirror the political norms and priorities that dominate the global and national gender and development discourse. The em-phasis on these values and qualities—particularly on the community's de-nunciation of harmful traditional practices—has been a major factor in se-curing for the community its status as a model among national and global policy makers and activists. The confluence between dominant global norms and the values promoted by the Awra Amba community suggests that "mod-els that affirm and extend dominant paradigms, and which consolidate pow-erful interests, are more likely to travel with the following wind of hegemonic compatibility or imprimatur status" (Peck and Theodore 2010, 170). In other words, Awra Amba has achieved its fame not only because it is a particular model *of* a village, but also because it is a model *for*, a prescriptive blueprint that affirms, extends, and carries dominant paradigms in the gender and de-velopment field. It is also interesting to see how Zumra's ideas and the val-ues and principles promoted by and through Awra Amba are not only closely aligned with national and policy norms and ideals but also change over time. In recent years, Zumra has, for example, been voicing a green rhetoric, em-phasizing the community's tree-planting efforts and their enthusiasm for sus-tainable gardening.

While Awra Amba first and foremost serves as a model *for* and model *of* gender equality, attracting global recognition and giving it status as a gender-equal, peaceful, and just society, the community also functions as a model in other ways. The Awra Amba community is, for example, a model *of* sus-tainable community tourism and is actively used and promoted as a model *for* others to emulate. Let me give an example. From 2011 to 2014, the Japan

International Cooperation Agency carried out a community development project in the Simien Mountains National Park in cooperation with the Ethiopian Wildlife Conservation Authority and the ANRS Bureau of Culture, Tourism, and Parks Development. The project's overall aim was to promote alternative ways of livelihood for people living in the park and to reduce their dependence on extractive agricultural activities in order to conserve the park. An expert who was involved in the project described how they used Awra Amba to encourage the people living in the park to develop sustainable community tourism: "We brought people from the Simien mountain village to Awra Amba so they could see how they could generate income and make handicraft products for the market, and for tourism. We took them there so they could understand how the Awra Amba community has been able to live from their weaving and from sharing their cultural traditions." This statement also reflects the Ethiopian government's policy focus on cooperatives and micro- and small enterprises as a key strategy in development. Having established itself in the market economy, Awra Amba is clearly perceived as a model in this regard. As a successful producer cooperative, where the means of production are communally owned and where members are fully committed to working for the cooperative, we can even say that the Awra Amba community is a model *of* both past and present state policies, in that the community reflects and represents the state's collectivist vision. As detailed in the previous chapter, producer cooperatives were first introduced by the Derg regime, and despite previous flaws and failures, they have in recent years reemerged as a development strategy of EPRDF.

The Ethiopian government has, moreover, recognized Awra Amba as one of many official model villages. Enaney, Zumra's wife, emphasized this aspect in one of our conversations:

> In public meetings, the government often refers to us using the phrase *"ende Awra Ambaoch"* (like the Awra Ambaians). The government is talking about good governance. They focus on maintaining peace and resolving disputes. Awra Amba is a model because we are doing all these things. In other communities, problems are not avoided. They have good governance-related problems. But, we are a model since we solve our problems through discussions.

Enaney's statement illustrates a key feature of model politics in Ethiopia. In order to become an officially designated model, a community must comply with government policies, and Awra Amba has, reportedly, implemented the various extension packages promoted by the Ethiopian state. A representative from the Wereta district's Women, Children, and Youth Affairs office emphasized this as a major reason why the government considers Awra Amba to be a model: "Awra Amba is a model because they know how to implement the packages properly. For example, when it comes to education, every household has accepted the obligation to educate their children. They have also implemented all the sixteen packages of the Health Extension Program (HEP). Each package has their own set of indicators and Awra Amba has managed to reach all the preset targets." The reference to indicators and targets in this statement is interesting and confirms the tendency, not only in the Ethiopian context, but within the global development discourse more broadly, to rely on numerical data to measure success, or perhaps more accurately, to assess whether things have been done "according to standard procedure or 'by the book'" (Zenker 2015, 104). In fact, as numerical representations, indicators play a key role as representative models (models *of*); they are assumed to be evidence of whether a prescriptive model (model *for*) has been successfully implemented.

While numerical models in the form of indicators are highly valued among policy makers and development bureaucrats and have been foundational for Awra Amba's status as a government-acknowledged model village, their representational power, particularly vis-à-vis a general audience, is much weaker than a well-narrated story. The official Awra Amba narrative is far more compelling, conveyed through the guides' oral narration, the subsequent tour of the village, and the immersive storytelling provided through Lyfta's virtual product *The Awra Amba Experience* (which I examine more in-depth in later chapters). This narrative is much more than an abstract model *of* conveyed by indicators and it is not a simple representation of the community in the conventional sense (such as a straightforward factual account of its history and a description of its location and structure). The fact that Awra Amba is a place one can visit—either online or in person—means that it is an experiential model that provides its audience with a sense of being part of something "real." This model has clear affective qualities; visitors can easily associate with it, become emotionally attached to it, and project on it their own desires for good community life. This is a key feature of the virality captured by the concept of viral assemblage.

The Awra Amba model embodies the norms and values envisioned by Zumra and his followers; the official narrative and the tour generate powerful lived-in experiences that have been vital to the model's virality. In fact, these experiences are so powerful that many of the visitors who arrive in Awra Amba or who engage virtually with the community via Lyfta's platform treat the tour and the narrative as true and full representations of the community's way of life. In other words, these carefully managed, profoundly immersive experiences come to stand for the community, hiding all the complexity and messiness of everyday life. This partly explains the tendency to portray the Awra Amba community as a utopian society. It is this perceived authentic reality that gives Awra Amba its prescriptive power as a model *for* that can be circulated as part of national and transnational development policies.

While Awra Amba is able to enact a narrative and give its visitors an immersive experience that closely aligns with Zumra's visions of how things should be—a model "of the proper, ideal pattern of social life" (Skorupski 1976, 164)—this is much less the case in the NESTown project. As I have shown, the development of maps and plans—of models designed to serve as guidelines for how to construct a new town—was an important part of the project.[11] But the NESTown Group's visionary experts also imagined that once constructed and successfully inhabited, the town as a model *of* their carefully crafted plans would be a living model *for* the development of similar urban settlements in other parts of the Amhara region. We have already seen that things did not exactly go according to the plans: the discrepancy between the intentions—sketched out in project documents, fancy digital models, and maps—and what actually happened on the ground is rather conspicuous, illustrating that "community building on paper [is] [. . .] an easier task than community building in reality" (Darley 2007, 149). This does not mean that it is impossible to design and develop physically coherent settlements. While the new villages that the Derg regime constructed as part of the villagization program in the 1980s "nearly always failed their inhabitants as human communities and as units of food production" (Scott 1998, 250), the actual construction of the villages was remarkably aligned with the plans.

The reason the Derg regime managed to both physically construct something that, to a considerable extent, reflected what was in the original plans and to create villages where people actually lived, was the strong commitment of an authoritarian regime to violently enforce their policies. In some areas

Figure 3.2   An example of an intentionally planned settlement in Bale Zone, December 2019. Photo by author.

of the country this even included mass executions of uncooperative farmers, burning of houses and crops, and theft and killing of cattle (de Waal 1991).

The Traveling Model

It would be easy to conclude that Awra Amba and the NESTown project are examples of successful and failed models respectively; the first as an example of a "real" model and the latter as an entity that unrightfully has been given model status. Such a conclusion would confirm the assumptions that underpin the wide and rather uncritical use of models in our contemporary world: that a model inherently carries within itself a successful implementation of policy into practice. This is why models that are deemed successful are commonly described as best practices that can be scaled up and emulated by others and why they are picked up and start traveling. The problem is that this assumes the model—a model *of*—is a true representation of the lived-in world. However, in Awra Amba's case, the model *of* that is conveyed through the tour and the various official narratives does not fully correspond to the lived-in world. Rather than being a full and neutral representation of the Awra Amba community's way of life, it is a model *of* that reflects particular normative ideals and ideologies, which include but are not limited to Zumra's visions and principles. The model *of* is, in other words, a reflection of the model(s) *for*. This is an important distinction that is crucial to understanding the role that models play in the global policy world. What becomes a model within this field, be it an organization, a village, a methodology, or a person, does so because of its ability to convey and enact powerful embodied experiences and affects and to project desires of what reality should be. This model, which always comes in the form of a success story, depicts an effective implementation or demonstration of a prescriptive model, and is, as Olivier de Sardan, Diarra, and Moha (2017) have argued, foundational to models in the global policy world. We may, therefore, say that a traveling model is one that fuses the model *of* and the model *for* in a particular way; that a traveling model emerges because of a particular entity's ability to construct and perform a model *of* that appears to be the real, authentic thing but that in practice reflects the model(s) *for*. In other words, the prescribed dimensions of the model are presented as purely descriptive, and thus neutral and given. This explains why, conversely, the model *of* also tends to appear as a model *for*—an example of how things are supposed to be or how things can be successfully implemented.

While a good story or a compelling narrative that strategically fuses the models *for* and *of* clearly plays a determining role in the creation of a traveling model, I believe that it is crucial to recognize the territorial and relational aspects of a model's mobility. Let me return to NESTown to clarify this point. First, it is important to underline that while the NESTown Group failed in its attempt to create a lived-in model *of* a rural sustainable town that also could serve as a model *for* others to emulate, this does not mean that they did not create a representation of their ambitious plans. Although incomplete and abandoned, the buildings and infrastructure the project has constructed reflect, at least to some extent, the project's plans. Hence, it is also a model *of*. In addition, through their web site,[12] academic publications (Angélil et al. 2013), various media articles,[13] and videos,[14] the NESTown Group has created a number of representations of Buranest. While these accounts acknowledge and detail some of the challenges the project faced and emphasize Buranest as a laboratory and an experimental space, they create imaginations of a nascent town. This is a model *of* that has attracted the attention of a few European-based media outlets and that seems, at least to some extent, to be circulating in architectural milieus. As a physical model *of*, Buranest is not particularly inviting, though. It does not provide a way for potential visitors to interact with a lived-in or simulated model, nor does it give visitors a positive, emotional experience. It is a model *of* that is best sustained on paper. This partly explains the silence and the lack of enthusiasm I experienced during my initial tracing of the NESTown Group's project. Had the project succeeded in creating an immersive, living model *of* that reflected the ambitious master plans, Buranest would most likely have become what Awra Amba is today: a widely promoted and popular model village and tourist destination.

An Idealized and Affective Model

In this chapter, I have attempted to deconstruct some of the parts of the Awra Amba model village. I have shown that the Awra Amba model, rather than being a given, static whole, is a viral assemblage of models: a place where different types of models come together in a miniature world. I have also argued that the model *of* Awra Amba—conveyed through the tour and various narratives—is not a model *of* the community's way of life, but of the confluence of various normative ideals and ideologies articulated through Zumra's visions and national and global policies. We have here an example of what Pierre Bourdieu (1977, 29) calls mistaking "the model of reality" for the "reality of the model." By saying that the model *of* is a reflection of the model *for*, rather than a reflection of the community's actual life, I do not imply that the tour and the official Awra Amba narrative are purely fictional. There are elements of truth in these representations.[15] But, as with all models, the official Awra Amba narrative is a selective and partial representation of the lived-in world. Being "ideal and perfect rather than real and messy" it is an example of "idealization" (Morgan 2012, 101). This form of model making has been described as "the process of picking out the relations of interest, and isolating them from the frictions and disturbances which interfere with their workings in the real world to give form to simpler and 'ideal' world models" (Morgan 2012, 21). In other words, it is a process in which certain desirable elements of the lived-in world are accentuated, while elements that may disturb or create complexity and ambivalence are erased or made invisible in order to create an ideal type or utopia. In the case of Awra Amba, the relations of interest—or what we perhaps could call "trademarks"—include the positive qualities, values, and achievements that are highlighted in the various official narratives and that resonate with the desires and expectations of various receptors, both national and international. These are the few relevant important parts that have been isolated from the whole and then exaggerated. The emotional and affective moments that this idealization generates have fueled the model's virality and its emergence as a highly respected traveling model.

To illustrate how the making of the Awra Amba model is an example of idealization, it is crucial that we turn to the invisibility of disruptive elements—to some of the parts that have been omitted. These elements have been erased or silenced because they can potentially subvert the official narratives and thus weaken, or at least relativize, their prescriptive and representational power. Nowhere are these silences more evident than in the hidden and partly contested history of the Awra Amba community.

Chapter 4
Alayhim—A Potential Disruption

"DO YOU KNOW a community called Alayhim?" When I raise the question, I am in the middle of a meeting with a government official in the Wereta district Women, Children, and Youth Affairs office. He has just finished a long speech praising Awra Amba and emphasizing how his office has actively brought people from other villages to Awra Amba so they can learn from Awra Amba's experiences. This initiative has produced significant results, particularly when it comes to gender equality, he claims. Considering the responses I have received when raising questions about Alayhim in Awra Amba, I am not really expecting much of an answer. The secrecy, contradictory information, avoidance, and stern, yet polite rejection I have experienced during my first week of fieldwork in Awra Amba has made me rather disillusioned. In the few informal conversations I have had with members of the community, they have constantly referred me to the members of the welcoming committee—that is, to the guides who are responsible for visitors. One young man, during a short conversation we had one morning, told me his mother was one of the founding members of the community, but when asked if he would be willing to introduce me to her, he responded: "It is better if you to talk to the guides and do your interviews with them. Some people may be afraid to talk. So the guides have been assigned to give interviews." Elders in the community, who normally are seen as the most important and reliable informants, have refused to talk about their background, claiming that they are not qualified to tell the history of Awra Amba or to give in-depth information about the community. The few persons who have been willing to speak with me have tended to provide scripted responses that are a mere repetition of the official Awra Amba narrative.

When I first arrived in Awra Amba, I was well aware of the challenges associated with doing research in Ethiopia, of "the secrecy which surrounds even the most apparently innocuous information, the multiple and contradictory accounts of any political event, and the extraordinary persistence even of myths which can clearly be shown to be fictitious" (Clapham 1988, xi). I assumed, however, that my long-term experience working and conducting research in southeast Ethiopia in areas with a history of strong political opposition, combined with my relatively good command of Amharic, would make it easier to establish trust and get access to "backstage" (Scott 1985, 27) unofficial discourses in Awra Amba. I was not at all prepared for the level of secrecy and control I experienced, and I started wondering whether this was a culture of secrecy peculiar to Northern Ethiopia.

"Of course, I know about Alayhim. It is a community in Alem Ber, a town situated fifteen minutes' drive from Awra Amba." The official's unexpected response to my question draws me back into the energetic research mode I had been in when I arrived in Awra Amba a week earlier. As I had been preparing for fieldwork, browsing the internet, watching videos on YouTube, and reading graduate theses written about Awra Amba by students from universities in Ethiopia, I had found myself increasingly captivated and fascinated by the community and its history. Yet, the consistency and homogeneity in the way the Awra Amba story was told, and the rather one-sided focus on it as a success and a utopia in the various accounts I came across, had made me eager to explore Alayhim firsthand. My research interest had been further piqued when I had come across a brief reference to the community in a thesis written by a student from a local university that described it as a "Muslim sect"[1] to which Zumra allegedly had belonged (Seid Mohammed Yassin 2008). Having lived in a predominantly Muslim part of Ethiopia for a number of years, with an interest in the relationship between gender and religion and with a spouse who is a scholar of Islam in Ethiopia, I had been intrigued, from a research perspective, by the hint of a connection to a Muslim community.

A few hours after my conversation with the government official, I find myself sitting on a gigantic log, together with a group of elders from the Alayhim community. The children who flocked around us when we first arrived in Sinko, a small rural village a few kilometers from Alem Ber, are now busy playing jump rope. Boys and girls are jumping together. There is no gendering of the game. I turn my attention to some of the elders who willingly share their community's history.

Alayhim was established by Sheik Saide Hassan Bashir in 1949. Challenging institutional religious practices such as fasting and daily prayer, his teaching represented a radical break with the worldviews and religious practices of the neighboring Christian and Muslim communities. As summarized by one of the elders in the Alayhim community:

> Sheik Saide asked—what is the meaning of fasting? What is the meaning of prayer? Fasting in Alayhim is not for one month. Every person has to fast, but it is not time dependent. Fasting in Alayhim is not connected with food—it is about living a good life—to not steal, lie, or do bad things. Prayer is not something to be done five times a day. Every action is connected with prayer— when you wake up, eat, or walk, you should pray. Through life you have to pray—prayer is about being conscious in all what you do. According to Sheik Saide—there is no difference between Muslims and Christians. We are all the same.

In addition to focusing on love, mutual understanding, and unity regardless of ethnic and religious identity, Sheik Saide preached the importance of working together and of supporting the poor and the needy. He also emphasized equality between men and women. Believing that *ando ke ando bebelt yellem* (one is not more important than the other), he among others opposed Sharia laws that gave men stronger property rights than women in case of divorce. His rather liberal values made him a controversial figure, particularly among the Muslim population in the area. Charged for not following what was considered to be the true Islamic religion and accused of being supportive of the political opposition, he was imprisoned multiple times during the Haile Selassie and the Derg regimes. He passed away in prison in Gondar sometime in 1981.

"Zumra was not only a member of our community; he was a trusted follower of Sheik Saide and the person who was closest to him." Foziya,[2] one of the two female elders who has committed her time to answer my questions, is clear in her response. I have just pointed out the striking similarities in the teachings and values they attribute to Sheik Saide with those now promoted and performed by the Awra Amba community. "What you see and hear about in Awra Amba today are ideas derived from Alayhim. It is Sheik Saide's philosophy." The elders continue their story, detailing how the Sheik's death generated questions and conflicts over leadership and ideology and how this eventually led to divisions within Alayhim. Those who supported Zumra, his newly voiced rejection of *du'a* and *dhikr* (supplication and prayer to Allah), and his emphasis on a strict work ethic joined him in establishing Awra Amba, while those who believed in a continuation of the religious rituals remained with Alayhim.

The same evening, I am back in Awra Amba, in the small, simple, but clean room I have rented in the guesthouse. As I sit on my bed, which is neatly covered by textiles produced by the Awra Amba community, I write in my field notes: *After a week of fieldwork in Awra Amba, it was a relief to come to Alayhim. It was great to feel welcomed and included and to have free access to information. The contrast between the two communities is remarkable. In Alayhim, people seemed to be speaking freely.* This conclusion was not only rooted in the informal interview I had had with the elders when we first arrived in Sinko. Following our conversation, the elders had invited us for coffee. Foziya had enthusiastically taken me by the arm and carefully guided me through the village to a small thatched hut, which she, as we arrived, had explained was their mosque. "It is Friday, and time for prayer," she had said, before she had invited me to sit down and join a circle of women. In a moment, one woman had passed me a scarf, which the elderly woman sitting next to me had arranged in a motherly manner so that it properly covered my hair. Seated on a pillow, only partially able to follow the quick chatter in the room, I had good time to observe. A long curtain divided the hut into two separate areas. I had bent sideways to peak behind the curtain to get a glimpse of the men's section and to make sure that Belay, my research assistant and an Orthodox Christian, was okay. The men were small-talking and chewing khat.

But it was in the women's section, visible the very moment you entered the hut, where things were happening. After we all had been served a piece of bread and a cup of coffee, Foziya entered the middle of the circle. The women stretched their hands forward with palms up, signaling that they were ready to receive blessings, and started chanting "amen." A little hesitant, I imitated them. Foziya then turned to each of us one by one, kneeled, and took our hands in her hands and kissed them before uttering a blessing. It was a mystical, almost sacred moment that took me ten years back to the day when I had been blessed by a dozen local Muslim women in the small rural town in the lowlands of Bale where my family and I had been living for almost two years. As I began to make final preparations to leave the town, I had invited a group of women—many of whom had become my friends—for a farewell party. Their blessing came as a surprise and it had been a very emotional and touching moment.

The ritual activities in the small, intimate space of the mosque, which I later realized had many of the signs and elements characteristic of a *zar* session, "the beliefs and practices associated with a particular type of spirit" (Kenyon 1995, 107), called me back to the present. Following Foziya's blessing, the women started passing around a small woven basket filled with khat leaves. After a few minutes of chewing and chatting, a woman brought a white beaded necklace that she put around Foziya's neck and a *gabi*—a white, handspun cotton blanket—that she wrapped around her. Then, Foziya started chanting. Soon the rest of the women followed her, alternately repeating the same phrases over and over again, as she continued leading them in prayer.

Alayhim Salatu'llah
Alayhim Salamu'llah[3]

No sounds came from the men's section.

Hidden Relations

How can we best make sense, respectively, of the alternative narrative that the members of the Alayhim community shared with me and the contrasting fieldwork experiences I had in the Awra Amba and Alayhim communities? One could argue, on the one hand, that it is likely that the stories that members of the Alayhim community told were colored by the fact that they live in the shadow of Awra Amba, a community that has been able to build their reputation as a successful and self-sustained model village. As I have already hinted, and as Chapter 8 reveals, Awra Amba's status as a model village has given them advantages that other communities do not have, including benefits that often follow when one is recognized by both the Ethiopian state and the international donor community. It is therefore likely that the openness and what at first glance may appear as an unconditional hospitality in Alayhim may have been influenced and fueled by their interest in receiving proper recognition. My status as a *ferenji* and the assumed economic possibilities that are associated with this identity in a country that is heavily aid dependent, may not only have colored the ways they welcomed and treated me but also the stories they told. The motivation of the various actors with whom I have been interacting during my research is certainly something that has been on my mind. While this is a methodological challenge to which there is no straightforward solution, my approach has been to listen to the multiple stories and voices with an open mind, while at the same time privileging stories that are consistent and confirmed by multiple, independent sources.

The historical links and the ideological similarities between Awra Amba and Alayhim, are, as already shown, not recognized in the official Awra Amba story. In fact, when I started asking questions about Alayhim during my first week of fieldwork, many of the Awra Amba community members—some of whom turned out to be close family members of Sheik Saide—claimed that they had never heard about the place. Some community members even displayed signs of uneasiness and fear when I mentioned Alayhim. I soon understood that I was crossing a line—that I was talking about something that should not be talked about. The secrecy and containment associated with Alayhim was evident in a conversation I had with a representative from the ANRS Bureau of Culture and Tourism who, when I first asked him about Alayhim, claimed he had never heard about it. When he realized that I had visited Alayhim and knew about its links to Awra Amba, his response revealed that he was well aware of its existence. In a rather confident and somewhat offensive manner, he concluded our conversation: "You will never be able to prove that there is a connection." In this way, he indirectly signaled the importance of keeping the relationship between the two communities hidden. During my second fieldwork, several community members, including Zumra and individuals who a year earlier had denied any knowledge about Alayhim, confirmed but downplayed this relationship.

How are we to make sense of the secrecy and the silencing of Awra Amba's historical connection to Alayhim? Can it tell us something about Awra Amba and its status as a model? It is worth mentioning here that studies of other idealized communities have revealed similar practices of secrecy and control. According to Helen Jarvis (2017, 125), who conducted research in the Danish Freetown of Christiania, "the practice of steering guests and external enquiries to a 'representative Christianite' is widespread." Drawing on Scott (1990), she argues that "hiding unpleasant stories is widely recognized as a 'hidden transcript' of resistance, a survival strategy of informal urbanism in a life lived under pressure" (Jarvis 2017, 125). Secrets and lies are also, as Luise White (2000, 15) has argued, "extraordinarily rich historical sources. [. . .] [They] signal that what has been declared secret, what has been deemed worthy of a lie or a cover story, is more significant than other stories and other ways of telling." They are "explanations about the past that are negotiated for specific audiences, for specific ends" and they "reveal a shifting terrain of ideas about danger, about risk, about importance, and about the public meaning of those conditions" (15). I will in the following sections argue that the invisibility of the Alayhim connection in the official Awra Amba narrative and the various efforts made to deny and conceal the links to a religious past are not only closely linked to Awra Amba's model status. The silencing also represents a key element of model making, and is, hence, part of what makes Awra Amba a model.

Model "Making"

Fields such as science and economics offer perspectives on how models come into being that also are applicable to models and model making within the policy world. These fields can help us elucidate the silences, evasions, and concealments behind the making of Awra Amba as a model. Let me illustrate my point by turning to the Edgeworth Box, a mathematical model developed by economists in the late nineteenth century. In her book *The World in the Model: How Economists Work and Think*, Mary S. Morgan[4] (2012) reproduces an account of the Edgeworth Box given by Professor Arnold Merkies as part of his retirement lecture at the Free University of Amsterdam in 1997. In this account, Merkies uses an artistic visualization he developed in collaboration with Koen Engelen to show how model making is a process of simplification, isolation, abstraction, and idealization.[5] I will use Merkies's illustrations to show how we can apply these concepts to understand how models come into being within the policy field.

First, model making is, as illustrated in figure 4.1, about simplifying and looking closely at some detail of a complex world (Morgan 2012, 101). This is, as has been shown by phenomenology, a natural part of the human cognitive process. It is the way in which we cope with the complexity and the plethora of stimuli we encounter as part of being in the world.

We then isolate a small part of the world. In figure 4.2, we can see how two individuals, each with their unique characteristics, have been selected as the model's key elements. The possessions that surround each of them provide information about two individuals who have different interests, educational backgrounds, and professional lives. However, these possessions tell

Figure 4.1. Zooming in. Reproduced with permission from Arnold Merkies and Koen Engelen.

Figure 4.2 Isolation. Reproduced with permission from Arnold Merkies and Koen Engelen.

us little about the wider social, economic, political, and cultural contexts in which the two are situated. We see in this illustration the beginning of how "the real world is shorn away" (Morgan 2012, 101).

In figure 4.3, we see an even more radical isolation and simplification of the two persons and their possessions. We are now looking at a woman who holds two bottles of wine and a man who is standing next to a pile of cheese. This is a simplified version of the lived-in world, where each person is left with only one commodity. It is a world where "goods become shadows and people lose their detailed character" (Morgan 2012, 101); where disruptive elements or noise have been eliminated or filtered out (Dalmedico 2007).

In Merkies's final illustration (fig. 4.4), where the two individuals are invisible and only the two commodities remain, we see a complete simplification and idealization. Made to explain and predict commodity exchange, this is a model where the complexities of the lived-in world have been "idealized away" (Morgan 2012, 279). Here, it is important to bear in mind that what has been deducted or taken away is not pre-established; these processes are partly political—influenced by the interests and worldview of those who construct the model. Model making as idealization is, in other words, dictated by or influenced by a specific paradigm—what we also could call the controlling model—that determines what is considered salient and what is not.

I do not suggest that Merkies's analysis of the Edgeworth Box can be uncritically adapted to model making within the policy world. Yet, these illustrations and the discussion of model making as a process of simplification, isolation, abstraction, and idealization point to some characteristics that are also highly relevant for how policy models come into being. The extraction of "miracle mechanisms" and erasure of context is, for example, something that Olivier de Sardan, Diarra, and Moha (2017, 72) discuss as a key feature of the traveling model: "The model is manufactured around a causal mechanism that is considered by experts as an explanation for the success of the founding experience. This mechanism is supposed to guarantee the intrinsic effectiveness of the model, regardless of the new contexts in which it will be implemented. It will be disseminated in other contexts by networks combining experts and decision-makers and supported by international institutions." Hence, in the same vein as in the sciences and economics, model making within the policy world is about idealization. This is, as I have already indicated, a selective process, where certain desirable elements of reality are

Figure 4.3 Eliminating noise. Reproduced with permission from Arnold Merkies and Koen Engelen.

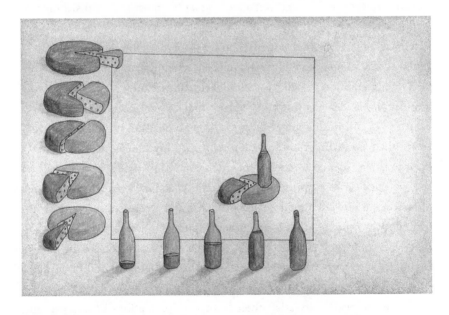

Figure 4.4 Idealization. Reproduced with permission from Arnold Merkies and Koen Engelen.

accentuated, while elements that disrupt or create complexity are erased or made invisible to create an ideal type or utopia. I would like to emphasize that the process of model making, to varying degrees, is a result of deliberate acts consciously undertaken by rational subjects. As "an always unstable assemblage of organic, social, and structural forces and lines of flight that at once shape and are shaped by their milieus" (Biehl and Locke 2017, 8), even a pre-planned, carefully designed model such as the NESTown project will always be in a process of becoming. In other words, models are not completed, homogenous products that can be uncritically exported without friction from one location to another. In order for us to understand what goes into model making, it is pivotal to explore the myriad processes—both intentional and unintentional—and the agents, materials, and conditions that are involved.

Religion—A Contested Issue

In this chapter, we have seen how model making, as a process of idealization, implies an erasure of elements that may disturb a highly simplified, clean model. And I have argued that in the Awra Amba case, Alayhim and its historical connections to Awra Amba are among the most salient disruptive elements that have been filtered out or eliminated from the model. But why, and for whom, is Alayhim potential noise? Why is it so important that Awra Amba's connection to Alayhim remain in the shadows?

First, in addition to being a potential threat to Zumra's legitimacy as the founder and leader of a just and gender-equal community—an aspect I will return to in full in Chapter 8—the Alayhim connection complicates a well-established, powerful origin story. It disturbs the myth of foundation that has been constructed around Zumra: that Awra Amba emerged spontaneously on its own because of Zumra's charismatic and visionary leadership. This idea of pristine origins, of a model without a past and a context, is key to establishing Awra Amba's status as an authentic and compelling model—a model that deserves to go viral. Keeping the Alayhim connection out of the picture is important to maintain the existing model *of* and to prevent potential audiences from realizing that Awra Amba is actually a model *for*, a contingent assemblage put together to satisfy their desires and projections. This is, perhaps, the most pressing reason why Alayhim has been thrust into the background. But one could also argue that the secrecy and silencing that surrounds Alayhim is linked to the fact that it is a Sufi-inspired Muslim community. It is here we must understand that religion, and particularly Islam, is a contested issue, not only in the Ethiopian context, but also in the global gender and development discourse. Let me first turn to the latter.

Feminist activists and the women's rights movement have often treated religion as an antithesis to gender equality and women's empowerment. This rather negative, suspicious attitude toward religion is not limited, however, to feminist and women's rights actors. It is to a considerable extent part of the modern policy regime. I showed in the previous chapter how model villages and other technologies of modern biopower emerged out of pastoral power, and how religious practices that were originally associated with pastoral care for the soul and salvation became secularized. A "series of 'worldly' aims took the place of the religious aims" (Foucault 1982, 784), and sociopolitical authorities were no longer grounded in God but in the rational activities of the modern bureaucratic state. In a context where the legitimacy of policy ideas and models is determined by scientific knowledge and rationality, the continued presence of religion in the public sphere becomes problematic; it is a sign of a stubborn traditional, primitive mindset that is not in line with modernist notions of progress and individual autonomy.

While one could argue that what has been termed the "turn to religion" (Butler et al. 2011) in our modern world challenges the secularization thesis—the belief that as societies progress, particularly through modernization and rationalization, religion loses its authority in all aspects of social life and governance—religion remains a contested issue. This is certainly the case when it comes to women's rights and gender equality.[6] In particular, Islam is commonly seen as a threat to the modern liberal feminist project. This has been fueled by Islam's contested status in the global scene, where the othering and depiction of Muslims and Muslim societies as violent and oppressive have been framed with special reference to women's rights and gender equality (Abu-Lughod 2002; Hirschkind and Mahmood 2002). As Lila Abu-Lughod (1993, 2009) has shown, the veiled Muslim woman is commonly cast as vulnerable, oppressed, and in need of salvation. While these generalized images of Islam, and of Muslim women in particular, have been challenged by feminist anthropologists (Mahmood 2005), the dominant global narrative remains that of the oppressed Muslim woman and of Islam as incompatible with secular, liberal values. The story of a Muslim Sufi sheik, living in the heart of the Christian-dominated highlands of Northern Ethiopia, who as early as the

1960s was a proponent of what could be called liberal, progressive values, is hence deeply disruptive for a movement that "has capitalized on conceptions of African savagery and Islamic anti-woman ideology" (Merry 2003, 58), and it partly explains why the process of abstraction and idealization takes place. Presenting Awra Amba as having an "immaculate conception" preserves stereotypes about Africa and Islam while advancing a model that is emancipatory and compatible with Western ideals of subjectivity. Simultaneously, because the model emerges locally, policy makers who promote it can argue that they are free from colonialist bias.

In order to fully grasp why Alayhim is a potentially disruptive element, we also need to pay attention to Islam's status in Ethiopia. Like Christianity, Islam has a long history in Ethiopia, where the relationship between the two religions has often been described as one of coexistence and mutual tolerance. Scholars of Islam in Ethiopia have increasingly challenged and problematized such a depiction (Desplat and Østebø 2013; Dereje Feyissa and Lawrence 2014; Abbink 1998). They have argued that Islam has always had a secondary status in Ethiopia and that the seemingly peaceful coexistence has only been made possible "because of an asymmetric relationship between Christians and Muslims, in which the former controlled the main political institutions and defined the latter as second-class citizens" (Østebø 2013, 1036). The regime change in 1991 and the new constitution of 1995 introduced "religious freedoms . . . at an unprecedented scale" (Haustein and Østebø 2011, 756). While this implied greater recognition of Muslims in Ethiopia and included state-led promotion and support of *neberu Islimina*—a term that "refers to a home-grown, native, or a traditional form of Ethiopian Islam" (Østebø 2013, 1042), of which Alayhim could serve as an example—the othering of Muslims by a Christian majority still remains in a country that commonly has been portrayed as an island of Christianity in a sea of Islam.

Islam's secondary status in Ethiopia, particularly in the northern, Christian-dominated highlands where Awra Amba and Alayhim are located, could therefore partly explain the secrecy and silencing of the link between the two communities. If the relationship between Alayhim and Awra Amba became known to the greater Ethiopian public, this could jeopardize Awra Amba's legitimacy as a national model *for* and *of* gender equality and sustainable development. The official Awra Amba narrative is colored by the "social and narratological expectations" (White 2000, 19) that Zumra and his inner circle of story tellers hold. Their imagined audience—from the Ethiopian government to NGO representatives and elites to tourists and visitors—determines what they tell and what they do not tell. Their narrative is strategic, reflecting a politically savvy leadership. As a former member of the Awra Amba cooperative once told me: "Zumra has always known how to position himself and adjust his ideas in alignment with political currents."

Here, one should also remember that both Christians and Muslims have historically looked upon the Alayhim community with great suspicion. As mentioned earlier, the imprisonment of Sheik Saide came as a result of considerable opposition against the Alayhim community from other neighboring Muslim communities. One could therefore anticipate that Awra Amba's legitimacy would be further jeopardized by the fact that Alayhim is a minority within a minority. To conceal historical links to Alayhim, a highly marginalized and at time persecuted community, could hence be a means of self-protection. The fact that Awra Amba once was an ostracized community makes it perhaps even more important for them to preserve the wide recognition the community currently holds. This raises ethical questions for me as a researcher. Is it unethical to write about and reveal this connection? If I do, whose interests do I serve? When I explore what being and becoming a traveling model has meant for Awra Amba in Chapter 8, I will strive to answer these vital questions.

But how and why did Awra Amba become a traveling model in the first place? These are the questions I turn to in the next two chapters.

Chapter 5
Modes of Transmission

IT IS HARD TO RECALL in detail how and when I came across Emily's[1] name and read about her involvement with the Finnish EdTech company Lyfta. Since it happened on an ordinary day, not during one of my many intensive fieldwork periods, I have not recorded it in my field notes. So, I have to rely on my headnotes. Thinking back, I believe I first read about Emily on Twitter. One day in spring 2018, I received a message from Twitter, one of those nudging emails that the company sends out about popular tweets by people with whom, according to its algorithms, I am closely connected. Out of pure boredom (I am not particularly fond of Twitter and not an active user), I ended up following a link to an article tweeted by Lyfta's CEOs and producers Paulina Tervo and Serdar Ferit. My arbitrary hanging out on Twitter was not a waste of time. It was how I found out that *The Awra Amba Experience* had entered American classrooms.

The Awra Amba Experience is an interactive, web-based documentary that follows the "click here and go there" logic (Aston and Gaudenzi 2012, 127), allowing users to visit and explore the village on a digital device such as a computer, phone, or tablet. It is one of twenty-five storyworlds that currently exist on Lyfta, a digital learning platform that contains immersive educational stories and lesson plans intended for use in K–12 education. Inspired by Lyfta's overall aim—to foster global citizenship skills and empathy—these stories are designed to stimulate and generate discussions on a wide range of topics linked to the SDGs. Lyfta, which is a subscription-based platform, is currently used by more than 350 schools in the UK, Finland, and the United States. Since its establishment in 2016, the company has received numerous awards, including the 2017 UN World Summit Award for Education and Learning. *The Awra Amba Experience* is Lyfta's flagship product and grew out of Paulina

Tervo's documentary with the catchy title of "Awra Amba—Utopia in Ethiopia," that was released in 2010.[2]

"It was Rachel,[3] a young woman who worked for a non-profit organization in DC, who introduced me to Awra Amba," Emily tells me when I, six months after I first came across her name on Twitter, meet her for the first time on Zoom. She is an associate professor of education at an American university who is passionate about educating teachers on how to best incorporate social studies and global issues into the school system. "I met Rachel at an academic conference a couple of years back. She came up to me after I had given a presentation on how to integrate global issues into elementary education. We shared an interest in the SDGs as a framework for elementary school teaching and learning, so I gave her my business card," Emily explains, before she details how she, a few months later, received an email from Rachel about a team of filmmakers who were documenting the story of Awra Amba, "an outside-the-box village" in Ethiopia. Rachel's description of and enthusiasm for Awra Amba as a potential model for social, economic, and environmental sustainability intrigued Emily. "So, I got in touch with Lyfta's producers, and while attending an SDGs conference in Finland in fall 2017, I even had the chance to meet with them. Shortly after, I was piloting Lyfta with teachers and students at elementary schools in my area."

The networking at an academic conference between two women, a relationship established through a shared passion for teaching global justice and sustainability to American children, and an algorithmically generated email related to my Twitter activity, offer a glimpse of the ways in which models and ideas travel in an increasingly transnational and digital policy world. In this chapter, I explore the vehicles and infrastructure—the multiple pathways and the networks of actors and vectors—that have facilitated the spread of Awra Amba as a transnational model for gender equality and sustainable development. To use an epidemiological term, we can refer to these pathways and networks as the traveling model's *modes of transmission*. Just as a virus does, the model moves and spreads in multiple, complex, and often unpredictable ways. A virus may, for example, be transmitted from person to person through direct contact; by biological vectors such as insects; through air, water, or food; or via material things such as a doorknob or a syringe. The messiness and multimedia that frequently characterize a virus's modes of transmission are good to think with when analyzing what has facilitated Awra Amba's virality.

In the first part of this chapter, I explore the role that various human actors play in spreading and translating the Awra Amba model. In addition to detailing how conventional policy actors, and in particular expert communities and professional groups, act as vectors, I discuss the role that non-conventional policy actors play in circulating, mediating, and translating the model. While it certainly is crucial to identify the various actors who are involved and to analyze the role that they play in the policy world, a one-sided focus on "who mobilizes policy" (McCann 2011, 113ff.) is, however, problematic. In addition to narrowly defining certain typologies, models, and conceptions of what constitutes policy, a categorization and analysis of various policy actors could easily prevent us from analyzing "the social processes that constitute policy transfer" (McCann 2011, 111). As I intend to show in this chapter, the different actors who contribute to the spread of the Awra Amba model are deeply embedded in relational, fluid, and complex processes that bring together multiple and heterogeneous elements—human and non-human—"in particular ways and for particular purposes" (McCann and Ward 2012, 328). In other words, they are part of the messy processes and constellation of actors, things, desires, and unpredictable events and relations that constitute the Awra Amba viral assemblage.

Policy Actors and Translators

Who picks up and mobilizes policy ideas and models? This question has been much explored and debated within policy studies. The traditional policy literature emphasizes the role that "transfer agents" (Stone 2004, 545ff.) and "global policy advocates" (Orenstein 2003, 273) play in circulating policy ideas and models. Several scholars have attempted to categorize these agents into typologies. Diane Stone (2004) identified three sets of actors that drive these processes: states, international organizations, and non-state actors. A more comprehensive framework for analyzing policy transfer—a term commonly used to describe how national policy making elites "import innovatory policy developed elsewhere in the belief that it will be similarly successful in a different context" (Stone 1999, 52)—has been developed by David P. Dolowitz and David Marsh (2000). They identified nine main categories of political actors involved in the process: "elected officials, political parties, bureaucrats/civil servants, pressure groups, policy entrepreneurs and experts, transnational corporations, think tanks, supra-national governmental and non-governmental institutions and consultants" (10).

Critical policy studies and anthropological studies of policy mobility also tend to have a strong focus on the role that experts and professional groups play in picking up and spreading policy ideas and models. This is, for example, reflected in the traveling model literature:

> A model always has at its root a founding experience (a success story) somewhere in the world, which international experts seize on to spread it beyond its original context. The model is manufactured around a causal mechanism that is considered by experts as an explanation for the success of the founding experience. This mechanism is supposed to guarantee the intrinsic effectiveness of the model, regardless of the new contexts in which it will be implemented. It will be disseminated in other contexts by networks combining experts and decision-makers and supported by international institutions (Olivier de Sardan, Diarra, and Moha 2017, 74).

The role that experts play in circulating traveling models is also highlighted in the works of Richard Rottenburg and his colleagues (Behrends, Park, and Rottenburg 2014a; Rottenburg 2009). While they acknowledge that various individuals can be mediators or carriers of a model, they maintain that carriers "are best represented by professional groups or experts who appropriate a model and relate it to their understanding of both the model's origin and the intention, and the situation into which it is supposed to be immersed" (Behrends, Park, and Rottenburg 2014b, 14). This does not mean that they disregard the agency of non-human actors. According to Rottenburg (2009, xxvii), the models themselves "acquire an agency of their own precisely because they are disseminated and duplicated and in this process come to be endowed with an authority to define the best solution to a particular problem." This latter point illustrates that although the traveling model literature and the conventional policy literature maintain a strong emphasis on human actors as the model's carriers or vectors, the two bodies of literature differ significantly in terms of how they conceive of the model and of what happens when a policy idea or model start traveling.

The conventional policy transfer literature assumes that policies and models are static, value-neutral products of rational and intentional decision-making processes, and that they move from point A to point B in a linear manner. Anthropologists and scholars situated within the emerging field of critical policy studies paint a much more complex picture (Shore and Wright 2011; Peck and Theodore 2010), paying attention to the agentic power of the model and the changes that emerge as it starts traveling. Not only does the travel change the model, but, as the model is disembedded and re-embedded, its place of origin and the location in which it is newly implanted also change (Behrends, Park, and Rottenburg 2014b). These changes are, as we shall see in Chapter 8, often unexpected and unintentional and may even contradict the ideals and norms that gave the model its status in the first place. Inspired by science and technology studies, particularly its attention to "practices of knowing and practices of ordering the world . . . [as] inseparably interconnected and mediated by social and material technologies" (Behrends, Park, and Rottenburg 2014b, 2), anthropologists who employ the traveling model as an analytical category see translation as a key feature of these processes. In fact, Behrends, Park, and Rottenburg (2014b) argue that the model, as "an element of an ontological, epistemic, normative or material order" (3), "cannot be transferred without being translated" (2). Translation, as the creative work to adapt a model to a new set of circumstances, thus becomes a precondition for policy mobility. Just as a text in English must be translated to Amharic for a speaker of that language to understand its meaning, a model also must be translated to the local conditions if it is to make sense for those among whom it is implemented. Reflecting the linguistic turn in anthropology, translation is viewed as a context-dependent, power-laden process of interpretation and negotiation that is subject to contestation. The ideas about translation reflected here are far more nuanced than the instrumental approach that is dominant in policy circles—that a good model is good for all times and places and that, therefore, there will not be any friction moving it from one place to another.

Expert communities and professional groups have certainly played a key role in disseminating and circulating the Awra Amba model. As shown in Chapter 3, representatives from international NGOs and the Ethiopian government played a crucial role in discovering Awra Amba and its potential as a model for gender equality and sustainable development. But Awra Amba is not only a site that attracts development practitioners, experts, and state bureaucrats. Actors in the educational sector have, for example, played a pivotal role in circulating, validating, and legitimating the community's ideas and way of life as a model or best practice. Public and private universities in Ethiopia organize tours to Awra Amba on a regular basis. A visit to Awra Amba is, for example, included in the curriculum for students who study tourism at the University of Gondar. They are taught and encouraged to incorporate a stop in Awra Amba when they, as future tour guides, travel with tourists between Lalibela and Gondar, two of the major tourist sites in the area. Furthermore, in 2011, Jimma University awarded Zumra an honorary doctorate degree, acknowledging his role as the founder of Awra Amba, his "progressive thinking," and his "contribution in creating a betterment in the lives of the community at grass root level."[4]

Academic institutions and educators are not only engaged in promoting and legitimizing the Awra Amba community and its values; they also act as translators and mediators. One of my interlocutors, a highly educated Ethiopian man in his forties who has lengthy experience working with international NGOs and in the educational sector both in Ethiopia and internationally, and who invited Zumra to speak at an event at Addis Ababa University (AAU), framed his engagement with Awra Amba in precisely such terms: "I see my contribution as building a bridge between Awra Amba and academic institutions. When I organized the lecture with Zumra at AAU, my objective was to create a stage where the Awra Amba community could share their knowledge and their lived experience, and where the university—students and faculty—also could question it." Similarly, researchers from the Sociology Department at the University of Gondar have, in addition to conducting research in Awra Amba, been involved in a project aimed at mediating between Awra Amba and its neighboring communities. In an interview with Public Radio International (PRI),[5] Ashenafi Alemu, one of the sociologists, described how the project brought together people from Awra Amba and members from the Christian and Muslim communities that surround the village and facilitated increased understanding between Awra Amba and its "hostile neighbors."[6] Taking for granted the unquestionable "goodness" of Awra Amba, we can here see how the involvement of expert communities and educators moves beyond translation and mediation and toward advocacy—defending the values of the model vis-à-vis its detractors and critics.

Indeed, it is important to acknowledge and analyze the role that expert communities and professional groups play in legitimizing, translating, and circulating models. Yet, a one-sided focus on these actors prevents us from exploring local actors or those who do not explicitly belong to the policy world. For example, Zumra himself does not fit nicely into any of the categories of policy experts and professional communities that commonly feature in the policy literature. Yet, as the founder and charismatic leader of the Awra Amba community, he plays a decisive role in promoting and circulating his community as a policy model. Together with his wife Enaney and other members of the welcoming committee, he conveys the Awra Amba story and communicates with the many visitors who arrive in the village. Since, as we saw in the previous chapter, this is a narrative of pristine origins, told by a figure who, in addition to being perceived as having extraordinary characteristics, is considered visionary and perhaps even prophetic, it is a compelling one that is likely to "infect" those who encounter it. A young Ethiopian woman who, as part of her work in an international NGO, has been involved with the community, highlighted these aspects when she described her very first visit to Awra Amba: "We spoke to Zumra, and we went around and visited the community. It exceeded my expectations, just talking to Zumra and seeing his thought processes and how he thinks; what kind of visionary man he was. Both me and my friend were really impressed and felt instantly that we had to do something to support."

While Zumra is the most visible figure and representative of Awra Amba, one should not underestimate the role of his wife Enaney. Some of my informants even argue that she tends to be the more outspoken of the two, particularly during public events. She is responsible for the community's public relations and plays a key role, negotiating and managing the community's partnerships with state and non-state actors. Her communicative skills and assertiveness were clearly evident during our first encounter. She is a powerful, well-positioned, and influential woman, and as we shall see in Chapter 8, it is unlikely that Awra Amba would have existed the way it does today had it not been for her and her father Kibret Siraj.

When it comes to making Awra Amba known beyond Ethiopia's borders, Paulina Tervo (hereafter Paulina), the Finnish-born film producer and co-CEO of Lyfta, has been most influential. A young man who used to have a central position in the cooperative described her role as follows: "She wrote about

Awra Amba on her website and was even interviewed by BBC. A lot of journalists and tourists would see her website, and a lot of people who wanted to know about Awra Amba would contact her first. She was one of the very first foreigners who came here, and she has visited our community multiple times." Paulina, who is a good example of a non-conventional policy actor, arrived in the community as a tourist in 2004, only a few years after the community had become a tourist destination. Capitalizing on her background as a filmmaker, she has spent the ten past years spreading the community's story and ideas, first through her documentary "Awra Amba—Utopia in Ethiopia" and more recently through her work with *The Awra Amba Experience* and Lyfta.

The Mobilizing Power of Things

While it is important to identify and analyze those who mobilize policy models and ideas, a one-sided focus on human actors and institutions risks overlooking the multiple material and sociotechnological relations and networks in which these actors are embedded. We also need to consider the role played by non-human actors and the mobilizing power of things such as a song, a newspaper article, a website, a YouTube video, a tweet, a mobile application, or, as we shall see below, Zumra's hat. Of course, as products of human creativity, these sites and objects are not disconnected from human actors. Yet, they may also act independently and beyond the control of their creators. This is why the notion of assemblage is helpful in elucidating various forms of agency.

Let us examine some of the material things and technologies that constitute the Awra Amba assemblage, starting with a more careful examination of Zumra. The traveling power Zumra holds as the community's founder and charismatic leader is not limited to him as a person or to the ideas and personal qualities that he presents to various national and international audiences. His appearance, particularly the green hat that he always wears, is also an important part of the heterogeneous assemblage of things, people, ideas, and technologies that make up the Awra Amba traveling model. In my first formal interview with him, I was curious to know more about the hat's history and meaning. I had only seen it worn by Zumra and another elderly man who often functions as his proxy. Interested in exploring whether the hat served as a symbol of authority, I asked Zumra why they were the only ones wearing it. Zumra downplayed the hat as a potential symbol of exclusivity and authority:

"We wish that all could wear it. In fact, everybody can wear it. There is no differentiation." But he also linked the hat and its history to the time when he, as a thirteen-year-old boy, was excluded from his family and wandered from place to place to attract followers: "I often slept near trees. I loved those trees. I wear the hat, in order to remember the trees. The hat sends a message about the importance of trees. Let's cover all land with green trees. Whoever accepts this idea can wear the hat." Zumra's comments reveal how the hat is nested in a web of multiple relations and meanings. While downplaying the role of the hat as a symbol of authority, thus echoing the community's ideas of equality and democracy, he also links the hat to the history of how he, as an ostracized wanderer, struggled to attract followers. Hence, he establishes it as a reminder of humble origins and a symbol of his role and legitimacy as the community's founder and leader. Zumra's expressive praise and love for trees also speak of a close relationship to and appreciation of nature. Here, it is interesting to note that his call to "cover all land with green trees" fits well with the green wave discourse that is so integral to contemporary political discussions and movements for sustainable development. One could, moreover, speculate whether his praise for trees is reflective of a deeper and more religious-oriented relationship, as the tree is a common symbol in many religious traditions.

Zumra's green hat is a key symbol, not only for the Awra Amba community and its status as a model for equality and sustainability but also for Zumra and his role as a leader. As a mark of distinction, uniqueness, and authenticity, the hat is an important material object in the Awra Amba assemblage, facilitating the model's circulation. We could perhaps even say that the hat is an un/intentional branding icon. A scene from a short film that documents Zumra and Enaney's participation at Slow Food USA's Terra Madre Salone de Gusto, a conference held in Turin, Italy in 2016, is illustrative in this regard.[7] In the scene, we see Zumra and Enaney standing in the lobby of the conference hall. Zumra's bright green hat makes them stand out clearly in the crowd. One of my interlocutors, an Ethiopian American woman who has invested much time and resources in the community, also attributed her initial contact with Awra Amba to Zumra's and Enaney's physical appearance. "I was at the Hilton Hotel in Addis Ababa and saw them standing in the lobby. They didn't look like the typical Hilton visitors. They really stood out in that context, so I approached them." Borrowing from Louis Althusser's (1971, 115) work on ideology, we may say that the hat serves to "interpellate," to call forth attentive subjects and, as such, it has a clear promotional function. Thus, Zumra's hat demonstrates the material "substrate" that is necessary to disseminate a model, an infrastructure that the literature on policymaking and circulation, even that which takes into account the role of translators and mediators, tends to ignore.

We should keep in mind, however, that the hat itself does not convey anything special. For example, if it were disconnected from Zumra, lying on the floor, people may not even recognize that it is a hat.[8] While the hat's properties would remain the same—its shape, color, and texture—its capacity to convey uniqueness and authority is lost. But, placed on Zumra's head, it is one of several elements that compose a larger whole—an assemblage. For example, Zumra and his hat can be compared to the "man-animal-weapon, man-horse-bow assemblage" (Deleuze and Guattari 1987, 404). Just like the nomad warrior with his fast-moving horse and bow, an emergent whole that is part of a larger assemblage of warriors (the nomad army), Zumra with his green hat is an assemblage—perhaps even a branding assemblage—within the larger Awra Amba assemblage.

Given Awra Amba's status as a peaceful, utopian community, reputed to be exempt from conflicts, it may seem paradoxical to compare Zumra with the nomad warrior. But the nomad warrior analogy is, of course, not to be taken literally. Deleuze and Guattari used the example of the nomad warrior to illustrate how assemblages are dynamic and made up of heterogeneous elements from "different realms of reality: the personal, the biological, and the technical" (DeLanda 2016, 68) that interact and form new wholes with emergent properties and collective abilities. Zumra's role and his legitimacy as a leader of the Awra Amba community are conditioned on material, technical, and human relations. Zumra would not have been able to establish the Awra Amba community by himself. The recognition of others has sustained his position and the community's model status. This recognition would not have emerged had it not been for the land on which the community resides, the community's infrastructure, and the story of a unique, gender-equal community that allows for visitors to engage in immersive experiences.

To think of and analyze Zumra as an assemblage is useful since it allows us to "capture the complex interactions between levels" and "the nested set of assemblages" (DeLanda 2016, 69) that make up the Awra Amba model. In addition to revealing the reductionism inherent in analyses that one-sidedly focus on the role of human actors in mobilizing and spreading policy models and ideas, the analytics of the assemblage allows for the recognition of the multiple identities and material and human relations that make up what, at first sight, may appear as a homogenous whole or a single actor. Let me explain by examining the role of Salem Mekuria, another actor in the Awra Amba assemblage.

Salem Mekuria is an Ethiopian American film director and a professor emerita in the Art Department at Wellesley College, Massachusetts. She is also the author of the photo essay "Awra Amba: A Model 'Utopian' Community in Ethiopia" found in *Global Africa: Into the Twenty-First Century*, an introductory textbook to African studies. In an earlier draft of this chapter, I had placed my description of her engagement in the section that details the role researchers and academic institutions play in spreading and translating the Awra Amba model. But Salem's engagement with Awra Amba is not limited to her role as an academic. As a film director, she has produced two shorter documentaries about Awra Amba, both available on Vimeo.[9] She has also initiated fundraising activities—both within and outside Ethiopia—for various development schemes implemented in the village. She is, for instance, involved with some of the architects behind the NESTown project, who, as described in Chapter 3, plan to construct a second model town in Awra Amba. In an interview with her in 2019, Salem Mekuria described herself as having a mediating role: "I am involved to make sure that the Awra Amba community has a central role in the planning and the design of the new model town." Fluent in both Amharic and English, she exemplifies how members of the diaspora, as bicultural mediators, often take on the role of translators or brokers. Based on her multiple identities, engagements, and relations, we could say that Salem illustrates what it means to be a Friend of Awra Amba. This is also how she self-identifies. As a Friend of Awra Amba, Salem is another example of an assemblage within the larger Awra Amba assemblage, in the sense that she plays multiple roles, linking various networks that promote and disseminate the model to diverse audiences. She is, however, not the only one who identifies as a Friend of Awra Amba. In fact, the majority of my interviewees who, following a visit to Awra Amba became involved in promoting and supporting the community, claimed they were part of the Friends of Awra Amba group. The group is difficult to pin down, as it is not a formalized organization nor is it a close-knit network. In fact, several of those I have talked with do not know about each other. The majority of those who label themselves as Friends of Awra Amba are Ethiopians, mainly urban elites who reside in Addis Ababa or in the diaspora. A Facebook group promotes activities organized by Friends of Awra Amba, but apart from offering information about different initiatives, such as an art workshop organized for children in Awra Amba in the summer of 2015 and various fundraising schemes, both in Ethiopia and abroad, the page does not reveal much and does not have a clearly identifiable administrator. The group has more than 900 unidentified followers.

Many of the individuals who identity as Friends of Awra Amba hold formal positions in NGOs. Some of them have used their positions and their networks to raise financial support for Awra Amba. For instance, members of Friends of Awra Amba facilitated Zumra and Enaney's trip to the Slow Food USA conference in Italy in 2016. Others tend to emphasize their role as volunteers and downplay their positioning in the NGO community. One of my interlocutors, who is employed with an international NGO, emphasized that he, in his interactions with the community, always made sure he comes as a private person. "As Friends of Awra Amba, we understand that care should be taken in order to maintain its authenticity. I never attempted to support them with funding from NGOs, and I did not want to join them as an employee of an NGO. I joined them in my own personal capacity." This does not mean, however, that his support was only ideological and moral in character. By the end of the interview, he revealed that he had actively participated in various fundraising activities. Yet, the emphasis on authenticity reflected in his statement reveals a paradox that makes the traveling model possible: while Awra Amba enters multiple global and transnational "lines of flight" (Deleuze and Guattari 1987) through the activities of various policy actors and various media platforms, it presents itself and is perceived as a local reality, a model *of* devoid of all the contaminants of international capital and media. This assertion of local autonomy and grassroots origins is critical to its authority as a utopian model.

Mediascapes

While assemblage thinking allows us to recognize how heterogeneous elements from different realms of reality come together in a messy and multi-relational, sociotechnological network, the role that the media have played in circulating the Awra Amba traveling model deserves particular attention. As I already have indicated, a diverse array of media technologies and outlets have facilitated the spread of Awra Amba as a transnational model for gender equality and sustainable development. In the following section, I look deeper into some of these media outlets, both digital and printed.

In Ethiopia, Awra Amba's dissemination among the general public has been facilitated by various national broadcasting channels and through pop culture. We have already seen that in the early 2000s the government-owned TV channel aired the first Awra Amba documentary, making Awra Amba known throughout the country. Zumra has also been a guest in national TV programs, including the talk shows Arhibu and Who's Who. Furthermore, in 2006, a popular Ethiopian singer, Ahmed Teshome, released the album Eyorika, which featured a song about Awra Amba.[10] The song, which became a hit, tells the story of a young man from Addis Ababa who has fallen in love with a girl from Awra Amba.

The song is full of references from the Awra Amba official narrative, plays on key imaginaries commonly associated with the community, and offers nothing but praise for Zumra and the community's values. For example, in the song, the young man promises to bake *injera* and spin cotton—activities that are commonly performed by women but have become the trademark of the gender-equality model that the Awra Amba community has become known for. In addition to praising the egalitarian and democratic values that Zumra promotes, the lyrics also convey an idealization of the simplicity and authenticity of rural life versus the meretriciousness and conflictive nature of city life. Awra Amba is a place where love and peace prevail, where people express their emotions and ideas freely, and where there is mutual and intra-religious understanding. The way Zumra is portrayed in the song is a paradox, however. Not only is he rightly presiding over this peaceful traditional place; he is also the one whose acceptance and blessing will pave the way for the young couple's love and unification. In other words, it juxtaposes a gender-equal place with an all-powerful patriarchal authority.

The extent to which this song has played a role in circulating the ideas of the Awra Amba community in Ethiopia, can, however, be questioned. My research assistant, Belay, did not realize that this popular song was about Awra Amba until I asked him for a translation. He had heard it many times, but even after working alongside me as I conducted fieldwork in Awra Amba, he had not realized that Ahmed Teshome was singing about Awra Amba. Another friend of mine had the same reaction when I showed her the music video on YouTube. "I know this, but I never paid attention to the lyrics," she said in surprise. She claimed that the song, typically played during weddings, at dance parties, or on the radio, was not the type of song that called your attention to the lyrics. While it is not possible to draw a firm conclusion based on these two individual reflections, they do indicate, however, that musical forms and rhythmic elements can be vectors in the circulation of models and ideas.

Promotional materials of a more conventional character also constitute part of the Awra Amba assemblage. The ANRS Bureau of Culture and Tourism has, for example, produced a DVD and developed brochures and small booklets that detail the community's history, values, and lifestyle. When I met with a government official in the Department of Cultural Heritage and Tourism Development in 2015, he emphasized the office's continued support and involvement in the community: "We have done a lot to develop Awra Amba as a tourist site. We have trained them on how to handle tourists and developed promotional materials in order to attract tourists. I am not sure how available these materials are at this time, though." While the government's promotional efforts, as illustrated here, may have had limited reach due to inadequate resources and a weak distribution program, other informational sources have had a far more important impact, at least when it comes to attracting international visitors. As early as 2006, Awra Amba was listed and described as a place worth visiting in the Bradt *Ethiopia* travel guide,[11] which will likely remain popular as long as internet connectivity is as limited and unreliable as it is today. That being said, social media applications such as Tripadvisor are becoming increasingly relevant as sources of information for tourists planning to visit Ethiopia. For example, during my first fieldwork in Awra Amba in 2015, I met a young couple from Israel who said they had learned about Awra Amba through a WhatsApp group for Israeli backpackers traveling in Ethiopia. Awra Amba is also listed on Airbnb and figures as a destination on the web pages of domestic and international tour operators. Additionally, as I mentioned in the Introduction, there are numerous web articles and travel blogs that detail the community's history and emphasize its unique qualities.[12]

When it comes to the spread of Awra Amba through social media platforms, YouTube is the most effective and far-reaching carrier. Several documentaries, a BBC interview with Paulina, and the Arhibu episode that features Zumra are available here. YouTube is also the platform Paulina used when she first released her documentary "Awra Amba—Utopia in Ethiopia" in 2010. Almost ten years later, in June 2019, the film had been viewed over 130,000 times. The launching of the documentary through YouTube was, as illustrated in this excerpt from an interview Paulina gave on Collabdocs,[13] a strategic and deliberate move:

> I didn't have a distributor or a broadcaster, so it was very much thinking outside the box, how can I distribute this film. I had tried all the obvious channels, so I then thought, well, if we release it globally, on a day that everybody's thinking about women's rights . . . so we released it on International Women's Day. I phoned up YouTube and asked if they would be able to put it on their front page for that day, which they then did. Through that launch, which we publicized a lot, we got lots of hits and that generated quite a lot of discussion.

The same day, the film was screened at the Frontline Club in London, a gathering place for journalists, photographers, and people interested in independent journalism that encourages freedom of the press and freedom of expression worldwide. In the first Skype interview I had with Paulina in 2015, she described the event as jaw-dropping. The venue had been packed and the Q&As that followed the screening generated a lot of discussion. "The film only lasted for 30 minutes, but the debate went on for almost two hours. We were finally thrown out from the locale." According to Paulina and her partner Serdar Ferit, it was during this screening that they realized that the Awra Amba story could be used to discuss what they call "universal topics." In the years that followed, they freelanced and worked on other projects in order to survive, but *The Awra Amba Experience* became their number one priority, what they in numerous interviews describe as their "passion project." Here, we see how the transmission of a model is not simply an intellectual or technical process of dissemination, translation, or mediation. Rather, it involves affects and desires, dimensions of mobility that are at the foreground in assemblage theory and social epidemiology.

In June 2019, I discovered a more recent YouTube phenomenon that appeared to be spreading much more rapidly and to a potentially broader audience than Paulina's documentary. I was in the middle of writing this chapter when I decided to explore whether there had been more recent Twitter activity related to Awra Amba. Using the hashtag #AwraAmba, I came across a posting from early May 2019 containing a link to a YouTube video titled "One Good Cult." In a nine-minute travel documentary, Evan Hadfield tells the story of Awra Amba. In less than one month, the video reached more than 70,000 views, contributing significantly to Awra Amba's virality.[14]

Evan Hadfield is the son of Canadian astronaut Chris Hadfield, who became famous when he, as Commander of Expedition 35 on the International Space Station, chronicled his life onboard a spaceship using social media applications such as Twitter, Facebook, Tumblr, and YouTube.[15] Evan entered the spotlight as the manager of his father's social media campaign, and this piqued his interest in sharing human stories. In 2017, he launched the YouTube channel Rare Earth together with his father. With more than 700,000 subscribers, the channel, which in addition to travel documentaries, hosts videos featuring Chris Hadfield's space-related videos, has a well-established community of followers. Hadfield has been described as "the most social media savvy astronaut ever to leave Earth."[16]

While Evan Hadfield's (2019) video has very limited footage from Awra Amba—in the comment section beneath the video the producer lets us know that the cameraman he had hired "got day-drunk and threw away everything from this entire week"—it more or less stays true to the dominant narrative of a "truly self-sufficient and undeniably prosperous" community. Yet, Hadfield's reporting also reveals skepticism and ambivalence, as illustrated in this excerpt:

> A group that defies local customs, dismisses local gods and centralizes around the idealism of a single person, will always come across to others as, in a sense, waiting for the other shoe to drop. While researching this episode, it was virtually all I could think about. When visiting the town, it was the first thing my eyes were looking for. But standing there, nothing seemed amiss. Under all the rocks I lifted and the carpets I unswept, there seemed to be nothing there except normal people looking to lift themselves out of poverty. Everyday Ethiopians, living everyday Ethiopian life. Despite living at odds with the world around them, these are not a people hiding from it. They are doing their utmost to grow, thrive and inspire the next generation of like-minded Ethiopians. It is hard not to see this as inspiring. Awra Amba is a clear model for success. There is no question about that. But even now, at the end of this episode, after lathering on minute after minute of praise, it is

hard for me to truly feel comfortable seeing this place as it is presented. Communes rarely last for long and deep down, in my heart, I know there are no utopias.

Hadfield's reflections and his characterization of Awra Amba as an example of a "good cult" has generated a lively discussion among his community of followers on his YouTube channel.

Hadfield's Awra Amba documentary and its distribution to new audiences through digital media channels such as YouTube and Twitter illustrate how the Awra Amba model, as an assemblage, "forms a rhizome with the world" (Deleuze and Guattari 1987, 11); a multiplicity of constantly expanding connections between heterogeneous, random, and sometimes even hidden elements. Just as "a virus can [. . .] take flight, move into the cells of an entirely different species" (10), the Awra Amba model moves into unexpected terrains, establishing new, partly arbitrary connections. These connections and relationships are neither static nor stable, and they vary in intensity. While those who self-identify as Friends of Awra Amba are committed to the Awra Amba community, return for multiple, longer visits, and have established network-like relations with others in the group, Hadfield's connection seems to be of a more fleeting character. We could perhaps say that his relationship is an example of an instrumental mediascape, an appropriation that allowed him to produce a compelling video he could post on his channel. As such, Hadfield's connection to the Awra Amba community is short-lived, an example of one of multiple relationships established through his travels. In addition to being foundational to the production of his videos, these connections strengthen the ties he has to his existing followers, allowing him to establish new ones.

Kinetic Elites and Relations of Power

As I have shown above, the assemblage of actors, technologies, practices, and events that shape and facilitate the circulation of Awra Amba as a transnational, traveling model, is complex and fluid. This makes it difficult to trace the different elements that constitute what I have termed the Awra Amba assemblage: the multiple flows, relations, and disconnections, the different translations and mutations, and the nature and the reception of the various audiences. Just like a virus, Awra Amba has specific modes of transmission that facilitate its circulation. And just like a virus, the model village appears to pop up everywhere, searching for and finding new and unexpected hosts.

We are certainly not dealing with a closed network in the sense of clearly defined actors and elements that come together for a common, predetermined ultimate goal. Nor is the making and circulation of Awra Amba as a model a mechanical process that can be elucidated once and for all from the perspective of a sovereign expert or policy maker. Characterized by contingency and affect, the Awra Amba assemblage—as both a constellation and a process—is messy, fluid, and not fully predictable.

This does not mean, however, that power relations, inequality, and differences do not exist, or that there is no ordering within this fluidity and unpredictability. The modes of transmission offer relatively stable pathways that in addition to enabling and constraining its circulation also produce power relations. Deleuze and Guattari introduced the notion of assemblage as part of the poststructuralist move to destabilize the idea of predetermined hierarchies and fixed teleologies and to "remove subjective [that is, excessively humanistic] notions of agency from our ontological worldview" (Legg 2011, 128). While their theoretical contribution was a constructive move that allows us to think of complexity in a more dynamic and holistic way, their antistructuralist thrust should not be overemphasized. Elizabeth Grosz (1994, 167) has pointed out that "a world without strata, totally flattened" does not exist. Rather, we encounter a world of hierarchies in which "the hierarchies are not the result of substances and their nature and value" but of different modes of organization. In the Awra Amba case, these hierarchies can best be captured through the concept of the "kinetic elite" (Costas 2013). These are actors whose mobility and positioning facilitates interaction with multiple audiences and across spaces, allowing them to spread and capitalize on the model's success in ways that other actors in the Awra Amba assemblage do not. As yet another assemblage within the Awra Amba assemblage, this is an exclusive assemblage, which, in addition to being prone to governing and scaling, functions as the model's "travel agency" (Olivier de Sardan, Diarra, and Moha 2017, 76). The travel agency is a useful allegory, since it in addition to emphasizing the role that particular actors play in terms of facilitating and promoting visits to Awra Amba—be it to the physical village or online—implies a recognition of the fact that Awra Amba, as a traveling model, generates and attracts economic capital and investment.

Let us first take a closer look at the kinetic elite as it exists within the Awra Amba community. Zumra and his wife Enaney are key figures here. Their role as kinetic elites have taken them to places and venues inside and outside Ethiopia, allowing them to connect with and become part of a global group of actors. In addition to frequent travels to the capital, they have traveled to France and Italy. Moreover, in December 2015, Zumra participated in the launch of Ethiopia's HeForShe campaign, where he and a select number of prominent leaders, including the former Prime Minister Hailemariam Desalegn, the CEO of Ethiopian Airlines Tewolde Gebremariam, and the retired Ethiopian long-distance runner and Olympic gold medalist Haile Gebreselassie, were officially designated as the HeForShe campaign's "Champions for Ethiopia."

In addition to Zumra and Enaney, Awra Amba's kinetic elite consists of a handful of relatively young community members, all well educated and with good English skills. While these actors are less publicly visible in Ethiopia, they are in positions that provide them opportunities to network with national and international actors. Furthermore, their language skills enable them to operate as translators in these forums. In 2014, Gebeyhu, a young man who, at the time, held a key administrative position in the cooperative, traveled with Zumra and Enaney to France. "We were invited by Robert Joumard," he told me when we met in 2018. "He is a French scholar who has written about Awra Amba. Our trip was facilitated by and paid for by some kind of activist organization. We were in France for about nine days, and during that time we participated in and presented our ideas at ten difference conferences. Some days we would speak at three different venues. We stayed in Robert's home for most of the time and had all our meals at peoples' private homes." Gebeyhu also worked closely with Paulina during the filming of *The Awra Amba Experience*, and, together with his wife, Gebeyhu is featured in one of the documentaries. The positions these young community members hold as part of the kinetic elite appear to be temporal. For example, after my first fieldwork in Awra Amba in 2015, Gebeyhu left his position in the cooperative in order to continue his education in Bahir Dar. A year later, Getasew, another young man and close relative of Zumra's family, returned to the community after having completed a degree in agriculture from Mekele University and became the chairman of the cooperative. More recently, Zumra and Enaney's eldest son, Ayalsew, who graduated from Addis Ababa Science and Technology University in 2020, has gained a more prominent role as part of the kinetic elite. In August 2019 he participated in the Young Women's Regional Consultation on Beijing + 25, held in Abidjan. Organized by UN Women, in collaboration with Oxfam and the UN Economic Commission for

Africa, the conference drew participants from all over Africa and the African diaspora. A month later, Ayalsew and his father were also among the invited keynote speakers at the 2019 Social Enterprise World Forum (SEWF) hosted by the British Council in Addis Ababa. SEWF is the leading forum for international exchange and collaboration in social entrepreneurship and social investment. More than 1,200 participants from fifty countries around the world attended the conference.

The members of Awra Amba's kinetic elite have been, and continue to be, key vectors or carriers, spreading and maintaining Awra Amba's status as a transnational model for gender equality and sustainable development. In addition to gaining further recognition for the community as a model village, their travels facilitate connections and networking with representatives from the Ethiopian government, the business community, transnational organizations, and both national and international NGOs. This does not mean that other members of the community do not participate in transmitting the model. By participating in the community's daily activities, which selectively have been incorporated into the official tour, a large number of the community's members actively engage in the preservation of Awra Amba as a utopian society. In the daily acts of modeling the community's prescribed way of life, they are successfully "cast as entrepreneurial and capable of managing their own development" (McFarlane 2009, 563). They are central to the scenes and narratives, but they tend to be background actors and not protagonists. In other words, while they do not physically travel to participate in international and national events through which knowledge of Awra Amba is disseminated, they are not powerless. Being part of the Awra Amba community, and enacting a narrative that fulfills the expectations of visitors from all corners of the world, they perform in a story that serves as an inducement, a form of power that Colin McFarlane (2009, 565) describes as "both manipulative and associational. It is manipulative in that it is presented as a neutral set of facts and constitutes a simple message with extensive spatial reach. It is associational in that it involves an attempt to constitute a common agreement or shared will." As members of the community, these actors benefit, at least to some extent, from these manipulative and associational activities, since these activities serve to maintain Awra Amba's status as a model—a status that, as we shall see, comes with material resources. However, we shall also see that rank and file community members do not receive the lion's share of the wealth generated in Awra Amba, raising questions about the community's status as just and equal. In comparison with the kinetic elites, community members participate only to a limited extent in the processes that facilitate the model's mobility and flow beyond Awra Amba proper. This mobility differential creates, or perhaps it is more correct to say, perpetuates, a stratified society and challenges the narrative of the utopian, egalitarian community on which the model rests.

While the concept of kinetic elites is useful in terms of fleshing out some of the unequal power relations that exist among members of the Awra Amba community, the term can also be extended to external actors such as Lyfta's producers. In fact, if we look at how other scholars have used the term kinetic elites—to account for the "super mobility" (Adey 2008, 1326) of various categories of global workers, such as consultants, corporate elites, and even academics—it may make more sense to apply it to actors such as Paulina, Serdar, Evan Hadfield, and myself. While our engagement in and relationship with Awra Amba may vary in quality and intensity, we are, by virtue of our activities, networks, and travel, nevertheless part of the Awra Amba assemblage, contributing to the circulation of the model and benefiting from its status. Based in the global north, yet also frequent travelers, we are all well educated and have access to resources, technologies, and networks that Zumra and the rest of Awra Amba's leadership do not have. This fact points to the power differentials that exist among the various actors who constitute Awra Amba's kinetic elite. While Zumra and Enaney may be powerful actors within the Awra Amba community, their mobility is to a considerable extent relational and dependent on the goodwill and inclusionary practices of other and more prominent national and global actors. It is important to recognize differentials within any assemblage in its shifting ramifications rather than just assume that all components and actors are equal—as some agents favorably located in the contested hierarchies would want us to do. This allows us to recognize, as Foucault has famously argued, that "power is everywhere," everywhere in the sense that it does not issue from a single centralized location like a fixed object that some actors have or lack, but it emerges from myriad social relations.

Beyond Human Policy Actors

In this chapter, I have explored some of the ways that Awra Amba has spread as a model for gender equality and sustainable development. I have shown how Awra Amba's virality has been facilitated by a sociotechnological network of actors, things, and processes. The Awra Amba case illustrates that the exchange of ideas between conventional policy actors during physical visits to model cities or model projects and at conferences, workshops, and seminars remains important in terms of facilitating a model's virality. Nevertheless, the case also exemplifies how important it is that we look beyond conventional policy actors and infrastructure. We live in an increasingly globalized and digitalized world where new actors, partnerships, modes of interactions, and technologies constantly emerge. This has changed the ways policy ideas and models travel. It is particularly important to explore the role played by the creative industries and new markets, here exemplified by the EdTech industry and YouTube, and recognize their political influence and their disciplinary power. By producing and circulating particular narratives and facilitating experiences, these fields "articulate fundamental organizing principles of society" (Shore and Wright 1997, 7), legitimizing and promoting particular policy ideas and models.

While a focus on modes of transmission, pathways, and infrastructure provides nuanced answers to what facilitates the circulation of models and ideas in our contemporary world, it does not tell us much about why a particular model or idea gains its status and starts traveling in the first place. What is it that makes a model attractive? Why are some models picked up, while others are not? What is it that has compelled the various vectors and carriers in the Awra Amba assemblage to spread the community's stories and values? In the next chapter, I turn to some of the stories I gathered from those who have been "infected" and hence are transmitting or circulating the Awra Amba model. A careful examination of these stories reveals an important aspect that the existing literature on policy mobility and traveling models has overlooked: the role that desire and emotions play in fueling a model's virality.

Chapter 6

Going Viral

IT IS A RAINY, cold, and windy fall morning in Helsinki, Finland's capital. I am about to arrive at Lyfta's headquarters after a thirty-minute brisk walk through a city that screams of innovation. After stepping out of the last plane from Oslo the night before, I was quickly reminded of Finland's status as a design nation. "If I were to see one thing during my stay in Helsinki, what should that be?" I asked the elderly woman who sat next to me in the shared taxi I had taken in order to avoid arriving too late at my Airbnb. "Only one thing!" she exclaimed. I seem to have offended her national pride by suggesting that this is all I have time for. "You should visit Amos Rex, our new art museum. It opened last month, and in the first two weeks, it had more visitors than they would have anticipated for a whole year. It is a place of innovative and digital art. Of modern design," she concludes.

The rain that pours down as I am on my way to my first offline meeting with Paulina and Serdar this morning does not stop me from exploring a city that clearly takes pride in its history of creativity and design. A block away from my Airbnb, I pass by the Design Museum. Established in 1873, it is one of the oldest museums in the world and tells the history of some of Finland's contributions to innovation: the brightly colored and worldwide celebrated patterns of Marimekko, the three-legged Aalto stool, Nokia—the world's leading mobile phone manufacturer in the early 2000s—and last, but not least, Angry Birds, the game that made the world go crazy in 2009. Two days later, when I drop in for a brief visit, a plaque at the museum details the immense impact this innovative video game had on Finland's economy and image: "Finland is no longer the country of thousands of mobile phone engineers that created Nokia, but also a Nordic miracle of innovation where courage, creativity and capability for renewal come together in ways that continue to break down the boundaries of design." As I approach the address

Paulina has sent me in an email, I walk through the city's design district, where every second small business seems to have the word "design" incorporated into its name. It is here—at the heart of a city that in 2012 was awarded the UNESCO City of Design Award—that *The Awra Amba Experience* has its home.[1]

"I came across the Awra Amba community in 2004. I had just finished my master's degree in documentary film making and was in Ethiopia visiting with my aunt," Paulina explains before taking another mouthful of the salad she has put together from the lunch buffet. We are sitting at an Italian restaurant only a block away from Lyfta's office. It is less than two hours since I walked into the office—a small, cozy, inviting place with a big window facing the street and pictures of people from Awra Amba on the wall—and met Paulina for the first time in person. After introducing me to Serdar, who is also her partner in life, and four other members of Lyfta's production team, Paulina had invited me to sit down for a tour of their website and an almost completed version of their new, updated product: Lyfta 2.0. "As you know, the current version only contains *The Awra Amba Experience* and two other story-worlds," Paulina had explained as she navigated the new interface. "Lyfta 2.0. will allow you to explore and visit the whole world." She had opened a page that displayed a globe at the center and had showed me how you could swirl, zoom, and click on the globe to enter the place you would like to visit. She then had moved to another page that contained a bright red passport. Lyfta 2.0. would, according to Paulina, be much more user friendly than the first version—both for teachers and students. The new, Netflix-inspired interface would provide teachers the opportunity to create tailor-made lesson plans, with the passport serving as a way to track an individual student's travels and his or her progress on key learning objectives. "Our vision is to foster a new generation of global, empathic citizens," Paulina had explained. "The children will be able to travel and explore stories from around the world. Once they complete the questions and activities their teachers have assigned them, they will receive a summary and light-colored stamps in their Lyfta passport that show the different life skills and the Sustainable Development Goals they have mastered. It will also give the children a track record of where they have been and what they have learned and help them understand and recognize the skills and values they have gained." I had asked her if *The Awra Amba Experience* would stay as it is today. After all, the Awra Amba story is what inspired the launch of Lyfta, and it is the story I am most interested in. "Yes, of course. It will be an integrated part of Lyfta 2.0," she had affirmed.

"I first heard about Awra Amba from a friend of mine, a Finnish girl who, at the time I visited my aunt in Ethiopia, lived in Bahir Dar," Paulina continues as Serdar joins us at the table. With his short-cut, sleek, dark hair, and big, brown eyes, he is a clear contrast to Paulina, who is blond and has blue eyes. Born to parents who immigrated to the UK from Turkey, Serdar grew up in a working-class, poor neighborhood in the eastern part of London where his father worked as a primary school teacher. A comment from Serdar's father inspired the couple to establish Lyfta. One day, after having seen *The Awra Amba Experience,* he had asked them whether they had shown it to children. The response when they first tested it out in a classroom at a school in Ipswich, UK had been, according to Serdar, "so inspiring that we haven't looked back since. Lyfta was born."[2] The students had been so captivated by *The Awra Amba Experience* that they had refused to go on their break, and when asked questions about what they remembered from their virtual visit, "they answered every single question correctly and very eloquently—so much so that they brought their teacher to tears in front of us."[3]

Back at the restaurant, Paulina continues the story about how she came across the village: "My friend knew I was interested in issues related to gender equality and women's rights, so she asked if I wanted to come with her to see Awra Amba. We drove to Awra Amba and visited for approximately two hours. Zumra was not there at the time, but it made a huge impression on me. I was amazed by the way we were welcomed. I couldn't stop thinking about them; I simply could not forget what I had seen." Paulina passionately continues the story. She explains how the community's way of life and their values made so much sense to her; how they gave her hope at a time when she was becoming more and more disillusioned by the actions of Western governments around the world and frustrated with the negative images of the developing world that were circulating in the popular media. She could not stop talking with her friends and her family about what she had seen and experienced in Awra Amba. In 2008, four years after first visit, Paulina returned to Ethiopia and started filming.

Persisting Rationalistic Biases

I have introduced Paulina's story here because her first visit to Awra Amba and her subsequent involvement shed light on questions that have been mostly ignored by the policy mobility literature. Why do some models go viral, while others do not? What makes a model attractive? What has gathered the various vectors and carriers into the Awra Amba assemblage and compelled them to adopt and spread the community's story and values?

As we saw in the previous chapter, assemblage theory provides valuable perspectives for understanding the unruly nature of an increasingly transnational policy world. Inspired by assemblage thinking, a growing body of critical policy studies has challenged the rational and linear assumptions that have dominated traditional approaches to policy studies. And yet, if we carefully examine the rhetoric and analyses in many of these studies, they appear stuck in a conceptualization of policy mobility as a process that is primarily about exchange of information and ideas or about the translation of language and meanings between (rational) human actors. This is particularly reflected in a strong focus on policy learning and policy mobilization, often framed as if they are active, intentional, and conscious processes that take place "through networks and flows of people, places and projects" (Jarvis 2017, 117). I concur with Helen Jarvis's assessment of the existing scholarship on policy mobility. She argues that by focusing on knowledge exchange and information-sharing infrastructure in the form of organized conferences, policy tours, seminars, workshops, and circulation of policy documents, this literature "reinforces a restricted definition of influence and impact" (118). Such a narrowing leads to a simplification of processes that are not only complex and often arbitrary but also conditioned on and facilitated by desire and emotions. In other words, although much of the recent literature recognizes the non-linearity and processual and relational character of policy making and circulation, it unreflexively retains the rationalistic bias of orthodox approaches. I find this particularly evident in an article written by a group of policy mobility scholars situated within critical geography (Baker et al. 2016, 459ff.). First, phrases such as "how policy and knowledge are mobilized" and "the ways in which people move ideas" reflect a conception of policy mobility as a controlled, intentional process driven by human actors. Second, the authors pay considerable attention to policy tourism sites as places "where learning takes place"; where policy actors "gain knowledge of new policy ideas."

I do not deny the role of human actors in fueling and circulating policy ideas and models. Nor do I contend that knowing and learning about new ideas or policy models is a deleterious process. I recognize that encountering new ideas and models is a crucial element of policy innovation, mobility, and translation. However, learning about something, or gaining knowledge of a particular policy, does not necessarily mean that you adopt it and put it to work in a new context as if it were a neutral instrument. As is the case for a virus—in order for a model to become infectious, to be taken up by a cell— it needs a receptor with certain characteristics. There needs to be an association—an element of recognition and interaction between the model and the entities by which it can potentially be picked up. In other words, the circulation of a model relies on an encounter with receptive agents or environments. We can say that, like a virus, the model and its receptors and promoters "summon" each other in the relationship. This relationship does not mean that the model has to be a perfect fit; it is enough for the model to have an attractive element that is recognized and desired by the receptive agent.

Richard Rottenburg's (Behrends, Park, and Rottenburg 2014a; Rottenburg 2009) work on traveling models does, to some extent, move away from the knowledge-exchange perspective that dominates much of the policy mobility literature. He argues that in order for a model to be picked up, it needs to have an aura—"something which is convincing and appealing and at the same time invisible" (Behrends, Park, and Rottenburg 2014b, 18). This appeal is contingent on a number of aspects. First, Behrends, Park, and Rottenburg (18) argue that the number of times a model has been adopted increases the likelihood of it being picked up again. A high number of adoptions suggests that the model offers "a superior way of doing this." The adoption and circulation of a popular model is, hence, not a matter of deliberate rational planning but an act of imitation. Second, the way a model is delivered matters; "a person or corporation with a certain charisma can for example convey ideas better than someone else" (18). Zumra's role as a founder of the Awra Amba community and his communicative skills and personal qualities clearly illustrate this aspect. Zumra exudes charisma and is surrounded by a compelling aura, and this has, with no doubt, been important for the establishment and circulation of Awra Amba as a traveling model. While our first meeting was filled with tension and suspicion, it did not take long before I myself was captivated. For example, in my first formal interview with him, his responses to some of my questions were framed as critical and philosophical counter questions, making me speechless—as illustrated in the following exchange:

ME: Some will say that Awra Amba is a place with no religion.

ZUMRA: These are people who have not understood what religion really is. You may even have heard them say that "the Awra Amba believe in work."

ME: So, how do you see the relationship between work and religion?

ZUMRA: Let me ask you a question. What do you mean by religion? Those who are not able answer this question may say that there is no religion in Awra Amba. My mother told me that I asked about religion when I was two years old. She did not reply to my question. Now, I am still waiting for your answer.

ME: What is religion depends on who you ask.

ZUMRA: But now I have limited my question to you.

Finally, a model's aura and appealing qualities depend on the "ontological, epistemic, normative and material orders of the receiving site" (Behrends, Park, and Rottenburg 2014b, 18). This latter point suggests, as I have alluded to above, that the environment or context with which the model interacts matters.

With these three conditions, Behrends, Park, and Rottenburg (2014b) acknowledge the role that non-rational elements play in facilitating a model's travel. Yet, a rationalistic perspective remains in the framework they offer, reflected in their use of rational choice theory.[4] In what follows, I move beyond the rational bias to demonstrate that it is particularly fruitful to think of policy mobility and the traveling model as viral assemblage: a complex, fluid, and sociotechnical process and constellation of actors, things, and unpredictable events that have affective and contagious qualities. In the previous chapter I paid particular attention to the modes of transmission—the infrastructure—that have facilitated Awra Amba's circulation. My focus in this chapter is on the role that emotions and desire play in the Awra Amba viral assemblage.

Let us briefly go back to the incident described in the beginning of Chapter 5, to the day I learned about Emily, her involvement with Lyfta, and her effort to implement the company's product in American classrooms. Reconstructing the multiple, unforeseen elements that facilitated and spurred this encounter will demonstrate the fruitfulness of the concept of viral assemblage in understanding how ideas and models travel. Had it not been for my boredom, which is linked to my desire for entertainment and my possession of and use of an iPhone, the algorithmic technology used by Twitter to predict my preferences, and Emily's business card, I may never have learned about or met Emily in the first place. This incident sheds light on how virality is "located in an epidemiological space in which a world of things mixes with emotions, sensations, affects and moods" (Sampson 2012, 4). The coming together of these heterogeneous elements in partly accidental microevents is a good illustration of the form of virality that Sampson derives from Tarde's theory. Feelings, affect, and desire play an important role here, bringing things and people together through involuntary and arbitrary encounters or "vibratory events" (7).

While much of the critical policy mobility has drawn inspiration from assemblage theory, there has been limited focus on the potential role that affect, desires, and moods play in shaping and fueling policy making and circulation. This is particularly surprising, since desire has been described as an essential component of assemblages (Müller and Schurr 2016; DeLanda 2016). I now return to a discussion and examination of Paulina's narrative and her engagement with Awra Amba and introduce and analyze the stories of some of the other actors who have played central roles in terms of spreading the Awra Amba model, with a particular eye for affective elements.

Enchanted

Paulina's first visit to Awra Amba and her initial encounter with the community was above all an emotional and deeply inspirational event. In fact, she was so amazed and surprised by the community and its values—so charmed—that she could not stop talking and thinking about them. Not only did the place take over her mind, this was a transformative experience, a profoundly affective, eye-opening moment that fueled her creativity and gave her life a new direction. "Struck and shaken by the extraordinary that lives amid the familiar and the everyday" (Bennett 2001, 4), we could say that Paulina was enchanted.[5]

What is it that makes Awra Amba stand out as extraordinary and enchanting? From a Nordic perspective—let's keep in mind that Paulina, in addition to being from Finland, spent years of her childhood in Sweden—the values and ideas conveyed by the Awra Amba community are not by any means astonishing. In fact, what Awra Amba offers is a model that Paulina is familiar with; it is a narrative that resonates and fits nicely with the secular, social democratic values and the gender equality models that the Nordic countries are known for. If we were to apply the virus metaphor here, we could say that what she experienced in Awra Amba "clicked" with a set of receptors—her conceptions of what constitutes a good society.

But how can the recognition of something familiar—of something that clearly resonates with her values—qualify as something extraordinary? Does it at all make sense to explain Paulina's reaction as enchantment? I shall here suggest that it is not the ideas and values in themselves that make Awra Amba stand out as extraordinary for Paulina. Nor is it the experience of the "vernacular lifeways" of an African, exotic "cultural village" (Comaroff and Comaroff 2009, 11). Paulina's fascination with Awra Amba surfaced because she encountered something familiar and something she highly values *in an unexpected place*. In other words, the exotic in the Awra Amba case is the unexpected discovery of the lifeways of "modern," liberal subjects who comply with the values and aspirations set forth by the MDGs, now SDGs, in what historically has been portrayed as an uncivilized and underdeveloped continent. As we will see in the next chapter, Paulina herself acknowledges the value of innovation and positive stories told from unexpected places. In fact, she believes that this is what gives Lyfta's narratives transformative power.

Paulina's reaction to and description of her first Awra Amba experience are not unique, however. In 2015, I met with the journalist who made the first documentary about Awra Amba and who for many years played an important role promoting the community. He described his initial interaction with the community in a similar way:

> I was really amazed by the community. The members were working twenty-four hours a day. They were living in grass huts, but the interior of their houses was the same as today. Their houses were clean. These were things that made me very surprised, so when I made the documentary, I used strong words and made some exaggerations. I felt so much happiness seeing the Awra Amba culture. People in this area, whether Christian or Muslims, are very conservative. So in comparison with these societies, Awra Amba was revolutionary. I would not have corrected or done any amendments to the documentary today. It reflected my feelings.

Similarly to this journalist's and Paulina's recollections of their first encounter, stories of others who visited Awra Amba were filled with powerful emotions, illustrative of the community's power to enchant. A young Israeli medical student who was backpacking in Ethiopia with her boyfriend described, for example, how they had become deeply touched during the guided tour of the village:

> It was fantastic! It is so special to find something like this in Ethiopia. You do not expect to find something like this, in a place like this; in Africa. Even in our part of the world, you do not find this. We told Zumra: "We have a stupid war going on in our country. If everyone lived the way you do, and accepted your values, there would be peace."

Let me here make a point that relates back to my discussion about models in previous chapters. We cannot separate the unexpected—that which surprises us—from our controlling models, our habitus, or the way we see the world. That which astounds us reveals unspoken and often unconscious assumptions. Many of these presuppositions are produced by the stereotypical images and narratives we encounter, particularly through the popular media. For example, the Israeli student's reflection and the way she speaks about Ethiopia and Africa rely on preconceived notions and images of the African continent as a place of war, inequality, oppression, and injustice.

A Western construction of Africa as "other" is less evident in the Ethiopian journalist's account. This does not mean, however, that his experience and storytelling are free from stereotypical assumptions. His admiration and framing of Awra Amba rest on and reify an image of rural Ethiopia as dirty, primitive, and conservative—of "being behind" (Donham 1999, xv) and stuck in the past. Filled with optimism and exaggeration, his narrative serves as a good example of "vernacular modernism": constructions of history that "separate the past from the present and reorient expectations toward the future" (xv).

While these stories, first and foremost, illustrate the role that emotions and affect play in fueling a model's virality, they also show the ideological and ethical confluences that exist between the values that these actors hold and what they experience and see in Awra Amba. A man who considers himself to be part of the Friends of Awra Amba group, a director for a well-known international NGO in Addis Ababa, described to me in 2018 how he had been moved by the community's values and philosophy. "I saw myself in them. Their philosophy and their ideas were always something I wanted." When I asked him what specifically attracted him, he mentioned two aspects: the community's emphasis on self-reliance and gender equality. There is also a clear element of recognition and resonance in his statement, something that is also present in Paulina's story when she describes how the community and their values "made so much sense to me." We could here also use the virus analogy and say that this shows that the traveling model—in the same vein as the virion, the non-living phase of the virus—has found a cell with the right receptor that allows it to enter. By emphasizing how he, in Awra Amba, found something he had always wanted, the NGO director furthermore reveals how his fascination was driven by desire. As we shall see in what follows, he is not the only one whose engagement and fascination with Awra Amba has been fueled by want and longing.

Desire

Aster,[6] a senior advisor for UN Women in Addis Ababa and one of Awra Amba's most committed and long-time advocates, meets me with a welcoming but apologetic smile. "I am in the middle of a Skype meeting with people at the UN Women headquarters in New York. I hope you don't mind waiting." She hands me a bottle of water that she quickly grabs from a nearby refrigerator, points me to a comfortable sofa with an accompanying coffee table stacked with brochures, and heads back to her online meeting. "Feel free to read about our work as you wait," she shouts as she hurries down the corridor. The next thirty minutes or so allow me plenty of time to skim through the brochures. They all focus on women's economic empowerment, and in addition to serving as a window into the Ethiopian government's and UN Women's priorities, they reflect the financial logics of the neoliberal ideas that dominate the global gender and development discourse. It is a discourse that, in addition to encouraging entrepreneurship and economic empowerment, seeks to unleash women as an "untapped resource" for economic growth and development.

Aster was one of the first members of Ethiopia's NGO community to come across Awra Amba. The story she tells about her first encounter with the community does not start in Ethiopia, however. It begins in Israel, which she had the chance to visit in 1994. "We were touring and visited a kibbutz," she tells me, when we finally sit down in her office for the scheduled appointment. "I became very fascinated by and interested in the way they were living in the kibbutz; how they worked together and how they all received a fair share, so, I inquired about the membership criteria. But when I learnt that you only could become a member if you were born Jewish, I was very disappointed. This was discrimination."

As Aster tells her story, I think back to the many Israeli backpackers I have met in Awra Amba who have told me that the community is known in Israel as the kibbutz in Ethiopia. "That is why Awra Amba is a very popular and famous destination in the backpacker community," a young woman told me one morning as I sat in Awra Amba's cafeteria eating breakfast. When I first saw her, and before I heard her speaking with her friends in Hebrew, I thought she was a visitor from Addis Ababa. Her looks were unmistakably Ethiopian, but her short hairstyle and way of dressing made me assume she was part of the capital's urban elite. "I left Ethiopia when I was five years old," she told me when I inquired into her background. She was among the 14,000 Ethiopian Jews airlifted out of Ethiopia by the Israeli government in less than one and a half days in May 1991 in what became known as Operation Solomon. "I am back for the first time in twenty-seven years and it feels great!" When the waiter comes to take her order a few minutes later, I can hear she has been able to maintain her Amharic. "It is a little broken, but at least it allows me to communicate with people," she laughs. She is not the only Ethiopian Jew to visit Awra Amba. During my fieldwork in 2018, I met a number of Ethiopian-looking visitors who spoke Hebrew. Their idea of the kibbutz as a familiar utopian community has attracted them to Awra Amba and made them receptive to its values and the experience it offers to its visitors.

I take a sip of the macchiato Aster has ordered for me—a common delight and courtesy to all visitors of non-governmental offices in Ethiopia—before I return to the scribbly pages of my notebook. I have written so fast in order to keep record of the details in her story that part of my handwriting is unrecognizable. I quickly look over some of the most scrawled words and add a few keywords as notes to myself in the margin before I return my attention to Aster. "My soul was searching for a place where human rights were respected, where there was justice and no differentiation based on class or gender. When I heard about Awra Amba, something clicked. There is something like this, in my own land!"

Aster's first visit to Awra Amba did not disappoint her. Together with a group of friends from Bahir Dar—an engineer, a journalist, and colleagues from the NGO community—she traveled to Awra Amba, where she met with Zumra.

> He came and greeted us, and I immediately knew who he was. I had seen a
> picture of him, wearing his green hat, in a brochure made by the Amhara

news agency. We sat down to talk and discuss in a small hut. You see, at that time, the community was poor, and there were only small grass-thatched houses in the village. They did not have enough food to feed themselves and could not offer us anything as guests. But as I listened to Zumra talking— I sat up a whole night listening to him—I said to myself: "This is what I have been looking for. I now have my own kibbutz."

Aster's description of her first encounter with Awra Amba and Zumra, as the moment she found what she had been searching and longing for, very explicitly illustrates the role desire plays in fueling a model's virality. But what is it that Aster desires? Why does she, a highly educated cosmopolitan woman who belongs to Ethiopia's national elite, express such an admiration for Awra Amba? Is she longing for the simple, rural life of the community? Does she envision herself spinning cotton eight hours a day for six days a week? Again, and as I emphasized in my analysis of Paulina, it is important to keep in mind Aster's background and positioning. For many years, she has been deeply involved in the gender and development field in Ethiopia. In this world, models—particularly models of gender equality—are objects of strong desire. They fit nicely into "the virtual world of dreams and expectations about development and the crude reality of actual development—or rather its absence" (de Vries 2007, 26). In other words, they give hope to the utopian desires that underpin and characterize the development field. One could therefore argue that Aster's story exemplifies how the Awra Amba traveling assemblage operates through the fuel of desire for utopias in a world of dystopias and widespread inequality. The predisposing conditions that enhance the contagiousness of Awra Amba are a frustration with current models and a fervent hope for new, more authentic, and perfect ones. Such a reading would feed into a conception of desire as being born out of lack; it assumes that we are "desiring what we do not have" (Colebrook 2001, 82). But the conceptualization of desire that is at the heart of Tarde's social epidemiology, and that we can also find in Deleuze and Guattari's assemblage thinking, moves beyond this rather instrumental, limited conception. Subjective aspects such as desire, passion, feelings, belief, and imagination are not secondary but are fundamental features of everything social. They are productive and relational forces that do not belong to or reside in "individual, interior spaces" (Ringrose 2011, 600). Hence, even in fields such as politics, economics, and science, often assumed to be governed my logic and rationality, subjective elements and social relations matter.[7] Desire is not limited to the explicit discursive expression of desires and wants that is mirrored in statements such as "their ideas were always something I wanted" (the NGO director) and "this is what I have been looking for" (Aster). Desire is a fundamental, albeit, perhaps, tacit aspect of everything we do. The desire we see expressed, not only in Aster's account but also in the other stories I have told here, is, in other words, not exceptional or an anomaly. It is not just a personal idiosyncrasy of a handful of my informants. The relative absence of these subjective aspects—of the spoken and unspoken, conscious and unconscious desires and passions—in the existing policy mobility and traveling model literature does not mean that they are not present in the process of model making and circulation. Rather, as I argued earlier in this chapter, this absence reflects rationalistic biases and neglect.

With this in mind, how could we best make sense of the expressions of desire and passion that surface in the stories I have shared in this chapter? To answer this question, it is pivotal that we conceptually explore desire. I have here found it useful to think with the two forms of desire that Tarde introduces in his work. Biological desire, the first and most fundamental of the two, is about survival. Born out of the "needs of organic life" (Tarde and Toscano 2007, 633), these desires are entwined with and reflected in the mechanics and everyday habits of eating, drinking, sleeping, and clothing ourselves. They are periodical: "they repeat themselves throughout the day or the year of the individual, at more or less regular intervals" (634). The hunger I felt as I was walking out of the hotel after a meeting with my research assistant is an example of this kind of desire.

Biological desire is appropriated and transformed by a second kind of desire, what Tarde (Tarde and Toscano 2007, 633) calls "special desires." They are "the economic translation" of the biological desires, and their origin is social. When I asked the guard for a restaurant recommendation, my inquiry was born out of my passion for a very particular kind of food; in other words, this reflected a cultural or social form of desire. Drawing on Tarde, Sampson (2012, 113) argues that this second form of desire—what he terms "cultural contagion"—revolves around events that "can [...] take on an imitative and spontaneous 'life' of their own." When a restaurant becomes popular or gains social recognition—which was why the guard pointed me in that direction when I asked him for his recommendation—or when something goes viral, such as a

YouTube video or the story of a village, it is this second kind of desire that is most clearly at play.

The division of desire into two kinds—biological and special—is certainly a bit risky. It suggests that there is a clear binary between what is biological and what is social. Here, it is important to keep in mind that the two kinds of desire do not exist independently of each other. While hunger certainly is grounded in our bodies' nutritional needs, it is also infused with social dispositions and demands. As "part of an inseparable and indissoluble continuum" (Sampson 2012, 24), biological and special desires are closely intertwined. Tarde's way of thinking about desire is useful since it positions desire as a fundamental feature of life. It is not something that only belongs to the psychological realm, linked to emotional sentiments such as love or passion. Desire is fundamentally present in everything we do and in every encounter we have with others. These encounters, and particularly the unexpected or casual meeting with a model or an example, generate new desires, driving us to create and invent or to copy and follow.

Paulina's story as well as the journalist's story very clearly illustrate how imitation and innovation are deeply embedded in and fueled by desires. Not only did their encounters with Awra Amba generate powerful emotions; these "desire-events" (Sampson 2012, 118) also inspired them to create and invent and to retell and adopt the community's story into the format of documentaries. These documentaries themselves have become contagious assemblages, generating new desires and innovations.

In the stories I have told in this chapter, the actors who in different ways circulate the Awra Amba model are driven by a desire for fullness, for pure love and ideal democracy and for a just, peaceful, and better world. As agents of social change, they do what they do because they have a calling or an inner desire to help or empower others. However, such commitments are, as Liisa H. Malkki (2015, 3–4) has shown in her work with Finnish aid workers and volunteers, seldom purely altruistic in nature. She argues that her interlocutors' involvement in humanitarian work and their desire to help was a form of self-care born from a need for "a human connection that help[s] them feel like real persons" and a desire "to be part of something greater than themselves."

Again, Tarde's way of making sense of desire is useful as it forces us to pay attention to the partly unconscious and unspoken desires that underlie every social field, including the global policy world. For example, we should keep in mind that stories of success—or successful models—are what sustain the development industry. These stories are what put food on the table for those who work within the industry. As several scholars have shown, models and the success stories derived from them are valuable commodities (Büscher 2014; Lund et al. 2017; Svarstad and Benjaminsen 2017). In other words, the model is an asset that, due to its perceived value, attracts the interest of actors who all, to some extent, rely on and capitalize on "selling success" (Büscher 2014). The model's perceived value also means, as we shall see more explicitly in Chapter 8, that the model attracts attention and recognition. This explains why Aster, in addition to expressing personal interest in Awra Amba and the community's values, also worked hard to convince the community to enter into a partnership with the NGO that she, at the time, was working for. Establishing a relationship with what she perceived to be a successful gender equality model would enhance the reputation of the NGO and would likely fulfill her personal interests and desires. In other words, models spread and become valuable commodities because they speak to our everyday biological and social desires, including our personal desires for success, mastery, and recognition. Abstract and universal desires for utopias are always accompanied by material causes and effects—by specific socially-conditioned desires. This confluence should not be understood as a personal moral flaw of the actors involved but as constitutive of the process of model making and circulation. Despite the avowed emancipatory claims, the models we pick up and spread as part of the "desires we invest in the Other" (Kapoor 2014, 1203) are neither neutral nor free from exploitation. They have causes and effects inflected with power, which a critical anthropology of policy must reflexively confront.

Why Models Go Viral

In this chapter, my aim has been to flesh out how the concept of viral assemblage can be used to explain why a particular policy idea or model clicks and starts circulating. The reason we pick something up and find it desirable and worth emulating is, as Tarde (Tarde and Toscano 2007, 632) argues, not because it is intrinsically interesting, pleasant, or agreeable; "it is because we desire it that we judge it to be agreeable, seductive, or interesting." To draw the lines back to the discussion about models in Chapter 3, we could say that the affect and recognition expressed in the stories in this chapter surface because the experiences that Awra Amba generate, as an immersive model, correspond to the controlling models the storytellers have—to their ethos (Geertz 1957, 424). The moments described in these stories are framed as if one has found what one has (unconsciously or consciously) been looking for. Similar to a virus, we embrace the ideas that we are already receptive to, that we recognize, and, hence, that we can easily relate to. We can also say that the Awra Amba experience—in both the real and virtual sense—latches onto the value systems and the desires of those who encounter it. This also suggests that a model's traveling power—its capacity to go viral—hinges on its existence in or relation to a particular place, institution, and/or group of people, which provides it with a capacity to facilitate and generate affective, contagious encounters. In other words, the traveling model not only travels but it also attracts travelers; it is both fixed in place and mobile. As Baker et al. (2016, 463) argue, "policy models are not generated abstractly in 'deterritorialized' networks of experts; rather, they emerge in and through concrete 'local' situations that constitute wider networks." This may not be as evident for standardized interventions as it is in the Awra Amba case. But if we look closer at the various models and best practices that are circulating, we will find that they often are closely linked to, and in many cases fueled by, their origin in a specific geographical location where they once were, or they are repeatedly put on display by groups or individuals who are either politically well-connected or have a certain charisma. As sites of "skilled practices" (Haraway 1990, cited in Behrends, Park, and Rottenburg 2014b, 2), these places become "culturally vibrant magnets" for policy tourism (Gonzalez 2010, 1397), recognized for their "power to export models and for inviting imitation by those who want to follow what is perceived to be a route to success" (Behrends, Park, and Rottenburg 2014b, 3). The circulation of policy ideas and models is, in other words, not an entirely rational process. In addition to relying on an encounter with receptive agents or environments, the process involves interests, desire, and emotions that strongly condition how we translate a model or an idea. What we pick up, copy, and hence circulate is a result of "semiconscious imitation" (Thrift 2008, 85) produced by biologically and culturally produced desires. This illustrates, as Sampson (2011, 8) argued, that it is "what 'we feel' about what spreads that becomes the most effectual contagion of all." Further, a virus and a cell interact in ways that transform both, producing the conditions for contagion and mutation. Through a process of assembling a heterogeneous-yet-efficacious concatenation of actors, vectors, desires, values, narratives, and physical and virtual experiences, the traveling model becomes "infectious," like a virus that not only transforms the cell but also has contagious capacity. This transformative capacity is important to stress: while Tarde's social contagion recognizes that the diffusion of collective representations and practices depends on initial recognition—that it needs a port or a receptor of entry—the notion of virality I suggest here emphasizes the agency of viral assemblages; that is, the ongoing transformative capacity that viral assemblages have on both the hosts and guests. Not only does the traveling model, as a viral assemblage, have the capacity to turn the host into a carrier who can reproduce the virus, it also incorporates the host into its circulatory assemblage.

Attention to the role of desire and an emphasis on semiconscious imitation as a driving force in circulating models and ideas do not exclude a recognition of conscious and deliberate human actors. While Tarde (Tarde and Toscano 2007, 631) emphasized how imitation together with affect and semiconscious desires are key characteristics of everything social, he also underscored that "there is not a single aspect of social life in which one does not see passion grow and unfold together with intelligence." Imitative processes are, in other words, not purely accidental or arbitrary. There are numerous examples of how imitative processes—such as the spread of a story, a model, or a product—are consciously and carefully steered. This is increasingly done in political campaigns, marketing, and the design industry, which use focus group-tested media strategies and devices to generate particular desires and emotions such as anger, outrage, fear, and ecstasy. As we shall see in the next chapter, when we further explore Paulina's and Serdar's work with *The Awra Amba Experience* and Lyfta, what is framed as an engagement born out of a desire to create a better world may also have exclusionary and iniquitous effects that often remain hidden under its idealization.

Chapter 7

Conditional Virality

IN 2019, on Father's Day, Serdar posted a rather personal article on Lyfta's web page. Inspired by a story he had heard while attending a learning festival the weekend before—one that took him on an "unforgettable emotional journey" and brought him to tears—Serdar's article is a tribute to emotions and fatherhood. In addition to describing precious, emotional moments with both his father and his son, he details how participants who attend Lyfta's workshops are deeply touched and even cry when they are introduced to the company's products. And then, he presents Muhammad, a Palestinian and widowed father and taxi driver who came to Finland in 1986, and who, together with his daughter Amina, are featured in one of Lyfta's story worlds. After detailing how he first met Muhammad, Serdar invites the reader to meet him and Amina, providing a link to a short, touching documentary. The invitation is not unconditional, however. "I am not sure how long we will be able to keep this online," Serdar writes before he wishes all fathers a Happy Father's Day.[1]

Serdar's Father's Day reflection illustrates how Lyfta's producers draw on the logics of affect and emotions in the framing of their products. Created with the purpose of giving the audience embodied experiences and feelings of actually being there, Lyfta's interactive documentaries exemplify a much broader phenomenon: the rise of immersive storytelling in an increasingly digital world. In the marketing of their product, Lyfta's producers emphasize how their stories have the power to foster compassionate and empathic global citizens by allowing the users to immerse themselves into the real life of others. This emotional and affective framing is evident in Paulina's and Serdar's description of why they decided to turn the Awra Amba story into an interactive documentary in the first place:

> Having spent several months in Awra Amba, we realized that Awra Amba's story is hugely important and multi-faceted, and that it simply could not

be told in a traditional, linear film. The best way to understand what Awra Amba is about is to visit them. This being out of bounds for many people, we have carefully crafted an immersive aesthetic and soundscape that evokes the feeling of being there in person. We have worked together with the community to build a space where people can experience their fascinating stories and draw inspiration and concrete solutions to make change in their own communities. An interactive format allows for free exploration, making it a perfect way for people to learn. All the stories within *The Awra Amba Experience* are designed to spark conversations, making it an ideal tool for educators, researchers and activists.[2]

While visiting Finland in fall 2018, I had the chance to participate in one of the many workshops Lyfta organizes for educators and teachers, during which the company's emphasis on empathy and on emotions became even more evident. The workshop was part of the Dare to Learn 2018 Conference—an international, annual learning festival attracting more than four thousand participants from sixty countries. Promoted as "a two-day playground for thinking big and creating wild" and aimed at rethinking learning, it is one of the largest educational events in Northern Europe. When I, on a sunny September morning, walked into the red-lighted foyer of the conference venue—an old cable factory turned into one of Finland's largest and most versatile cultural centers—and was met by a party atmosphere, I knew it would be a very unusual and different conference experience. Attracted by upbeat music, I quickly passed by numerous EdTech vendors that had lined up to showcase their products before I entered the main event hall. A long, red-carpeted catwalk served as the stage, with the audience sitting on bleachers along the sides or standing at its end. Tables or chairs were nowhere to be seen. "Definitely not a conference where I can sit with my laptop and take notes or follow up long-overdue emails," I thought to myself as I maneuvered among the standing audience, trying to find an opening that would allow me to catch whatever was happening with my iPhone camera. When I finally found a spot that gave me an open view of the scene, I realized I had arrived just in time for the opening speech. Dressed in a black Dare To Learn T-shirt and walking up and down the runway with a microphone in his hand, one of the organizers made his introductory remarks before Finland's Minister of Education, Sanni Grahn-Laasonen, emerged from behind a black curtain and was greeted with a high five to the sound of upbeat music. After talking about

Finland's role in and passion for global education and innovation, she ended her address with the following statement: "Finland wants to be a model country for global education."

A few hours later, I am sitting in a crowded room in the basement of the old factory, ready to attend the first of two workshops facilitated by Lyfta. With the words "Let the World Come to You. Teach Global Citizens with Immersive Human Stories," Lyfta's home page fills the screen in the front of the room, welcoming the participants. The room is packed long before the event starts, prompting Serdar to invite people to come in and sit on the floor. A few minutes later, he opens the workshop introducing Lyfta, his background as a filmmaker, and his role as a cofounder of the company. After he has given a brief introductory speech on the company's history, including how it all started with Paulina's visit to Awra Amba, he encourages the audience to actively use Twitter during the event. He then gives the floor to Katri Meriläinen, Lyfta's head of education:

"Lyfta's focus is on important emotional and social life skills," Katri starts out, clearly referring to the workshop's title "Tools for Making Sense of Life Skills. Emotions and Learning." "We aim to bring to life concepts that often are abstract to children," she continues as she circulates a page that contains fifty words that show "Lyfta's life skills." The list includes terms such as *human rights, respect, communication, active citizenship*, and *empathy and understanding others*. These are, according to Katri, core values that often are listed in curriculums but never assessed. "What is being assessed really shapes the way we learn. Lyfta's learning platform provides ways for students to understand, apply, and assess these skills," she concludes.

Starting from *The Awra Amba Experience*, Katri then guides us through the Lyfta platform, emphasizing how the company's documentaries provide children with the opportunity to meet all kinds of people from all over the world. As she opens a space in Dinnertime 360, one of Lyfta's storyworlds, and leads us to a dinner table in the home of Habiba, a Somali Finnish single mother and her seven children, she emphasizes that "the documentaries are all about perspective taking," that they have been created in order to generate an understanding of a concept or a situation from an alternative point of view. Using the mouse, she then shows us how, by clicking on one of the plates, you can get the recipe of the Somali dish and see how Habiba makes it. "If you use a virtual reality headset you will have a pretty authentic experience. You will be sitting at the table in front of one of the plates and meet Habiba and her children. In this way, we can give children an opportunity to get to know people they are not much likely to meet," Katri says before she clicks on Habiba and starts the screening of a three-minute documentary.

In the film, Habiba, who works for Finn Church Aid where she is involved in developing models for family support to prevent radicalization and social marginalization, talks about her experience growing up in Finland: "My mother never told me to choose whether I'm Finnish or Somalian. We were allowed to be just ourselves. At home, we never needed to think about it. When I was with Finns, I was that Somalian girl, and when with Somalis, the Finnish girl." The short documentary shows glimpses of her daily life, but the story Habiba tells is first and foremost centered around exclusion and racism. As we see her sitting on the bus wearing a pink hijab, she talks about how the general atmosphere in Finland has changed over the past five years: "In a bus, no one sits next to me, even if the bus is crowded. People would rather stand than sit next to me. I just think 'Well, good, more space for me,' but not everyone thinks like that. Some really do get depressed and wonder what is wrong with them. Especially young people." The documentary ends after Habiba, with tears in her eyes, talks about how she, because of her children, cannot afford to give up.

The documentary is well made, and I find myself touched by Habiba's story. However, when Katri asks us to form groups, discuss the film, and create an illustration about "perspective taking" that could be posted on Twitter and go viral, I find it difficult to focus and engage. The rest of the members in my group also seem hesitant and without much creative energy. Given the limited time we have been given by the workshop organizers—to both establish relationships with each other and complete the assignment—we fail in our half-hearted effort to produce something that could potentially go viral.

Katri's reference to "perspective taking," defined by Kimberley Chalbot Davis (2014, 9) as the process of "imaginatively experiencing the feelings, thoughts and situations of another" and considered a defining feature of empathy, reflects Paulina's and Serdar's overall vision: by telling positive, inspiring, and emotional stories that challenge the stereotypical images that are often produced by mainstream media, they aim to foster global, empathic citizens. Lyfta's producers assume that empathy is a skill that can be "cultivated in order to augment moral skills and promote ethical relations between people across social and geo-political boundaries" (Pedwell 2014, 47). This was what motivated Paulina when she, in 2008, returned to Awra Amba to film her first documentary. In May 2019, on the day of Lyfta's three-year anniversary, Paulina shared a reflection about her journey and the history behind *The Awra Amba Experience* and the establishment of the firm:

> We wanted to do our bit to change the world by sharing the story of Awra Amba. We had been invited by several universities to present it ([the University of]Cambridge and LSE [the London School of Economics] among them), screened it at numerous film festivals and negotiated a deal with *The Guardian* where they were showing parts of our content. We wanted to make an impact by offering a new perspective of a country that had often been portrayed in a negative light in mainstream media. We thought that by sharing a positive story, portraying people who are in charge of their own futures and showing innovation from an unexpected place would help people reconsider their preconceptions.[3]

But empathy is, along with other affective and emotional elements, not only the company's end goal; it is also a pedagogical tool. In fact, Lyfta's producers are explicit about the role that emotions play in their documentary productions: "At Lyfta, we believe that learning has to engage the whole child, including their emotions and social context. Positive emotions create motivation and motivation is the fuel for learning. We believe that we have found a very special formula to help educators nurture tomorrow's empathetic, global citizens—and we look forward to working with them to do that."[4] In an online article, Katri and Serdar describe the Lyfta learning experiences as "inherently interwoven with emotionally powerful and engaging human stories, which makes them memorable and easier to learn."[5] They also detail the company's pedagogical approach, citing, among others, Paul Ginnis (2002, 17), one of the longest-established education consultants in the UK and author of the influential guide *The Teacher's Toolkit: Raise Classroom Achievement With Strategies for Every Learner*: "Experiences that are multisensory, unusual, dramatic or emotionally strong are remembered far longer and in more detail." Influenced by research in neuroscience, Lyfta's producers moreover emphasize that

> experiencing inspiring stories (e.g., stories of other people's accomplishments, moral fortitude and determination in the face of difficulties and obstacles—which can be found in every Lyfta story) is likely to trigger a

powerful and intrinsic motivational force in learners that inspires them to take action.

The reference to neuroscience is neither incidental nor particular to Lyfta. Supported by research in psychology and neuroscience that explores the neural underpinnings of affect and emotions, "the affective priming of experience is fast becoming endemic to the study of social influence and methods of persuasion" (Sampson 2011, 8–9), and hence, it is not limited to the field of education. Neuromarketing, a fairly recent disciplinary field that draws on psychology and neuroscience to make sense of consumers' affective responses to marketing stimuli and predict their purchasing decisions has, for example, become increasingly popular, and empathy marketing has emerged as "the incandescent mantra in business and advertising circles" (Olson 2013, 61). As Sampson (2012, 105) has argued, emotional branding and marketing are increasingly and very consciously used by digital marketers: "Many of these new digital enterprises look to exploit new windows of opportunity by hooking up the microrelational flows of the consumer to emotionally persuasive purchase environments. Like this, the priming of consumer mood and flows of social influence produce new affective relations between people, products and brands, which can be cultivated and purposely steered."

Olson and others who have studied the widespread and partly naïve belief in, and framing of, empathy as an unquestionable good shed light on what happens when empathy becomes "an affective technology of global profit accumulation" (Pedwell 2014). In Olson's (2013, 61) words: "Market researchers and advertising experts are attempting to stand shoulder to shoulder with 'the better angels of our nature' in hopes this pose will increase sales. In short, putting oneself in another's shoes is a technique for selling them another pair." These perspectives are important to keep in mind as we continue to explore *The Awra Amba Experience* and how Lyfta frames and markets its product. Lyfta's use of empathy and emotions—both in the production and framing of their product—is an important element of the Awra Amba viral assemblage. The product's immersive qualities speak to the desires of educators and students alike, contributing to the model's virality.

Reinforcing Stereotypes

The Awra Amba Experience contains ten spaces: the clinic, the elderly home, the library, the school, a family home, the weaving workshop, the assembly hall, the finance office, the village square, and the visitor's center. Each space is a 360-degree environment that can be explored by using a mouse, a touch screen, or by looking through a virtual reality headset. If you click on the school building, for example, you will enter a classroom filled with students. As you listen to the buzzing sounds of the students' chatter and the clicks of chalk from the teacher's writing on the blackboard, you can move around the room, zoom in to explore particular details, or explore clickable objects that trigger various multimedia features. Each space sheds light on a particular theme and includes a short documentary featuring persons from Awra Amba. For example, in the classroom you can click on Tsegaynesh and "bring to life"[6] a young girl who has come from one of Awra Amba's neighboring villages to study at the high school. You can watch and listen to the story she tells about her childhood, how she struggled to continue her education, and how she, after escaping an early marriage, found a safe haven in Awra Amba. In fact, reflecting the community's status as a gender-equal model village, many of the spaces address gender-related issues. If you visit the family home, for example, you will meet a young couple who just had their first child. In addition to detailing the community's norms and values related to family life and sexuality, the short documentary follows the couple on a visit to the clinic, where they receive counseling about different family planning methods.

Interviews with students who have immersed themselves in Lyfta's story worlds suggest that Paulina's and Serdar's vision and pedagogical strategy have been quite successful. Students who are featured in Lyfta's promotional videos[7] describe their experience with *The Awra Amba Experience* and Lyfta's storyworlds in the following way:

> It's awesome, in a word. Being able to instantly teleport halfway across the world whilst staying in the same spot, and see how things are, for real. [. . .] In [the] real world we're glued to one outlook: we can only see what we see and feel what we feel. If we somehow allow ourselves to . . . interact our emotions and our viewpoints with other people's, then we can become better than if there was only one person.

> It's absolutely amazing. You can get lost in a completely different world.

> It drew me in.

As part of Lyfta's promotional material, these comments have certainly been selected for commercial purposes. For a limited period of time, I did, however, also have access to the platform, and this allowed me to test out *The Awra Amba Experience* with my students. While some of them struggled to navigate the platform and found it limiting and a bit slow, the majority had, just like the students in Lyfta's videos, a positive experience:

> My Awra Amba experience was unlike anything I have ever seen or heard of before. Throughout the video I kept having to remind myself that this is an actual place and not a movie that I am watching. I truly believe that Awra Amba is a representation of what our world should be more like.

> I thought that the whole experience of being able to see all the intricate parts that make up this village on the computer was a clever way of teaching people about other cultures.

> I very much enjoyed *The Awra Amba Experience*. I feel it was very interactive and informing. I enjoyed hearing from different members of the community and hearing their stories and experiences. At first I thought it would be very monotonous and would drag through however each member had a very important thing to say about their community. Also being able to see the community was incredible to me because we can explore this area while being thousands of miles apart. I think *The Awra Amba Experience* is extremely informative and I loved it!

> I have never experienced anything quite like it. I really liked the interactive aspect that allowed me to go into multiple different areas of the community and learn about each one in depth. My favorite part was being able to watch the videos in each area because I felt as though it gave me a sense of what the community and the people in the community were actually like.

At first glance, and based on these testimonies, it would be reasonable to conclude that Lyfta has succeeded in creating an immersive learning platform that challenges stereotypical images of various others, fostering a new generation of empathic citizens. Yet, a closer look and analysis of the stories they tell, particularly in the Awra Amba case, reveal problematic underpinnings. In fact, most of the documentaries in the Awra Amba storyworld reinforce common stereotypes and generalized images of Ethiopia as an undeveloped rural village. To further substantiate this argument, let us take a closer look at *The Awra Amba Experience*, exploring the virtual village and some of the stories offered to its online visitors.

The idealization of Awra Amba's values and the community's simple, rural way of life, combined with the construction and portrayal of life outside Awra Amba, turns the stories in *The Awra Amba Experience* into the stereotypical narratives that Lyfta intends to challenge. While Awra Amba is depicted as a peaceful utopia—a progressive island and a successful modernist and entrepreneurial project—the world that surrounds it is cast as its contrast, creating dichotomous worlds: When neighboring communities reportedly attacked Awra Amba with weapons, Zumra and his followers did not fight back but spent time playing volleyball; elders in Awra Amba are properly cared for and live a comfortable life, while elders outside Awra Amba live in hardship and are often abandoned by their families; in Awra Amba, the young choose who they marry at an appropriate legal age, while those who live in neighboring communities are forced into child marriage; and women outside Awra Amba are oppressed victims of harmful traditional practices and lack economic freedom, while Awra Amba is a haven for gender equality. There is, in other words, a clear othering of everything outside Awra Amba. Presenting the village against a starkly dark background of violence, prejudice, and iniquity serves to heighten not only its uniqueness but also its uncontested legitimacy as a model for the viewer's desires for justice and empowerment.

It is certainly not my intention to deny that injustice and inequality exist in Ethiopia. But the gross generalizations that are used to tell Awra Amba's story and the failure to situate complex issues such as, for example, early marriage within a larger historical, cultural, economic, and political context exacerbates dominant images of Ethiopia as a rural, war-ridden country, where harmful traditional practices flourish and girls and women are universally oppressed and are victims of violence. There is, in addition, another tension inherent in the idealized portrayal of Awra Amba that aggravates the stereotypical image of Ethiopia as an uncivilized place. While Awra Amba, from a (Western) liberal point of view, may appear ideologically progressive, the village's infrastructure and architecture and the various material and symbolic artifacts that make up the village are rather simple. Considering that Awra Amba is portrayed as a successful, self-sustained, entrepreneurial community, an outsider who visits the village via *The Awra Amba Experience* could easily be misled into thinking that this is what development and progress looks like in Africa; that this is how far they have come, and perhaps more importantly, that this is only how far they can come.

An audience who is familiar with Ethiopia or similar contexts may see the problems and challenges these stories pose. A young, American elementary school teacher, who has used *The Awra Amba Experience* with fourth grade students in the United States, expressed concerns about Lyfta's stories in an interview I had with her after a visit to her school. Having spent a year teaching at a school in another African country, she was worried that *The Awra Amba Experience* could exacerbate and reinforce stereotypical images: "If I am only showing them this part of Africa, am I reinforcing the stereotype of all of Africa as this small village? Am I portraying this community as it should be portrayed?" She talked about how she had used her experience working and living in Africa to balance the image her students had of the continent and the perceptions that she thought were reinforced by *The Awra Amba Experience.* "I showed them pictures from the school I worked at and I said 'Look, this is in Africa too.' And the students said 'Oh, wow. You had desks, a library, and even a laptop?'" Realizing that stereotypical perceptions and images of Africa are prevalent, even among adults and fellow teachers, she was clearly troubled: "I worry, having been to and experienced life in Africa as a white American . . . coming back here and hearing so many white Americans say: 'Oh, did you live in a hut?'"

While this young teacher can contextualize Lyfta's stories and use them as an entry point to share her experiences of life in one of Africa's most vibrant, modern cities—she would pull up pictures that showed she had a bigger house while living in Africa than in the US—some of the other teachers I observed and talked with did not have the knowledge and background to critically assess and contextualize the stories. Just as the young teacher argued, they were unknowingly buying into the stereotypical images that *The Awra Amba Experience* rely on and thereby reinforce.

As the producers of *The Awra Amba Experience*, Paulina and Serdar play a central role, constructing the dichotomous narratives and hence creating the othering described above. The way audio and visual effects are used in the documentaries makes it hard to believe that this othering has been completely unintentional. For example, when the different protagonists talk about how people outside Awra Amba live, the tone and mood of the music tend to change, becoming darker and more dramatic. Similarly, in two of the documentaries there is an interesting yet troubling use of a particular scene that is used as an illustration when the narrator is talking about Awra Amba's neighboring communities: the naked, dusty, scarred legs of a man wearing shorts and rubber sandals that have been made from old tires. This visual effect appears when Tsegaynesh—the young girl featured in the documentary about the high school—talks about her ex-husband and when Zumra tells the story about their hostile neighboring communities. In the Ethiopian context, particularly from the viewpoint of the country's urban elites, these are the feet of uneducated, poor, primitive peasants. While I disapprove of and deeply disagree with the assumptions of backwardness that underpin such perceptions—my experience living among rural pastoralists in the southeastern lowlands of the country have taught me that physical appearance and lack of formal education do not mean that people are ignorant or lack sophisticated knowledge—for outsiders, these images serve to cement dominant images of Africa, and particularly rural Africa, as uncivilized.

The othering and the dichotomies that characterize the documentaries in *The Awra Amba Experience* are produced not only by Lyfta. Members of Awra Amba's kinetic elite—particularly Enaney and Gebeyehu—worked closely with Paulina and Serdar when they were planning and shooting the footage for *The Awra Amba Experience*, and the othering we see in Lyfta's documentaries is clearly present in the stories that members of the Awra Amba community tell their visitors on a daily basis. By contrasting their way of life to outside communities, they underscore the community's position as an exceptional model village. This othering also serves to legitimize Awra Amba's model status. It is, in other words, not only Lyfta—as outside entrepreneurs—who extract value from the marketing of Awra Amba's difference and particularities. As we shall see in Chapter 8, insiders—most notably members of Awra Amba's kinetic elite—also benefit from the othering that goes into the branding of the Awra Amba model.

The construction of an exceptional model through various levels of othering enhances the market value of the Awra Amba story and the community's positioning within what John Comaroff and Jean Comaroff (2009, 24) have described as the "identity industry." They discuss and exemplify how ethnicity and identity have been commodified and have entered the global marketplace through, among other things, the establishment and branding of cultural villages. With its entry into the commercial EdTech industry, Lyfta has contributed significantly to and benefited from the commodification and branding of Awra Amba's values and the community's cultural identity. Yet, as Comaroff and Comaroff (2009, 23), borrowing from Mazzarella, argue, this is not a "one-way process of abstraction."

While othering at multiple levels and in different ways clearly serves to legitimate the model and increase the value of the Awra Amba story, hence fueling the model's virality, the commodification and commercialization of the village, its values, and its history also pose limitations to the model's virality. This is clearly reflected in Serdar's above-mentioned blog post in which he, after encouraging the reader to explore the short documentary that tells Muhammad's story, warns that it may only be accessible for a limited period of time. The conditional and temporary hospitality Serdar conveys suggests that there are certain limitations to Awra Amba's virality—that its spread and contagion are neither universal nor unlimited. Just like a virus, the traveling model does not spread unconditionally. Its infectiousness depends on a favorable, hospitable environment—on open access. As will be clear in the following section, there are economic, technological, and ideological barriers that prevent unlimited and uncontrolled transmission. The model's travel is, in other words, not frictionless.

Exclusive and Limited Virality

After Paulina and Serdar established Lyfta and became part of the EdTech industry, it has become increasingly difficult to access the platform and *The Awra Amba Experience*. During the first year Lyfta was on the market, one could sign up as a guest and get limited access for a month. This would allow one to enter the village, explore its overall layout, and get an overview of the potential spaces one could visit. But only one space, the weaving workshop, was open. The limited access was clearly a marketing strategy—a way to get potential users hooked and convinced about the value of purchasing the product. My first visit to *The Awra Amba Experience* certainly spurred my curiosity. Yet, it quickly turned into frustration when I scrolled down the page that provided more detailed information about the cost of a Lyfta subscription: a one-year institutional subscription is 1,600 Euros for a small school, 2,500 Euros for a medium school, and 3,400 Euros for a large school.[8]

As indicated in Serdar's Father's Day reflection, access to *The Awra Amba Experience* and the rest of Lyfta's storyworlds is not free and unlimited. In the UK, where Lyfta has partnered with Connecting Classrooms through Global Learning, an international program funded by the British government and implemented by the British Council that supports teaching and learning about global issues, the company offers free Continuing Professional Education for primary and secondary schools. This comes with a period of a free Lyfta subscription. Such arrangements are not available in the US or in Finland where teachers rely on an institutional subscription to get access. Teachers at schools in the US, particularly in public schools, raised this as a major concern when I visited them. Their initial access had been facilitated by a research initiative at the College of Education at a nearby university. None of them believed their schools would be able to invest in an institutional subscription once their license expired.

I first had full access to *The Awra Amba Experience* in the summer of 2018 following my second Zoom interview with Paulina. At that time, I was in the early phase of writing this book, and I realized that a focus on Awra Amba as a traveling, viral model, would require a focus on Paulina's role. More than three years after our first interview, I reached out to her again, curious to learn more about her work. "I don't have access to the full platform," I told her, when she made a reference to the role Enaney plays in one of the documentaries. It was clear that she assumed I had explored the *The Awra Amba Experience*. The next day, she had sent me an email with a link to a Windows version of the app that allowed me to download *The Awra Amba Experience* on my personal computer. "It would be amazing if you could show it to people in Awra Amba when you visit next month. If you download it on your computer, you will only need internet access for the few minutes it takes you to sign in," she had told me as we had rounded up our conversation the day before. During the interview, she had explained that the Awra Amba community had not yet been able to see and virtually explore *The Awra Amba Experience*. She had forwarded a mobile phone version of the app to one of Awra Amba's younger members, a young man who had been in touch with her over Facebook and had shown an interest in seeing the final product. But the app had not worked. "It is a product that does not work on every kind of device," Paulina said. "And it requires much bandwidth."

When I arrived in Ethiopia in September 2018 with *The Awra Amba Experience* on my laptop, one of the first things I did was to contact one of the members of Awra Amba's kinetic elite who lives and works in Addis Ababa. He is well educated, and when I met him in 2016, he identified himself as a mediator between Awra Amba and various national and international actors. This made me assume he was well informed about *The Awra Amba Experience* and the more recent establishment of Lyfta. But after spending an hour exploring the platform, he took off his headphones, turned toward me, and said: "I had no idea this existed. I knew they had produced a documentary. A friend of mine who lives in Belgium saw it when it was screened at a film festival. But I did not hear about this." I asked him whether he thought it had been discussed with people in Awra Amba. "There may be people in the community who are better informed than I am. If this has become a commercial product, there must be an agreement with the community. Perhaps there is an agreement. But I don't know .... There must be a legal representative from the community who knows about this. There has to be a legal contract," he said, while also acknowledging the opportunity Lyfta's product provides for the community. He talked about how it would facilitate the spreading of the community's ideas and values to all humans and to every corner of the world and about how the program would generate discussions—even at universities. But he also spoke in an emotional, almost disturbed tone about all the community has sacrificed. "Many visitors are coming. Researchers like you are coming, and the village is an official tourist attraction. The community members have the right to know that this has become a commercial platform. And they should also get some benefits."

A few weeks later, I am sitting in the welcoming center together with Zumra, Enaney, and their eldest son, Ayalsew, ready to connect to *The Awra Amba Experience*. The room, which since my last visit has been painted in a bright green color, is filled with anticipation as Ayalsew fiddles with his phone to turn on the hot spot. A few minutes later, we are all crowding around my screen as I navigate the interface, explaining the different features of the program. As the three first-time visitors see themselves and other community members on the screen, they chuckle and comment on things that have changed since the time it was filmed. And when an elderly woman, the protagonist in a documentary about compassion, uses an unwrapped mosquito net to decorate the wall in her room, they all burst out in laughter.

"I expect that you, in your book, represent our community in the same way Paulina has done," Zumra jokingly concludes when I shut down my computer. I have enjoyed the lighthearted atmosphere and the laughter that has filled the room, yet Zumra's comment disturbs me. It reminds me of the day when, a few weeks earlier, I had returned to Awra Amba for a new round of fieldwork. When Zumra had entered the welcoming center accompanied by Ayalsew, he had been uptight. "I remember you and your last visit," he said in a resentful tone. "I remember we had a disagreement." I had not been prepared for his harsh and unwelcoming attitude. While we certainly had discussed my research, I never thought of our relationship as fraught with disagreement. When I had tried to find words to smooth the conversation, Zumra had constantly interrupted, setting conditions for my research. "You have to promise to send your manuscript to us for approval," he had said as he picked up a report written by Robert Joumard, the French scholar who had invited them to France, from the bookshelf. "Do you see this?" he had asked. "When Robert first wrote about us, he got many things wrong. But after we gave him feedback he corrected his mistakes. This is also what you should do." We had a long and difficult conversation where I tried to explain that because my book project is about how the Awra Amba story has spread all around the world, I do research that involves a lot of people and that I could not let them check everything I write. After much back and forth, I had promised to send them the parts of the manuscript that detail Zumra's philosophy and the Awra Amba story.

"I have greetings from Paulina," I had then said, hoping her name will cheer up the tense atmosphere. But Zumra's response was not what I had expected. "I am not at all happy with her," he said. "She has broken her promises. She promised us a lot, but she has not followed up. She never gave us a copy of her documentary." In the days that followed, it became clear that what once may have been a close partnership between Paulina and Awra Amba, is no longer so. "The last time we met was in France in 2014," Gebeyhu, the young man who used to have a key role in the cooperative, told me one day.

> At that time, she said she was in the final stage of producing the new documentary. She told us that she planned to show it to children in schools, and that she would invite Zumra to London for the inaugural screening, where he would be given the chance to talk and share his ideas with a lot of different people. But things did not go as she had planned. She later told us that it would require a lot of money to invite Zumra to London, and that they had not been able to secure funding.

When I asked him if he had heard about Lyfta, he shook his head. In fact, no one in Awra Amba knew that their story had entered the EdTech market.

Zumra and Gebeyhu may be part of Awra Amba's kinetic elite, but they are not immune from being subjected to exploitative and exclusionary practices.

The fact that *The Awra Amba Experience* is a viral model and a commercial product that circulates through global electronic media yet is unknown and not available to the community's inhabitants themselves, or elsewhere in Ethiopia, is clearly a paradox. It illustrates, as Jana Costas argues (2013, 1468), that "discourses and practices of mobilites [. . .] can be 'contradictory' and 'sticky'"; that global flows are not "open-ended" and unlimited, but go "hand in hand with closure" (Geschiere and Meyer 1998, 602). The virus metaphor is, again, useful here, since it illuminates the conditional hospitality and mobility that characterize our increasingly digital and transnational world. The flows and mobilities that emerge in the Awra Amba case point to an exclusive form of virality. It is a virality that includes, welcomes, and benefits some while excluding, exploiting, and oppressing others; a virus that preys on some and feeds others. In the viral assemblage, not all components circulate with the same intensity and extensity and not all agents in the various networks have access to its materials and the resources it generates. These power asymmetries, which are, in the Awra Amba case, perhaps most clearly on display through the exclusionary and partly exploitative practices that have followed in the wake of Lyfta's entry into the global, commercial EdTech market, illustrate the limitations that are inherent in what is often erroneously perceived to be an unlimited and uncontrolled viral flow.

The limited virality and conditional hospitality surface not only in relation to Lyfta and the company's products, however. It is here worth mentioning that although a wide range of national and international actors have enthusiastically and uncritically embraced the Awra Amba model, the reception among people living in neighboring communities has been lukewarm at best. In the conversations I have had with people from the villages next to Awra Amba, the most frequent explanation for why they reject the community's way of life relates to religion. "If we were to be like Awra Amba, how can we keep our religion? How can we celebrate our holidays if we have to work the whole time?" a young farmer argued. In a country where religion and religious practices are institutionalized and deeply woven into people's everyday lives and social relations, Awra Amba's way of life is not at all appealing. As I will discuss more in-depth in the next chapter, this aspect not only limits the acceptance of people outside Awra Amba, it also inhibits Awra Amba's younger generation from seeking membership in the cooperative.

There is, additionally, another potential factor, not openly stated, that could explain why Awra Amba has a limited appeal in the Ethiopian context. This relates to the community's status as a weaving community. As in many other areas of Africa, artisans, such as weavers, are often considered to occupy a marginal social posision. They are perceived as polluted and often experience shunning (Lyons 2014). Awra Amba's status as a weaving community, along with its historical connection to another marginalized group, the Alayhim, are factors that potentially further limit the model's virality in Ethiopia.

Ambivalent Empathy

My main focus in this chapter has been on the central role that affect, particularly empathy, plays in Lyfta's productions and in their promotional and pedagogical practices. While the policy literature generally ignores the role that emotions and affect play in fueling the virality of policy models and ideas, this is, as we have seen here, not at all the case for actors situated within the digital and creative industries. In addition to drawing on affective elements for marketing and pedagogical purposes, these actors very purposely tap into these elements in the production of new, commercial, digital commodities.

Paulina's and Serdar's motivations and their affective engagements may have transformative potential. Yet, a closer reading of the company's products and partnership with the Awra Amba community illustrates the "ambivalent grammar of empathy" (Pedwell 2014, 67). To cultivate a constructive form of empathy is clearly not as straightforward as one may imagine. Through a close and contextual reading of *The Awra Amba Experience*, I have shown how the cultivation of empathy, particularly when it fails to account for historical, cultural, and political context, may even sustain and reproduce "that very difference that it may seek to overcome" (Ahmed 2004b, 30). This is perhaps reinforced when empathy and emotional, immersive stories, become commodities that not only reproduce but also depend on idealizations, which, as we saw in Chapter 4, entail processes of exclusion and erasure. The increased commodification of empathy calls for a careful consideration and a contextual and situated analysis of "the rhetorical and pedagogical functions of empathy" (Kulbaga 2008, 507).

Lyfta's entry into the EdTech market sheds light on the "ambivalent relationship between empathy and transnational capitalism" (Pedwell 2014, 3). The exclusionary processes and exploitative relationships that emerge when empathy becomes a commercialized commodity and a marketing technique challenge assumptions of empathy as an unquestionable moral good. We cannot assume that empathy is a universal capacity that can be nurtured and developed as "an affective 'solution'" (1) and a key to social justice, respect, and equality. This is not to say that empathy cannot promote good actions or be the basis for increased understanding of the suffering of others. My point is instead to emphasize how important it is that we not treat empathy in the abstract as an unquestionable, good virtue and that we also consider empathy as a polyvalent affect that can have a dark side. Just as a virus turns and redirects the machinery that is vital for the cell to function normally, producing more of the virus that eventually undermines the cell, so too can empathy, which is key to sociality, become a source of predation.

In this chapter, we have seen some of the unintended consequences and the exclusionary practices that *The Awra Amba Experience* and Lyfta's products have generated. Now, let us return to Awra Amba proper. What has becoming and being a model meant for the Awra Amba community? What are the ways in which the community has benefited and capitalized from its status? And what does the model status hide? These are some of the questions I explore in the next chapter where Elsabet,[9] a woman who once held a prominent position in Awra Amba, serves as the chapter's protagonist.

Chapter 8

Being a Model

"WILL YOU WRITE about Alayhim in your book?" Elsabet asks in a hopeful tone. As always, she has welcomed me warmly into her home. She had not expected me today; she did not even know I was in the country. I had been trying to call her for several days, without luck. "My phone broke," she explains after the warm embrace I receive when I apologize for arriving without notice. "I do not think it is possible to write a book about Awra Amba without mentioning Alayhim," I assure her. She smiles as she bends over a pot of bubbling *shiro*, a spicy, smooth sauce made of chickpea flour. A staple everyday Ethiopian dish considered poor man's fare, it is my all-time favorite. "A lot of people in Awra Amba will be glad if you publish the book," Elsabet continues, stirring the sauce. "Perhaps as much as half of the community." Her mother, who sits on a mattress on the floor spinning cotton, nods her head. They want their story to be told.

Elsabet lives in a one-room rented house in the town of Alem Ber, together with her mother, her aunt, and her youngest son. The small house is located in a neighborhood where the majority of the population belongs to the Alayhim community. "My parents were followers of Alayhim, so I knew Sheik Saide Hassan from the time I was a child," Elsabet told me the first time we met. Born in the early 1970s during the reign of Emperor Haile Selassie, she was a small child when the Derg regime came to power in 1974. At that time, her family lived in Grar Minch, a green, lush, and peaceful place located halfway up the hillside of one of the mountains that surround Alem Ber. Unless someone told you, you would not know what is hidden in the mountain. When I, on a warm summer day in 2017, hiked the dusty, swirling paths that take one to the place, crossing creeks and passing through fields that had been prepared for another season of rain, my two guides—one of the community's leaders and his son—had pointed to what looked like a small forest in the mountain side. "Do you see the big trees?" they had asked me. "That is Grar Minch, the place where Sheik Saide Hassan resided and built a mosque." An hour later, we had arrived in Grar Minch, where I had been surprised to find an old, two-story building. As I had climbed the fragile staircase that led up to the crafted wooden veranda that partly surrounded the mosque's second floor and provided access to a big room, I had been reminded of a time in my childhood when I had taken weekly piano lessons with Mrs. Svetlana—a Russian pianist who lived in an old house in the Piazza neighborhood in Addis Ababa. Her house had probably been built in the early 1900s. While the mosque certainly appeared as a simpler version—or a model of the old Addis Ababa-style houses—the influence of that period's urban architecture was unmistakable.

There is not much of a settlement left in Grar Minch today. During the villagization program the Derg initiated in the mid-1980s, the Alayhim community was forced to leave Grar Minch and settle in new, government-designed villages. "Some left to Alem Ber or Sinko. Others followed Zumra," Elsabet reports. She is an articulate woman, and even after her brother enters the room, she is the one who does most of the talking. But, once in a while, her mother and brother add details to the story. "My family followed Zumra because we believed he was Sheik Saide's successor," her mother explains, as Elsabet leaves the room to pick up a big serving tray from the backyard that she had left drying in the sun when she had finished cleaning the dishes earlier that morning. "I had developed a close spiritual relationship with Zumra, so I became one of the founding members of the farmer producer cooperative that Zumra established in 1985," the old woman continues. "It was a well-functioning producer cooperative and we owned much land."

But Zumra's strict treatment of their neighbors—he would, according to Elsabet's mother, charge those who failed to keep their cattle from entering the fields 100 ETB—created tensions. The neighbors became increasingly hostile and started opposing Zumra and his followers, alleging that they were affiliated with the TPLF. "That is when we left for Bonga," Elsabet concludes as she carefully pours the thickened, steaming *shiro* sauce atop the *injera* before placing it on a small, three-legged stool that she puts in front of me. "*Bi!* Eat!" she says, as she tears off a part of the *injera*, folds it around a mouthful of *shiro*, and puts it in her mouth. "It is good. Eat!" she repeats.

For many years, Elsabet and her family lived in Awra Amba and were dedicated members of the cooperative. But then, on July 19, 2008, Elsabet was unexpectedly and without warning expelled from the community. "It remains the darkest day of my life," Elsabet says. "I used to be very happy and was living a good life in Awra Amba. I had been with the community through harsh and difficult times. We had struggled to survive, but because we worked together we were very productive and made great improvements. But that day, everything changed." The day was not only dramatic for Elsabet and her family. One of the community members who finally confided in me in 2018 described it as "the day the community broke." He detailed how some of the people in the village had physically removed Elsabet from the community. They had come to her house, loaded all her things on a truck, and had driven her and the rest of her family to Alem Ber, one of the neighboring towns. The decision to exclude her, which was made by Zumra and Enaney, had not been discussed in any of the committees or in the general assembly. In fact, the decision had limited support, and many of the community members cried when she left.

In talking with me and sharing her story, Elsabet was motivated by her sense of the injustice to which she had been subjected. "I am telling you my story because I believe that it may bring change. I would not be interested in giving you information if I did not think it could serve a purpose—to correct injustice. If we keep silent about the injustices that have happened in Awra Amba, the things that happened to me may also happen to others." While Elsabet's narrative clearly is colored by the hurt, stress, and marginalization that she and her family suffered as a result of the exclusion, her story is by no means a one-sided condemnation of Awra Amba. Since the first day I met her, Elsabet has reminded me of how important it is to recognize both the strengths and the weaknesses of the community: "When you do your research, you should identify both the good and the bad things."

I have written this chapter, detailing what becoming a model has meant for Awra Amba, with Elsabet's advice in mind. But before I turn to a discussion and analysis of the impact the model status has had on Awra Amba and its community members, let us first go back to the time when Zumra and his followers returned from exile in Bonga; to the time when Awra Amba was an unknown, small, and struggling community.

Recognition

As we saw in Chapter 1, according to the official narrative, the Awra Amba community was established by Zumra in 1972. Elsabet and other members of the Alayhim community strongly contest this and claim that Zumra at that time was still part of Alayhim. What *they* say was established in 1972 was a co-operative initiated by Sheik Saide; a cooperative that Zumra revitalized later as a response to the 1985 villagization program. This cooperative, which was situated in Gibra, about six kilometers from Awra Amba, is the cooperative that Elsabet's mother joined and the one they left behind when they fled to Bonga around 1987 or 1988. This means that Awra Amba—the place it is to-day—was established much later than the official narrative suggests.

When Zumra and his followers returned from Bonga in 1992 following the fall of the Derg regime, the land they had previously cultivated had been oc-cupied by their old neighbors. Not only did Zumra confirm this in interviews, but he also detailed the process of how the community attained its current landholdings. They first received a small piece of land from Kibret Siraj—Zumra's father-in-law—who has never been a member of the Awra Amba community but who resides, together with other members of his family, in a fertile area adjacent to Awra Amba. The community also filed claims for additional land, and during a land-distribution reform that took place in the southern areas of the Amhara region in 1997, the government granted small pieces of land to individual members of the community. This land was pooled into the association's common landholding, which, according to the official narrative, amounts to 17.5 hectares.[1]

Elsabet describes the first years they lived in Awra Amba as a difficult time. "But we had love for each other. It was this commitment and our hard work that made us known in the first place," she says. With a background in Alayhim, many of the community members had weaving skills, and shortly after they returned from Bonga, they constructed a weaving workshop. While Sheik Saide had emphasized that men and women are equal and had stressed the importance of not imposing extra obligations on women, Zumra intro-duced, according to Elsabet, a new idea: they should all work together; women could weave and men could also make *injera*. Along with the community's insistence on being self-reliant and in charge of its own development, this change in the gender-specific division of labor was what first caught the at-tention of representatives from the Ethiopian government, the media, and the NGO community.

According to Elsabet, the screening of the first Awra Amba documen-tary on ETV had a significant impact on the community. In addition to be-coming an official tourist destination, the community drew the attention of numerous NGOs and government institutions. At first, Awra Amba resisted any form of support offered by the government and the donor community. Aster, the UN Women senior advisor I introduced in Chapter 6, who came across the community in the late 1990s when working for an international NGO, described how hard it was to convince Zumra to accept external support. "I told him that we had funds available for the community, and if they accepted, it would help them achieve their goals in five years instead of ten," she said in an interview in 2018. In her opinion, Awra Amba would know how to utilize external support effectively. The community's accomplishments would triple what other communities achieved, according to her.

Zumra's hesitation and initial rejection of external support speaks of a strong-willed and independent leadership. And Awra Amba has, without doubt, taken ownership and set clear conditions for donors and outside involvement. This has, according to Zumra, been key to the community's success:

> It is our motivation and self-confidence to do things ourselves that contribute to our current achievements. We were [. . .] running from below [working from the bottom up] to plan and do things for which we are today known to be successful, with nobody from outside to assist us. Of course, if you do not plan by yourself, it is like to travel on the road that you do not know. . . . If you ask me about where the plan comes [from] it is from the community. Plans for our activities are prepared by the participation and discussion of all community members (Getu Demeke Alene 2011, 59).

Zumra and other members of the community's elite consistently emphasize Awra Amba's independence and claim that the community has no interest in being associated with a particular organization. Yet Awra Amba is not self-sustained and its achievements are not independent of external funding. The village has received substantial support in the years since it became publicly known. This is not immediately evident to visitors. Compared to many other communities in Ethiopia where NGO presence in the form of cars, offices, and signs is often visible, Awra Amba's many partnerships are not particularly evident. There are only two signs that speak of partnerships with external donors: one, which is posted at the Awra Amba turnoff, announces that the Organization for Rehabilitation and Development in Amhara, in partnership with the Solar Cooking Foundation, a Dutch NGO, has implemented an

Integrated Solar and Water Pasteurization Project in the community. I found the other sign lying on the ground behind one of the buildings. It told me that the Amhara Development Association (ADA), in partnership with an American philanthropic foundation called Glimmer of Hope, had constructed the community's health post. ADA also donated the first mill to the community.

The institutional, material, and visual absence of NGOs, coupled with what appears to be partnerships with private actors and informal groups such as Friends of Awra Amba, make it hard to track down the external support the community has received. But when one explores the various accounts of the community that exist on the internet, it is evident that Awra Amba has received financial and material support from a number of NGOs and foreign donors. In 2003, the Ethiopian Business Development Services Network and the Amhara Regional Micro and Small Enterprises Development Agency constructed a new weaving production hall in Awra Amba, donated four modern weaving machines, and arranged a two-month skill-training workshop for the weavers supported by the Swedish International Development Cooperation Agency (SIDA) and Deutsche Gesellschaft für Technische Zusammenarbeit. Paulina and Serdar, Lyfta's CEOs, also conducted a crowdfunding campaign that supported the construction of the community's high school, and a Belgian NGO, Heber Solidarité Ethiopie, worked together with the community to reconstruct the kindergarten, which the organization also furnished and equipped. Heber Solidarité Ethiopie's website reveals its role in stocking the library:

> During one of our visits, we found that the elementary and secondary school library was poorly equipped and lacking basic school books, those of the Ethiopian State Program. They were too expensive for some children to buy. We have equipped the work room with enough of these books for children to borrow or work on site. We received a complete list of what was needed and have already been able to buy hundreds of them.[2]

One of the more recent initiatives has been spearheaded by Salem Mekuria, the Ethiopian American filmmaker I mentioned in Chapter 5. In 2017, she organized a fundraising event in Martha's Vineyard, Massachusetts in the US for the installation of a solar-powered water delivery system in Awra Amba.

While Awra Amba has received considerable support from international and private donors, the most substantial investments have come from the

Ethiopian government. "Following the first screening of the documentary on ETV, we became very popular, particularly among the various local and regional administrative bodies of the government," Elsabet recalls when I ask her to reflect on how the community's status as a model for gender equality and sustainable development impacted the community. "They started to offer us trainings, and we also received certificates and medals for introducing different schemes." These were not, however, the only ways in which Awra Amba received assistance from the Ethiopian government.

One day during my first fieldwork in 2015, as I visited a health center in one of the neighboring towns, I suddenly realized how Awra Amba stood out and received preferential treatment regarding basic infrastructure. "There must be some very powerful people in Awra Amba," a young nurse concluded as our tour of the facility was coming to an end. We were standing on the edge of a deep, black hole—a new well—that had been dug as an attempt to solve the health center's water problem. The health center still lacked the budget to purchase and install the equipment that would be necessary to pump up the water. It had been more than four years since the facility had been inaugurated and the first health workers arrived, yet there was still no water or electricity on the premises. Without these basic services, and with an almost inaccessible road—a few hours earlier my driver had given up maneuvering the four-wheel drive Toyota Land Cruiser up the steep and stony road that led up to the health center—it was no surprise that so few patients were present. With clear reference to the, at the time, increasingly authoritarian nature of the Ethiopian government, the nurse sighed when she described how people in the health center's catchment area were too afraid to complain about the lack of absolute necessities such as water and electricity. "If they complain, it will be taken as a sign of political opposition. So, people keep silent," she said, as we were about to depart. Shortly after, we returned to Awra Amba, to a place that is easily accessible by car, where there are electricity and phone services 24/7, and where two drilled wells provide water for the community. Part of the village even has piped water, and the ANRS Bureau of Culture and Tourism has installed common bathrooms with showers next to the guesthouse. When compared to some of the neighboring communities, the accumulation of resources and the well-developed infrastructure in Awra Amba is striking.

While Awra Amba maintains its image of a successful, self-sustained model village, it continues, at the same time, to present itself as a vulnerable

and marginalized community due to limited access to land and the hostil-
ity that neighboring groups historically has displayed toward them. This representation can be called into question, however. The relationship between
Awra Amba and the neighboring communities has improved significantly,
at least on the surface. This is partly due to the Ethiopian government's pro-
tective measures and active promotion of Awra Amba. In addition to being
a well-visited tourist attraction and a model community that the Ethiopian
government and local and international NGOs have embraced, Awra Amba
has become an important trade hub. There are several shops in the village:
one shop where tourists and visitors can buy Awra Amba weaving products;
one typical *suq*—a small shop selling basic items such as sugar, pens, note-
books, and soap; one shop where hardware and household items are sold;
and one shop selling corrugated iron sheets. Awra Amba has also established
shops in the neighboring towns of Wereta and Alem Ber and in Addis Ababa
where they sell their weaving products. In addition, the community runs four
mills, and the cooperative has a large grain store and an Isuzu truck enabling
them to be involved in the larger Ethiopian grain market. In recent years, the
community has established a cooking oil factory.

Awra Amba's infrastructure and its success as a producer cooperative are
partly a result of the community's hard work and commitment. However,
higher officials at both the regional and the federal level emphasize the government's investments in its commitment to Awra Amba. For example, the
Ethiopian Roads Authority constructed the two-kilometer gravel road that
leads up to the community, and the Ethiopian Electric Light and Power Authority provided the electrical grid and infrastructure. A top official in the
Ethiopian Ministry of Culture and Tourism, who has known and followed
Awra Amba since it was first recognized as a tourist destination and model village, concluded in an interview that the community is given preferential treatment due to the value it has for both the region and the country as a whole.

The community's story and its success have also attracted representatives
from the Ethiopian political elite. In a photograph that is on display in Awra
Amba's museum, Elsabet, who, until she was expelled, was part of the welcoming committee and worked closely with Zumra, stands next to Dr. Te-
dros Adhanom, a former Minister of Health (2005–2012) and Minister of Foreign Affairs (2012–2016), now the Director-General of the WHO. "A lot of

prominent people came to visit," Elsabet told me one afternoon as we were flipping through her photo album. She stopped at a picture of herself together with well-known politicians. "Genet Zewde [former Minister of Education], Teffera Walua [former Minister of Capacity Building], and Berket Simon [former Minister of Communication] all came on the same day. Following their visit, three students were offered scholarships from the Ministry of Education," she explained.

The availability of resources, the recognition, and the preferential treatment that has followed Awra Amba in the wake of its popularity as a model village arguably speak to a much broader phenomenon in the national and transnational construction and circulation of policy models. I have seen many of the features described above follow other entities that have gained status as models or best practices. One example is Tostan, an American human rights organization founded by Molly Melching in 1991, which is at the forefront of the global movement against FGM/C. The organization itself and its methodology—the Community Empowerment Program—have been recognized as models for others to emulate. For example, in 2013, only a few weeks after Hillary Clinton took office as the US secretary of state, she endorsed Tostan as a model for how "grassroots work supported by the United States Government" can affect real change in communities around the world.[3] In their award-winning book *Half the Sky: Turning Oppression into Opportunity for Women Worldwide*, Nicholas D. Kristof and Sheryl WuDunn (2010) devote one chapter to Tostan, presenting it as one of several models that can serve to emancipate and empower women. With more than thirty-five partners, including the Bill and Melinda Gates Foundation, United Nations Children's Fund (UNICEF), United Nations Population Fund, NORAD, and SIDA, Tostan's recognition and positioning within the international development and donor community certainly exceeds that of Awra Amba. Yet, a comparison of the two models reveals that they share some key features. They are led by a charismatic front figure, have received numerous awards and recognitions, have a strong media and internet presence, and have attracted the attention of members of the global elite, including considerable donor support. These similarities suggest that the confluence of heterogeneous factors and vectors that I have described earlier as constitutive of the Awra Amba viral assemblage have larger implications.

While the presence of a charismatic leader, strong media and internet presence, and global recognition clearly are interlinked, I would like to emphasize the correlation between gaining public recognition and increase in donor support. This is something that the authors of *Half the Sky: Turning Oppression into Opportunity for Women Worldwide* (Kristoff and WuDunn 2010, 227) explicitly highlight in their discussion of Tostan: "Tostan's work has gained praise from a host of international agencies and in 2007 it won the Conrad H. Hilton Humanitarian Prize and a UNESCO prize. The recognition has helped win Tostan financial support from private donors as well as from UNICEF and American Jewish World Service, allowing it to expand at a steady pace." The increase in donor support, the preferential treatment, and the increased publicity are key features that emerge in the wake of something or someone gaining status as a model. The impact that the model status has on the model itself is, however, unexplored terrain in the policy literature. While much has been written about what happens when a policy model travels and is implemented in new contexts, there has been limited research, if any, on what happens to the original model—to the place or the site that produced what became a traveling model in the first place. This points to a void that sociologists who have studied human role models have also identified. Harriet Zuckerman (1988, 125) has, for example, argued that researchers who have studied human role models as a sociological phenomenon have tended to treat them "as if influence flows only from those chosen to those who choose them." This reflects a rather one-sided focus on the impact that human role models—as tools or instruments for social and behavioral change—have on others. In other words, the underlying assumption is that human role models are invariably positive, or perhaps, when seeing them more skeptically, they are neutral, not making a difference one way or the other in the face of structural constraints. In failing to examine the multiple, often contradictory, and unintended impacts that the model status can have, particularly on those who serve as the model, the policy literature makes the same uncritical assumption.

Being chosen and publicly hailed as a model or as an example of best practices does have positive consequences. Yet, it is also clear that the model status comes at a price. In order to maintain its status as a successful model of and for gender equality and sustainable development, Awra Amba is under constant pressure to engage in representational and performative strategies that serve to control and stabilize the narrative that gave the community its status in the first place. Because this narrative meets the perceived expectations and interests of the actors who are in control of the model's recognition and the resources that come with it, it is essential for the model to sustain the narrative and suppress other stories or voices that may be perceived to contradict or depart from it. In other words, the narrative serves important normalizing and disciplining functions, creating and reifying particular collective and individual identities and maintaining the model's economic, political, and cultural capital. One of my interlocutors who works as an adviser for the Ethiopian Ministry of Culture and Tourism made this point clear during one of our conversations: "If Awra Amba wants to be attractive, they have to maintain the cultural things they have become known for. They have to do this in order to make sure that tourists and other visitors do not lose their interest." This pressure prevents community members from talking openly about the problems and challenges they face and serves to conceal unequal power relations, exclusionary practices, and injustices. This is why it is extremely important to pay attention to the impact the model status has on the model itself. In the Awra Amba case, an analysis of the unintended consequences can shed light on why a community, which is known as a model for gender equality and commonly portrayed as a peaceful utopia, could so callously exclude one of its members.

Exclusionary Logics and Practices

"Did you ever consider taking your case to court?" I ask Elsabet one day. She shakes her head and tells me how her mother had strongly discouraged her from doing so, saying that they should leave it up to Allah. "In Alayhim, we do not like to bring our grievances in front of government bodies. Among those of us who have been excluded from Awra Amba, there is only one who has taken her case to court," she says.

After I had first heard rumors about Elsabet's exclusion and later had met her, I was able to speak with and hear the stories of many who used to live in Awra Amba but who, for various reasons, now live in other places. Like Elsabet, some live in the Alayhim community in Alem Ber. Others have settled down in Wereta, in rural villages in the surrounding areas, or in Bahir Dar. Some have even moved to Addis Ababa and cities in other regions. The people who have left Awra Amba can roughly be divided into two categories: those who for various reasons have made a conscious choice to leave the community—permanently or for a short period of time—and those who have been excluded or have felt forced to leave. The first category consists mainly of people from the community's younger generation. They grew up in Awra Amba but left the community to pursue higher education. They are, generally speaking, well-educated, and while their parents may be cooperative members, they are not. Many of them speak warmly of Awra Amba as their home, cherish the community's values, and see themselves as ambassadors for the community. While some say that they may consider joining the cooperative in the future, the majority appear hesitant to do so. Each individual obviously has diverse reasons for not wanting to commit to the cooperative. Yet, I shall focus here on two major concerns that emerged in my conversations with members of Awra Amba's younger generation.

First, the Awra Amba codes of conduct require both spouses to be members of the cooperative. Although the community claims that they accept people from different religious backgrounds, new members not only have to go through a long trial period, but they also have to commit to and abide by the Awra Amba working schedule, which is, as mentioned earlier, from eight o'clock in the morning to five o'clock in the afternoon, Monday through Saturday. This means that while members of the cooperative may be allowed to have their own, individual religious beliefs, they will not be able to adhere to common practices associated with Orthodox Christianity or Islam, such as going to church or to the mosque or performing daily rituals such as the *salat*. I should mention that within Ethiopian Orthodox Christianity, religious observance is not limited to attending church on Sundays. Most Christians observe many saints' days and often attend church services and perform rituals on a daily basis. Life as a member of the Awra Amba cooperative is, in other words, not compatible with the two major religious traditions in Ethiopia.

The conditions set by the cooperative in terms of membership also narrow the younger generation's "marriage market," requiring them either to find a spouse among members in the community or to look for someone outside of the community who is willing to give up his or her religious practice. This appears to be a contentious issue among Awra Amba's younger generation. Some have hopes that the cooperative will open up and change the rules and regulations pertaining to this issue. A young man, a student at one of the top universities in Ethiopia who envisions returning to the community as a cooperative member, expressed his concern and hope as follows:

There are things in the community that need to be moderated. For example, the joint-membership principle—that both spouses have to be members of the cooperative—is too strict. I am not fond of this regulation. It does limit your possibilities, for sure. But this is a contentious issue, and difficult to discuss and change. Perhaps we may reach a compromise over time. If those of us who belong to the younger generation keep asking questions.

The second concern of those in the younger generation who have distanced themselves from the community voluntarily speaks to a more fundamental critique of Awra Amba and of the cooperative as a sustainable and viable form for organizing social life. "I do not want to become a cooperative member," another young community member tells me one day. "I have felt a pressure to join, but I want to be free. If I become a member, I would not be able to do what I want—to make my own choices and invest in developing my interests and skills." In the conversation that followed, he emphasized how much he loves Awra Amba, and how he, even though he does not see himself joining the cooperative, hopes to settle down and make a living there. "Many of my friends have similar concerns," he explains. "Most of them don't see this as a viable future, partly because the cooperative offers very limited job opportunities. Also, my friends know how things work and they do not want to be part of that. There is only half freedom in Awra Amba." The references to "half freedom" and "how things work" point to some of the unspoken and hidden challenges in the community of which, as we will see in the following section, exclusion is only one.

Gendered Exclusions

"The stories of Elsabet and others who have left the cooperative are complex," one of my interlocutors tells me one day when I ask him to comment on her story. He has good insight into the everyday life of the community, yet he has repeatedly told me that, even if he has lived in and been part of the community for many years, there are many things he is not able to trace to their roots. And he is right. It is not easy to get to the heart of these stories. While those who have been excluded willingly yet cautiously talk about their experiences, members of the Awra Amba community are very reluctant to talk about exclusion. In fact, during my first fieldwork period, most of the people I talked with said that they did not know about any excluded members. Exclusion was, as illustrated in the official story told during the guided tour, framed as a theoretical possibility, not as something that was actually practiced. But, when they realized that I had concrete information about people who had been excluded, some of the community members, including Zumra and others who belong to the community's elite, would mention and confirm the names of individuals who had been excluded and rather reluctantly talk about the process. Ayalsew, Zumra's eldest son, who in summer 2018 had taken the role of the community's English-speaking guide, did, for example, elaborate on this issue during one of our conversations. He emphasized that exclusion was a last resort, and that it would only be implemented if a member had failed to improve his or her behavior after receiving advice three times. According to him, "it is only exercised when a member acts against the purpose of Awra Amba or misrepresents the society in a way that the community does not want." During a conversation I had with his mother Enaney, she claimed that the community's grievance resolving committee, was idle.

> Our neighboring communities have many problems related to governance. During public meetings, the government will often refer to us and encourage them to follow our example. We are recognized as a model because of the way we solve our problems. We follow the golden rule, emphasize unity of ideas, and solve disputes through dialogue.

According to Enaney and other community members who were officially selected and assigned to talk with me, the community's conflict resolution mechanisms and emphasis on dialogue are not only an ideal—a model *for*, or an ethical framework for how things are supposed to be—the community's official representatives go as far as painting a picture of Awra Amba as a utopian community devoid of conflicts. While they acknowledge that disagreements and miscommunication might occur, they claim that these are rather minor incidents that would be solved during their daily discussions. They describe these negotiations as having a stabilizing function, serving to keep emotions under control and in turn making punishment unnecessary.

The construction of Awra Amba as a utopian community—not in the sense of an imagined community but of a model community that portrays itself and seeks to behave as a real utopia—is important as it serves to confirm that Zumra's philosophy has been successfully put into practice. One of his key postulates is that it is possible to create peace and heaven on earth. By controlling and eliminating bad speech and bad deeds, he claims that conflicts can be eradicated. The dismissal of any form of punishment is also part of Zumra's philosophy and a principle conveyed on one of the posters found on the wall in the welcoming center: "Punishment does not correct people, rather it causes revenge. What teaches people is out-casting." By juxtaposing punishment and exclusion as if they are categorically different, this statement fails to recognize the suffering and social and economic consequences that practices of exclusion produce. It is also a way to divert and remove dissent and conflict outside the community, thus maintaining the sense of unity and consensus.

Exclusion is not unique to the Awra Amba community. In fact, according to the Cooperative Societies Proclamation No. 147/1998, which provides comprehensive legislation for the organization and management of cooperatives in Ethiopia, "any member of a society [cooperative] may leave the society when it is decided by the general assembly to dismiss him from the society because of committing repeated faults." Religious or moral communities also tend to rely heavily on this form of disciplining, where exclusionary practices often are linked to ethical norms that regulate sexuality and intimate relations (see, for example, Wolff and Himes 2010).[4] So, too, in Awra Amba.

"The main reason for expelling me from Awra Amba relates to my daughter," Elsabet told me on the first day I met her. We were sitting in the car, continuing the conversation we had started a few hours earlier in a restaurant in Gondar. When I had finally been able to track Elsabet down and locate her living in Alem Ber, I had come to an empty and locked house. "She is in Gondar for a wedding," one of her neighbors told me. A few phone calls later, I was on my way to Gondar, a major historic town two hours from Alem Ber, with clear instructions about where to meet her. "My daughter was in tenth grade when we were excluded," Elsabet explained when we finally met. "Enaney, Zumra's wife, suspected that he would take her as a new wife, so she set out rumors about my daughter, accusing her of having a sexual relationship with a young boy. These were false allegations, so my daughter spoke back: 'Do not exclude me and my family, please check my virginity,' she pleaded. But they did not care to check it. And we were excluded."

While the Awra Amba community is hailed and promoted as a gender-equal community, and in many ways it appears to have a rather liberal and what some may term "progressive" stand on issues that in Ethiopia are highly contentious, such as early marriage and FGM/C, some of the community's norms and principles are rather conservative in character. For example, pre-marital sexual relations are banned, and divorce is only possible if there is a good cause. The document "Journey for Peace," produced by the Awra Amba community, lists four acceptable reasons for divorce: (1) if there is an incurable illness, particularly which prohibits sexual intercourse; (2) if uninterrupted nagging between the couple is manifested; (3) if sterility is manifested in one of the partners; and (4) if one of the couple violates the bylaws of the community (Awra Amba Community 2012, 30). The three first reasons resemble Muslim marriage laws, indicating the influence of the community's Islamic heritage. According to Awra Amba's bylaws, which are reflective of the Cooperative Societies Proclamation No. 147/1998, the general assembly decides whether a divorce is acceptable. While the community officially promotes monogamy and has set the age of marriage to eighteen and nineteen for girls and boys respectively, several community members have been married multiple times. Zumra himself has, for example, previously been married; some say four and others say as many as six times. Enaney's suspicion and fear of a potential remarriage may therefore not have been groundless.

Elsabet is not the only woman who has been excluded from Awra Amba. While it has been difficult to determine the exact number of exclusions, based on conversations with people inside and outside Awra Amba I generated a list of twenty-six names, of whom twenty-one are women. The high proportion of women on the list and the stories I have collected from some of them suggest that exclusion is a highly gendered practice. In the same vein as Elsabet, these women speak of practices of injustice and marginalization. I recognize the contradictory and perilous ethical implications of delving into this issue. Revealing information may lead to new exclusions and shunning of those I interviewed, produce further polarization within the community, and undermine Awra Amba's achievements that have made possible the flourishing of many of its members. These risks are real. But they are also worth taking, when there seems to be a pattern of exclusion that severely and unevenly affects women, in a community that has become a national and global model for gender equality.

The most common official rationale used to explain why certain members of the community have been excluded is that of "arbitrary divorce." This was the reason that Zumra gave when he, during one of our discussions in 2016, explained why a young woman and her family had been excluded. "We paid a tuition of 20,000 birr so she could go to Bahir Dar to study for her diploma in Computer Science. At the end of the day, she arbitrarily divorced her husband. Since arbitrary divorce is not allowed, the general assembly decided to exclude her." Conversations with other members of the community indicated a much more complicated story. They claimed that the woman requested a divorce from her husband when she heard rumors of him having an extramarital affair with one of Enaney's relatives. When her request for divorce was denied by the general assembly, she decided to leave her husband. This act qualified as arbitrary divorce and led to her exclusion. When her family contested the decision, they were also excluded from the community.

"I may not have been explicitly excluded, but they intentionally made my life difficult," another woman told Belay, one of my research assistants, when he met with her a few months after my first fieldwork. Her story tells of harsh working conditions and inflexibility when it came to work assignments. "When my husband passed away, I had to work day and night in order to cover schooling fees and living costs for my children. I frequently felt sick, and it became hard for me to handle the big weaving machines. I asked for another job assignment, but Zumra refused. They made my life so difficult, so I did not really have a choice. In order to improve my health, I decided to leave the cooperative." The inflexibility in terms of distribution of labor that her story illustrates deserves further explication.

Implicit Hierarchies

According to the official narrative, the community's Work Assignment Committee is responsible for delegating and distributing work among the community members. However, as I witnessed, the work is, in practice, assigned by Zumra or other members of his inner circle in a ritualistic event that takes place outside his house every morning. Zumra and Enaney's house is by no means extravagant, yet it has certain qualities that other houses in the community do not have, such as tiled floors and a veranda. It is located on the hillside above the center of the village at the end of a road that passes by the Security Committee's command post, just a few hundred meters from the village square. Surrounded by other buildings—a service quarter with rooms for Zumra's children, a private weaving workshop, and the house of Enaney's mother—the area in front of his house gives you a sense of being in a courtyard. Stacks of stones, some designed as half walls, frame the entrance to the property and the open space in front of the veranda. Despite its physical closeness to the center of the village, the place feels secluded and private. It is not part of the village tour and most visitors will likely never see the place.

My first visit to Zumra's house took place during one of the first days I spent in the community, at a time when Zumra and Enaney were in Addis. I was sitting outside the guesthouse, watching the workers from the weaving workshop as they were passing by after a long day of work. But rather than heading to their respective homes, they all flocked to the village square, where they stopped for a few minutes before they started walking up the hill to Zumra's house. I cautiously followed them and watched as they each respectfully approached his house. Tsiddik, an elderly man who is close to Zumra and who also wears a green hat, was seated on the veranda together with members of Zumra's household. As the community members approached the house, they turned to the people sitting on the veranda, bowed their heads, and greeted them before they each found a spot to either sit or stand. As I sat and observed the interactions between the community members and the people on the veranda, I felt as if I were attending a religious service. People came, sat down, showed their respect, listened, and left. Reflecting a clear hierarchical order, with the elders and close relatives of Zumra being the ones speaking, the whole event involved an embodied discipline and an inculcated way of conducting oneself before Zumra's family members and his close associates. "We get together to discuss things. It is a way of knowing everything," Tsiddik explained to me, before he made a brief speech to his audience in which he made a comparison between the work of Zumra and that of Jesus and the Prophet Muhammad:

> The Prophet Muhammad only worked for the Muslims and Jesus only worked for the Christians. Zumra has, however, since the time he started, worked for the global community. He came from a good, strong, and highly respected Muslim family that was dominating over the Christians in his area. If he wanted, he could have stayed there and led a good life. But because of his internal and deep-rooted interest in serving others, he suffered a lot in order to achieve his goal.

These events outside of Zumra's house take place every morning and evening on workdays. When Zumra is in the village, he is the one who plays the central role. In the morning, Zumra will inform the cooperative members about the day's activities and assign each individual specific tasks. In the evenings, they will report to him about the work they have done and discuss potential challenges they have faced.

"People accept that things are as they are and have even anticipated that this is the way things would be," one of the community members tells me, when I one day ask him how the community members are able to cope with all the visitors and tourists that arrive in the village. He explains that many of the cooperative members believe very strongly in Zumra and his philosophy and ideas. "Zumra wanted the whole world to know his ideas and his philosophy. So, his followers believe receiving visitors is part of his vision. They really respect him. And they also believe that there will be another one who comes after him. This is what they wanted in the first place." While the informant is hesitant when I suggest that Zumra appears to be a religious leader, many of the people I spoke with outside the community argued that the Awra Amba community treats Zumra as if he is their God. A journalist who has been following the community for a number of years claimed, "They believe that he is God. Not only God, but God Plus." Although members of Awra Amba, including Zumra himself, dispute such affirmations, the status Zumra holds as the leader and founder of the Awra Amba community, the mythical elements in his personal story, and the influence of his philosophy on the community's practices, norms, and self-representation show that Awra Amba is a community with clear religious characteristics.[5] More importantly, Zumra's elevated status and his leadership fly in the face of the image of an egalitarian, democratic society.

Democratic Shortcomings and Economic Inequalities

According to the official narrative and Awra Amba's bylaws, the general assembly is the community's ultimate decision-making body. When I asked one of the excluded women about the role of the general assembly—it had unanimously approved of her exclusion—she was very critical and questioned its actual decision-making power: "It is simply a formality. The decisions are made by Zumra and his wife. For example, many cooperative members were supportive of my case. Still, due to Zumra's and Enaney's strong arm, they could not decide in favor of me. If Zumra says 'yes,' all people say 'yes.' If he says 'no,' they also say 'no.'"

I had heard before that Zumra and his family were in control of Awra Amba—not only from Elsabet and the other women who have been excluded but also from people who have followed the community over time: journalists, tour guides, and teachers. They all had expressed their concerns with how decisions were being made in the community. The teachers, who are recruited from outside Awra Amba and employed by the government, are particularly well positioned, since they live in and interact with the community on a daily basis yet are not members of the cooperative.

"Awra Amba is a very democratic community on paper, but in practice it is Zumra and his family who is ruling," a teacher at the high school in Awra Amba told me one day. Belay and I had agreed to meet him at one of my favorite restaurants in Wereta. With cats roaming around our feet waiting for a piece of excess food to fall down from the table, it is not at all a fancy place. But the food is good. And the coffee, poured from a *jebena*, the traditional Ethiopian coffee pot, is not only as strong and sweet as it is supposed to be, it is also served with a small sprig of rue.[6]

Our initial plan had been to do the interview over lunch, but when I realized that the teacher felt extremely uncomfortable, I moved to another table, leaving him alone with Belay. As a government-employed teacher, he is not a member of the Awra Amba cooperative. Yet, he did not feel free to talk, and we ended up doing the interview roadside under a tree we found on a desolated stretch of the road back to Awra Amba. A few days earlier, another teacher had shared with us some of the challenges that teachers and other government employees were facing in Awra Amba. He had talked about how it had become increasingly difficult for government employees to find housing in Awra Amba. Teachers, in particular, were struggling after some of them had openly questioned the official narrative and what they saw as unequal distribution of wealth and resources. Suspected of transferring false information to guests and foreigners, many teachers felt they were disliked, and some had even been denied rooms to rent. As a consequence, several teachers had applied to be reassigned to other places.

"I came to Awra Amba two years ago," the teacher tells me when we finally sit down for the interview. "Before I arrived in Awra Amba I thought of it as an amazing place. I had heard about the community and considered their activities and accomplishments to be very impressive. But after living here and observing and interacting with people, I have become increasingly critical. I have seen the inequalities, the differences in living standard, and the unfair distribution of work. Zumra acts as if he is a manager, and the weavers, who are positioned at the lowest level in the hierarchy and who are not from well-off families, have many problems. Some of them live in absolute poverty."

Even before the teacher mentioned poverty, I had been mulling over the idea of it being a potential problem in Awra Amba. I had been puzzled and troubled by some of the numbers that the community presented as proof of their achievements. For example, one of the posters in the welcoming center provides an overview of the annual share each cooperative member receives. In 2011–12, the annual share of each individual member was 6,200 ETB. Seven years later, in 2018, I was told that the annual share the previous year had been even lower—only 5,000 ETB. This amounts to less than 200 USD. Considering that during this time period, Ethiopia has seen high inflation, an annual share of 5,000–6,000 ETB is extremely low. As Belay concluded, "It is nothing." It is also well below the poverty line of 1.25 USD a day. In view of the amount of time each cooperative member is required to work for the cooperative and the limitation this sets in terms of time available to generate private income, the annual share is troubling and raises a number of questions.

Members of the cooperative admitted that the annual share has remained flat and that it is low. They explained it with reference to increased capital investment:

> Yes, there has been no increment the last three years. This year, we bought a residential home in Addis. Every year, the community will discuss the options. And we may decide—it is better if we buy this. Even if 6,000 ETB is not enough, we believe that in the long run, we will benefit for taking out a small share. This decision is, most of the time, made through agreement. Also, most of the time, individuals will have their private income.

It is, however, not only the annual share that is surprisingly low. During my fieldwork in 2015, I was given access to the 2013–14 audit report that has been approved by the Wereta District's Cooperative Office. According to the report, the net total income available for distribution during that year was 1,206,000 ETB, 82 percent of which was distributed to the 164 members in the cooperative. The remaining 18 percent was left for investment. If all of the net income had been distributed to the members, the annual share for each would have been increased to 7,350 ETB (in 2015 this amounted to about 370 USD). Still, this amount is below the poverty line of 1.25 USD a day. The Awra Amba cooperative appears to be a thriving business community. According to government officials, the accumulation of resources in Awra Amba requires high-level security. So why are the net gross income and the annual share not higher?

Some of my interlocutors questioned to what extent the members in the cooperative have the resources necessary to overlook and understand the financial management of the cooperative. Although the Awra Amba community is rather unique in its focus on and investment in education, a significant number of the cooperative members are illiterate and do not have the necessary resources to examine issues of financial and administrative character. Some of the people I interviewed claimed that many cooperative members not only are excluded from decision-making processes but are also struggling. One of them shared the following:

> Many are suffering. But because they do not want to lose their share of the accumulated property, they cannot leave the community. The elite can easily live their lives. 6,000 birr is a very low amount. The people who are not members of Zumra's family have to get up early in the night to work for their private income, since the majority of the income goes to capital investment and infrastructure.

"From the outside, it looks like a fully developed Marxist society, but in practice, it is more like a feudal system. Zumra and his family are just like the *balabbats*," Belay concludes as we one day discuss how to make sense of our fieldwork findings. He was not the only one who made this analogy. The term *balabbat*, which refers to people who were appointed during the imperial era to serve as intermediaries between their people and the state, emerged in several conversations I had with people who critically reflected on the role and power of Zumra and his family. The *balabbats* often came from a powerful and exploitative family with significant rights of land.

While one may argue that this analogy is too simplistic, structural tendencies in Awra Amba indicate that the analogy to *balabbats* and Abyssinian feudalism is by no means far-fetched. Zumra and members of his family dominate, for example, positions that involve decision making and direct control of resources. They are in charge of the shops that the community runs and they occupy all the financial positions. Additionally, members of Zumra's and Enaney's families tend to be in positions that do not require heavy physical work. They are seldom seen working in the community's weaving workshop. Awra Amba is, in other words, a clearly stratified community. But it is perhaps the issue of land and property rights that most clearly makes the *balabbat* analogy compelling and worth exploring. This issue is also at the heart of the stories of those who have been excluded.

Precarious Property Rights

Land ownership in Awra Amba is communal. This does not mean that members of the cooperative do not have private property. Most of the Awra Amba cooperative members have, for example, private weaving machines and own their houses. With the establishment of the high school in the village, it has moreover become relatively lucrative to rent out houses. Many of the cooperative members have therefore invested in constructing additional houses with rooms that they lease to students and teachers. These houses are also considered private property.

According to Zumra and the chairman of the cooperative, members who leave the community cannot claim their share of the capital investments. They have the right to take their annual share and the private land that they pooled into the cooperative when they became a member. If the cooperative has invested in infrastructure on the land, exiting members will be given another plot as a substitution for the land they originally brought in when they became members. While these guidelines are in line with the Cooperative Societies Proclamation, the implementation of these principles is inconsistent in cases of exclusion. One of the women who was excluded for arbitrarily having divorced her husband claimed that an individual member's right to property is practiced rather capriciously:

> It seems to be different from person to person. In some cases, you see that people take their land back when they are excluded. In other cases, you see that people are denied access to their property, including land. If you see the case of my family, my parents were not even allowed to take their private property. I was also not allowed to take my share of the community's savings. Rather, they were asking me to reimburse the money that the association had invested in my college education.

This woman is the only one who has attempted to bring her case before a court. When she filed the case in the district court, many people intervened.

Members from the community tried to convince her to drop the case and to opt for negotiation instead. Some of the members in the community also threatened her. Community members and even representatives from the government argued that a court case, which implied public hearings, could have a negative impact on the community's reputation. This would be contrary to Awra Amba's image as a peaceful model community, void of conflict. The woman finally gave in to the pressure, and the court closed the case. Again, we see how voices and stories are silenced in order to preserve the authority and authenticity of the model.

In a similar vein, Elsabet's case sheds light on the effect that exclusion has on land security and livelihood. When she was kicked out of the community, she was in the final stage of completing the construction of a new house; the only thing missing was a transformer to install electricity. "I was among the sixty-four people who were given a piece of land during the land-distribution reform in 1997," Elsabet explains. "I was initially given a plot of land where the clinic is now, but at one point, I agreed to substitute that land with two plots of land on what was common property. One of these plots was right behind the library, and that is where I built my new house." When Elsabet was excluded, she was denied access to her property. Her house was locked, and since it was located on land that was considered common property, she was not allowed to sell it or rent it out. She is filled with regret when she speaks and retrospectively reflects on her decision to give up her original titled land. "If I had kept the land I was originally given, I could have sold that. Now, because the house is on common land, it is considered common property and I cannot sell it. The only thing I can sell is the corrugated iron sheets on the roof, but that would mean the same as destroying the house and everything I have invested." There is unmistakable bitterness in her voice as she talks about the devastating economic consequences the exclusion has brought on her and her family. But she has not given up. She has been and is still fighting against what she sees as an attempt by Zumra and his family to establish themselves as landlords in Awra Amba. While Elsabet can express her concerns freely and has nothing to lose by talking with me, the existing cooperative members are in a much more precarious situation. "They are afraid to talk," one of the high school teachers concluded. "Those who speak freely risk being excluded. And if that happens, they will be at great loss. Many of the cooperative members have invested much time and energy in Awra Amba.

They have contributed much in developing Awra Amba into what it is today. They do not want to lose that. In practice, they do not really have the option to leave, even if they wanted."

Elsabet's story and the gendered nature of exclusion in Awra Amba have significant implications for a community that is widely known as a model of and for gender equality. These counter-narratives are, in many ways, troubling, and if we were to adopt the assumption that underpins common approaches to models and best practices in the policy world—that a model is a successful implementation of a particular policy idea into practice—Awra Amba would not qualify as a model at all. Such an interpretation of the model is, as I have already argued, not at all compatible with model theory found within the philosophy of science and in economics, where it is widely acknowledged that models are not true representations of the lived-in world. As simplified, symbolic representations of complex systems, "all models are wrong" (Box 1976, 792). This does not mean that models are useless or that they are void of any positive qualities. First of all, models are analytical tools that are good to think with. They can serve as windows into particular historical and contemporary political situations and processes, helping us to comprehend the lived-in world. To further elucidate this, let me share one last encounter from my research in Awra Amba. Fasil,[7] my driver when I visited Awra Amba in December 2019, plays a key role.

Little Ethiopia

It is a bright and shiny morning after a long night of heavy, unexpected rain. The warm, golden rays of sun that generously flow over Awra Amba have quickly turned the muddy, slippery village into a picturesque paradise. As students hurry through the village on their way to school and Awra Amba's diligent community members stride the slope up to Zumra's house for the daily morning ritual, I am getting ready to leave Awra Amba after a final round of fieldwork. "*Negus hoi*," Fasil murmurs as we both climb into the car. "What did you just say?" I ask bug-eyed, not sure if I heard him correctly. "I said *Negus hoi*" he repeats, as he turns on the engine. It is less than a week since he picked me up from Bahir Dar airport when we met for the first time. "Why did you say *Negus hoi*?" I ask, as we leave Awra Amba behind us. Fasil pauses for a brief moment as he carefully maneuvers the car down the gravel road. He is a man in his mid-thirties and a skilled driver with more than fifteen years of experience working for various tourist companies. "Every morning and every evening they go up to Zumra's house. They treat him like a king." Keeping his left hand on the wheel, he then lowers his head, makes a bowing movement with his right hand and his upper body, and says "*Negus hoi*" in an overly, reverent tone. We both laugh. "When you say *Negus hoi*, you do not simply say *Negus hoi*," he continues, uttering the phrase without any intonation as if it is an everyday word. The term—which is akin to Your Royal Highness—calls for bodily reverence and veneration. According to Fasil, this is exactly what Zumra's followers are doing when they, as they approach Zumra, are holding their hands on their back and bow. "They are acting as if they were greeting a king or as if they were going to church," he concludes.

Fasil's remark reflected the analytical work that he had been doing while he was staying in Awra Amba and driving me to neighboring communities. His most succinct comment had come a few days earlier when we had visited Elsabet. We had spent several hours at her house where we had been served lunch and coffee. Elsabet's daughter—who now lives in Addis Ababa and who, as I described earlier in this chapter, was accused of having a premarital sexual relationship, leading to the family's exclusion—had also been present. She had just given birth to her second child and was spending the postpartum seclusion period—known as *aras bet*—in her mother's house. As Elsabet and her daughter told their story, Fasil had listened attentively, asking clarifying questions. He had been deeply troubled. As we were getting ready to leave, sipping our last cup of coffee, he shook his head, turned to me, and said, "*Tinnishua Etiyopia nat*" ("She [Awra Amba] is little Ethiopia").

By calling Awra Amba "little Ethiopia," Fasil summarized an argument that had been on my mind but that I had not fully articulated: that Awra Amba, in both a historical and contemporary sense, is a miniature model of the country's political culture (Vaughan and Tronvoll 2003). On several occasions, Fasil made comments that illustrated this point. For example, in our discussion of *Negus hoi*, he drew parallels between Zumra and Emperor Haile Selassie, arguing that Zumra and his family were acting in just the same way rulers in Ethiopia have been doing for a long time. Fasil's point and the relevance of his comparison to Ethiopia's historical, feudal past, became clear when, a few days later, I had walked up to Zumra's house to observe and participate in yet another evening ritual. Enaney and Zumra had been sitting in deep armchairs, with Zumra to the left and Enaney to the right of the door entrance. Wrapped in a white *gabi* with the green, yellow, and green-striped colors that are commonly associated with the flag of the old Ethiopian empire, Zumra spoke to the attentive community members, inquiring into their day's activities. Zumra and his wife reminded me of royalty, and it was impossible not to think of and draw parallels to Ethiopia's feudal past: to the relationship between the nobility and peasants during the reign of the Emperors Menelik and Haile Selassie and to the vertically stratified, top-down character of Ethiopia's political culture, which continue to hold a close grip on contemporary political dynamics.

As Fasil's analysis illustrates, models are valuable as analytical tools, serving as mirrors into larger political and social processes. They do not, however, offer a blueprint for how to order a complex lived-in world. This does not mean that models do not act or that they are of no use in the policy world. While gender inequality and injustice certainly exist in Awra Amba, and one may rightly question to what extent the dominant narrative reflects what de facto is happening on the ground, this does not automatically mean that Awra Amba is a failed model of gender equality and, thus, that it should be rejected tout court. Again, as I argued in Chapter 3, such a conclusion assumes that a model *of* reflects a successful implementation of a normative model—of the dominant ideological norms that circulate in a particular interpretive community of policy actors. It assumes a linear, managerial association between the prescribed and the representative model—between policy norms and practice.

Awra Amba has, with no doubt, had an immense influence on gender-equality discourses and policies in Ethiopia. It has, to paraphrase David Mosse (2003, 44), "succeeded as code or policy argument in the wider arena." As such, the Awra Amba narrative represents an alternative to the often one-sided and negative representations of gender relations in Ethiopia that tend to focus on harmful traditional practices and gender inequality. An expert at the Ministry of Women, Children, and Youth Affairs emphasized the benefits of having a home-grown model: "It is much easier for us to promote something that already exists in our country. If we, in our gender trainings, were to rely on stories and models from places in the global north, people would be much less receptive to our message. Awra Amba is a powerful example and has a much more convincing effect than what models of gender equality from Western societies could ever have." The trouble with this statement is not that it is overly optimistic about the inspirational and transformative power of Awra Amba—hope and desire for positive change are essential ingredients in development and policy-making—but that it uncritically reproduces narratives created and advanced by people in power, subsequently silencing voices, particularly those of women who are disciplined and excluded in order to reinforce the narrative.

While the Awra Amba gender-equality model has greatly inspired and influenced Ethiopia's gender and development discourse, the extent to which the "let women plow and men make *injera*" model—or the equality-as-sameness model—have transformed gender relations in Ethiopia is open for debate. In my earlier work, I have shown how rural men and women in other parts of the country negotiate and reject this particular model (Østebø 2015). Whether the model is practiced in Awra Amba can also be questioned. While it is true that women are involved in the community's productive activities, there is still a clear division of labor in the community. In the weaving workshop, where most of the cooperative members work, I have only seen two women who have occasionally been weaving. This does not mean that women do not participate in the weaving production, but most of the women are spinning, warping, or involved in preparing the weave, reflecting traditional gender-weaving practices in Ethiopia (Itagaki 2003).[8] There is also a clear division of labor in other domains. Many of the processes that involve food production, such as preparation of grain, lentils, and spices, are performed by women. I have only once seen a man making *injera* in Awra Amba, and he happened to be a young student who had come from one of the neighboring communities to study at the high school. When I asked an elderly man in the community whether men are fetching water and baking *injera*, he admitted that except for in times of crisis, men would not participate in these activities. One of the excluded women confirmed this: "When men are absent, women will plow to fill the gap. And if women for some reason are not present or if a woman is ill, her husband may bake *injera*. If it is necessary, he will do this, but it is not part of daily life. When it comes to plowing, this is very difficult for women. A woman will only plow when it is absolutely necessary."

These crisis-induced gendered practices are, however, not peculiar to Awra Amba. In fact, the model of gender equality that is at work in Awra Amba appears to be similar to what is found in other places in Ethiopia. Emphasizing the importance of working together in order to increase productivity, this model fuses ideas from global gender policies—dominated by an emphasis on gender equality as "smart economics"– with local gendered norms and practices (Østebø 2015).

In other words, Awra Amba is not as revolutionary as it claims to be. Instead of taking for granted the idealization advanced by official narratives and being enchanted by the prospect that Awra Amba is an authentic, existing model for the things we desire to see in development, we need to place the village in its proper historical, social, and cultural contexts. This implies examining the model at its margins, following the resistances at various points in the assemblage, and tracing the hidden threads and power configurations that link Awra Amba with larger political and historical realities in Ethiopia.

Conclusion

Infected

I AM SITTING at a fine-dining restaurant in downtown Helsinki. My short visit is coming to an end and I am euphorically writing up my field notes. "I guess I ended up here because I am overexcited on behalf of Lyfta," I open my entry. It is an excuse—an attempt to shake off the high-priced menu options the restaurant has to offer.

When I had started communicating with Paulina a few months earlier about the possibility of visiting Lyfta in Helsinki, she had mentioned that the firm had been nominated to participate in the Scandinavian semifinal of the Global EdTech Startups Awards (GESA)—the world's largest EdTech startup competition, which would be held at the Dare to Learn conference. After exploring the conference website, I decided to register, since this would allow me, as I describe in Chapter 7, to participate in Lyfta's workshops. During the final event of the two-day conference, Lyfta had, along with seven other EdTech companies, also been given four minutes to pitch their products. Paulina had been the last to enter the red-carpeted stage, where she introduced Lyfta as "a multisensory, immersive learning platform that is home to what many teachers and pupils say is the most powerful and engaging educational content they have ever experienced." When she finished her pitch, she joined me in the bleachers. "Who do you think is your strongest competitor?" I asked her as we were waiting for the jury to return with the results. She shrugged her shoulders, returning the question back to me. "I think you did a great job, but after all the buzz about the use of Artificial Intelligence (AI) to track and tailor individual students' learning during these past two days, I assume one of the companies that is promoting AI-based learning will win," I said.

So, when a representative from the jury, a few minutes later, announced Lyfta as the winner, emphasizing the company's unique pedagogical approach, its global scalability, and commitment to foster empathic global

citizens, I was initially surprised. Then, as I held up my iPhone to catch Paulina entering the stage to receive the award, my hands lightly shaking, I also
realized I was deeply moved. In fact, I was so touched that I had to use one of
my try-not-to-cry-tricks to contain my emotions. My excitement grew when
Paulina invited me to join her and the other members of the Lyfta production
team for a celebratory drink. "I am so happy on their behalf. It was great to see
a product that focuses on empathy win," I wrote in my field notes a few hours
later, not fully realizing that I, myself, finally had been infected by the Awra
Amba virus.

What was it that almost moved me to tears when Lyfta won, that tore
down my well-developed immune system and undermined the distance and
critical stance that had characterized my approach to the Awra Amba viral
assemblage? As I had researched Awra Amba, listening to multiple and partly
contradictory stories, and observing and learning about some of the unintended consequences associated with the community's model status, my re-
luctance to celebrate the model had grown. In fact, I have to admit that even
before arriving in Awra Amba the first time, I had been skeptical and resis-
tant to the hype around the community. Being a researcher within the field of
development, I had seen and heard too many well-rehearsed and performed
stories of success as well as hardship. Through my work as a development
practitioner, I had also been actively involved in constructing and staging
these stories, facilitating tours for donors and evaluation teams. For example, during the famine in 2000, I had been in charge of setting up and managing an emergency relief program in the southeastern parts of Ethiopia. After three weeks of intensive work, I had returned to the capital with pictures
of severely malnourished children—pictures that attracted the attention of a
major international donor organization. When higher officials from the organization's headquarters in London announced they were on their way, my su-
pervisor in Addis Ababa advised me prior to their arrival: "You have to make
sure we visit a village where they get a chance to see severely malnourished
children." Knowing the value of emotional moments and stories, I knew a lot
was at stake. A month earlier, I had been working in a village in the middle of
the Somali Region when a small airplane with journalists from major Norwegian newspapers had arrived. The visit had not been a success. The absence
of severe, malnourished children had disappointed them, and they had demanded to be flown to another site where many journalists and NGOs were

flocking. My preparations and carefully planned itinerary for the two British gentlemen from the donor organization, on the other hand, were successful. A couple of weeks after their visit, I was in charge of a major relief operation worth one million British pounds.

So, why was I finally infected by the Awra Amba virus? Why did I leave Helsinki passionate about Lyfta's product? An analysis of my own immediate reflections written in my field notes reveals that my emotional reaction to Lyfta's success and their victory during the Scandinavian GESA semifinal was linked to my identity and desires as an educator. I was, first of all, surprised by the jury's emphasis on Lyfta as a unique pedagogical tool for enhancing empathy, described by the jury foreman as a "twenty-first century skill we need at all age levels." Assuming that empathy was an unquestionable, uncontested moral virtue, first and foremost promoted through the humanities and fields such as anthropology, and unaware of the increased commodification and appropriation of empathy by the market, Lyfta's victory felt like a recognition of my own work as an educator and an appreciation of the values and virtues that I highly valued, but which, in an increasingly STEM-focused and profit-driven, neoliberal world, tend to be neglected. The fact that Lyfta defeated EdTech companies that promoted products that were clearly skewed toward the hard sciences further intensified my feeling of admiration. This is what I wrote in my field notes: *Considering all the focus on STEM, the jury's rationale—the emphasis on empathy—really got to me. So, I found myself so glad on their [Lyfta's] behalf. Perhaps more than that—on behalf of values that mean something. What really matters—is our ability to care for one another.* My enthusiasm, or perhaps we could even say infection, cannot be explained by the jury's praise and recognition of Lyfta as an empathy-enhancing pedagogical tool alone, however. Lyfta's short documentary also spoke to particular desires I have as an educator: *It is impossible to not be fascinated by Lyfta's stories. I have been thinking, the past few days, that their documentaries are exactly what I have been searching for in my work as an instructor. They are examples of everyday struggles, experiences and events, and they can be used to think critically about many things—also theoretically. This is what I, as a teacher, have been looking for.* This quote makes little sense without an understanding of my approach to learning.

Since 2014, I have been using Team-Based Learning (TBL) as a teaching strategy in my classrooms. TBL offers a comprehensive framework for how to organize and implement a "flipped classroom"[1] experience. It is, in other words, an example of a prescriptive model. In a TBL classroom, we spend most of the time on team-based activities that require the students to use or apply course content, theory, and knowledge to complex problems. To design these assignments is a time-demanding and challenging task. It requires that I, as an instructor, develop questions that relate to concrete, specific situations; that I identify or design cases or stories that introduce circumstances, conditions, and realities that challenge the students to engage with or apply theoretical concepts and content to particular situations—real or fictional.

Since I first started using TBL as my overall teaching strategy, I have been on a constant search for stories or scenarios that could be of relevance for my teaching. I have spent endless hours on YouTube searching for short films or documentaries, and every time I watch a TV series, I am looking for potential scenes. My reflection, which in the same vein as Aster's story (Chapter 6), emphasizes that I have found something I have been searching and looking for, and my emotional reactions to Lyfta's success and their victory during the Scandinavian GESA semifinal, were, in other words, also linked to my own teaching practices, to my identity and the wants and needs I have as an educator. Looking at Lyfta's product, from the perspective of an educator, I could see its value. As I participated in Lyfta's workshop and watched the documentaries in a room filled with other educators, I saw how I could use the documentaries and storyworlds to generate critical thinking and discussions among my students (albeit not in the prescriptive way suggested in Lyfta's lesson plans). For example, the documentary from Awra Amba's home for the elderly contains scenes that could be used to critically discuss theories of care, globalization, representation, and othering. This explains the conclusion I wrote in my field notes: *The Lyfta documentaries are perfect in length for use in the classroom. Even if they may not be true—regardless of the discrepancy between the "reality" and the stories told—these are powerful stories. Just like fairy tales, they can be used to teach us important lessons.*

I have included my own "infectious" experience here because it illustrates how emotions and desires are driving and motivational forces, instigating imitative, viral processes. The moment Lyfta was announced as the winner of the Scandinavian GESA semifinal, I got caught in a multisensory and affective encounter that allowed the Awra Amba virus to pass under my skin, turning me into a potentially contagious and passionate vector. In other words, this final vignette serves as yet another illustration of the usefulness of approaching traveling models through the lens of viral assemblage. As I have attempted to show throughout this book, this is a theoretical concept that allows for greater recognition of the affective and unpredictable nature of the complex situations and processes that make up our lived-in world. By sharing and discussing my own emotional reactions and my fascination with Lyfta's product, I also show how I not only am part of the Awra Amba viral assemblage or the larger modeloscene, but how I, in a conscious, self-reflexive move, also draw on and use my own emotions and experiences as a source of knowing. Hence, the story is also meant to illustrate what anthropology can look like when we approach and think of what we do as a viral assemblage.

Wrong and Useful—But for Whom?

So, what are the take-home lessons from the Awra Amba story? What is the relevance for policy makers and for the vast number of people around the world who use models to change the world for the better?

First, the Awra Amba story shows that models are *not* magic bullets. Models are *not* examples of success that can be scaled up easily and implemented in other places. The idealized model, commonly presented as a best practice, is invariably a simplification that reflects taken-for-granted norms and hegemonic political discourses. Because the model is highly simplified and idealized, it tends to mask complex social relationships and interactions and only partially mirrors what is actually happening "on the ground." One should, therefore, not assume that a model is an example of what works that can be scaled up and applied to other places without any friction. As David Mosse (2005, 17) argues, models "reveal and conceal, explain, justify, label and give meaning. It is through them that chaotic practices are stabilized, made coherent and validated for a project's various publics (donor managers, politicians, professionals); that progress is measured and success proclaimed; and that the gap between policy and practice is constantly negotiated away." Hence, it is highly problematic to unreflexively reify a fallible model—as all models are—into an infallible, neutral, universal one. No matter how much they appear to be emancipatory or seem to fulfill our desires for equality and justice, models are not unified, univocal, and fixed realities. As assemblages consisting of heterogeneous elements, models are unique, historic, and complex entities that evolve as they move and are implemented. They are highly political and imbued by power, and they emerge and are implemented in the midst of contestation, tension, domination, and resistance. Therefore, they have to be contextually situated and understood. Just as virologists and epidemiologists study a virus—as situated phenomenon with specific epidemic and endemic qualities and potentials—we have to approach traveling models as unique entities or constellations, situating them in the historical, political, and special contexts in which they exist. This means that we need to understand how the original model worked in its original place. We have to assess contextual factors that may have been detrimental to the model's perceived success. And then we have to be sure we understand the new context in which we would like to implement the original model. In other words, we have to consider the complexity and contextual factors that are at play at both ends: at the model's place of origin and at its new destination. The question is whether policy makers are ready to engage in processes of social change in ways that takes context and complexity into consideration. Models are popular and attract global attention precisely because they are perceived to offer easy solutions to complex problems. What anthropologists and studies like this one offer is precisely what policy makers do not want to hear: that complex problems require complex, place-specific, and carefully crafted solutions.

Second, the story about how Awra Amba went viral shows that the circulation of a policy idea or model is not facilitated by a narrow, clearly defined group of rational policy actors who, after learning about a model, simply pick it up and implement it in new places. The making and circulation of a policy model is a complex and partly unintentional and unpredictable process involving heterogeneous actors—humans as well as non-humans. Furthermore—and this is perhaps the most original contribution of *Village Gone Viral*—a model's virality is determined by its ability to generate emotional and immersive encounters with host or vectors who are captured by and attracted by the model because it carries with it certain elements that are desirable and recognizable. Just as for a virus, the model's travel and its contagious capacity are conditioned on vectors, hospitable environments, and receptive host cells. For a model to spread, it needs to find the right carrier or vector. It needs to click with a cell that has the right receptor. There needs to be an association—an element of recognition and interaction—between the model and the entities by which it potentially can be picked up. Similar to a virus, we embrace the ideas to which we are already receptive, which we recognize and, hence, to which we can easily relate. As illustrated in my own infectious experience, this is not an entirely rational process as it is often assumed by policy makers. It involves interests, desire, affects, and emotions that strongly condition whether we adopt a model or an idea. This means that the model does not spread unconditionally; the model's virality is somewhat restricted.

The fact that a model's virality relies, to a considerable extent, on recognition of something familiar actualizes what Sally Engle Merry and Peggy Levitt (2019, 245) have described as "the resonance dilemma." With a particular focus on how women's rights and ideas about gender equality are translated in various contexts, they discuss how we tend to embrace norms and values that are familiar, while we resist those that diverge from our existing normative frameworks. One could therefore argue that the model's transformative power is weaker than what we often assume. But one could also say, as I have done in some of my earlier work (Østebø 2015; Østebø 2018), that the translation and mutation that emerge when a model is introduced in a new place open up and bring new perspectives to the norms and ideas that, in the first place, underpinned the original policy model. In other words, the place and situation to which a model is introduced can also "speak back," challenging some of the assumptions and stereotypical images that underpin globally sanctioned models.

Finally, similar to viruses, models have both constructive and destructive capacities. George Box (1979, 202), the statistician who originally formulated the idea that all models are wrong, later expanded his claim to state, "All models are wrong, but some are useful." While the analysis and discussion of models and modeling practices I provide in this book are certainly critical in nature, this does not mean that I think models are useless. In fact, when I described earlier in this chapter my use of TBL—an increasingly popular, pedagogical model—I make it clear that I myself acknowledge that models are valuable tools. I am, in other words, also caught up in the modeloscene. Models may be fallible and even dangerous. Yet they are still useful in making sense of and acting in response to a complex world. Models showcase desires, possibilities, futures, and alternative ways of living and being in the world. They can generate constructive debate and negotiation. For example, Colin McFarlane (2009, 563) details how model houses in a particular project in India became "the basis for negotiations around the kind of houses people want to live in, a process in which the collective will must be weighed against individual preferences, and which is subject to a range of social and cultural specificities and alternations."

Even if a model is considered to be wrong or imperfect, it can have transformative potential, though not necessarily in the linear way that we tend to assume. We have, for example, seen how the Awra Amba community has benefited from being a model. The community's model status has led to increased recognition, preferential treatment, increased donor funding, and investments. Just as viruses, models can be both good and bad. Yet we should keep in mind that models and modeling practices are tools for ordering and controlling a complex world. As technologies of governance, they are powerful political tools that can be strategically manipulated and put into use, predominantly by people in power. While a model may be promoted as an emancipatory tool, it could easily be turned into a weapon of oppression in the hands of the powerful. When we encounter or use a model, it is therefore crucial that we approach it with a good dose of skepticism and ask the following: What does the model conceal and hide? What and whom does the model exclude and include? And perhaps most importantly, who benefits and who is negatively affected when a complex social formation is declared a model worthy of becoming viral? In other words, who gives the model its status, and who is it useful for? Here, it is pivotal that we recognize that models are a valuable currency vis-à-vis powerful, international donors. Models are commodities that, due to the political, economic, and cultural capital that surround them, attract the interests of multiple actors who rely on and capitalize on stories of success. This partly explains why the NGO community was eager to establish a partnership with Awra Amba. In a policy world where failed projects and social engineering initiatives are plentiful, the possibility of actually working with and establishing a partnership with an actor who can deliver on preset measurable goals—or perhaps it is more correct to say one who has the capacity and the power to perform in accordance with the dominating prescriptive models within the field—is therefore appealing. Establishing partnerships with models speaks to the "managerial optimism" (Mosse 2005, xi) that characterizes the transnational field of policy and practice. There are, in other words, strong economic interests associated with the model as a category and phenomenon in the policy world. This also creates a pressure to perform according to dominant policy norms. The model status may be a political and economic asset that benefits the traveling as well as the original model. Yet, the practices of exclusion and injustices that I have detailed in this book shed light on the political nature of models and modeling and the hidden power effects that gaining model status produces. The unintended consequences that the model status has on embodied models demand increased vigilance.

While pen-and-paper models and standardized interventions are framed and exist as utopian dreams or aspirations and as guidelines for an imaginary future, Awra Amba is an example of a model that exists in a real place. It is a model that consists of people who—due to the community's model status—are compelled to act as if Awra Amba is a real utopia and as if paradise on earth exists. It is this performance of an imaginary community that makes it particularly attractive and that also opens the door for the surreptitious emergence of power. This is a performance that does not take place on a stage away from the community members' everyday life. While parts of the village are hidden from the public gaze, a large part of the community's daily life is not only on display, but it is also included as part of the performance. The Awra Amba model is, in other words, not a closed system that runs parallel to the lived-in world—it is part of it. The pressure to perform according to a well-rehearsed and politically recognized narrative conceals power relations and silences the voices of the weak and marginalized; and since Awra Amba is assumed to be self-sufficient—and has become a national symbol of success—the community also escapes scrutiny and regulation. Not only does the community operate independently and undisturbed by the formal legal system, it also has to remain in that position, since anything else would disturb its model status. While the pressure to perform and conform applies to all members of the Awra Amba community, it poses particular challenges for the most vulnerable members of the community, since they participate in the model's travel agency in a limited fashion and hence have less access to the community's social, economic, and political capital. The community's status as a model limits their possible opportunities to question and challenge inequalities and injustices; it has shaped a village that only partly reflects the idealized model for a just and peaceful society depicted in common representations of Awra Amba.

As a critical anthropology of models and practices of modeling in the policy world, the story I have told here illustrates the need for a robust anthropology of policy that foregrounds the processual character of models and brings into focus the complex and contested contexts in which they are generated, circulated, transferred, and deployed. With a focus on relationality, emotions, desires, and unforeseen dynamics, the concept of viral assemblage facilitates a critical reading of traveling models—one that challenges the naïve instrumentality of traditional approaches to policy mobility. Since there are no innocent, totally emancipatory models that can be transplanted as panaceas for all time and place, it is crucial to understand the complex and multiple effects that models generate as they operate at and circulate through multiple scales, from the local and national to the transnational and global. In its effort to engage in reflexive and critical analysis, a critical anthropology of models pays attention to the exclusions and silencing that actors at the margins suffer—to the hidden dimensions of traveling policy models.

Notes

Introduction

1. For a discussion of Norwegian gender equality policies and models and their translation into practice in development projects in Ethiopia, see Hilde Selbervik and Marit Tolo Østebø (2013), "Gender Equality in International Aid: What has Norwegian Gender Politics Got to Do With It?" *Gender, Technology and Development* 17(2): 205–228; Marit Tolo Østebø, Haldis Haukanes, and Astrid Blystad (2012), "Strong State Policies on Gender and Aid: Threats and Opportunities for Norwegian Faith-Based Organisations," *Forum for Development Studies* 40(2): 193–216; and Marit Tolo Østebø (2013), "Translations of Gender Equality in International Aid: Perspectives from Norway and Ethiopia," (PhD diss., University of Bergen).

2. For an overview of the WEGE program see Heidi Holt Zachariassen, 2012, "From the Bottom Up: Lessons About Gender Mainstreaming in the Andes from Digni's Women Empowerment and Gender Equality (WEGE) Programme," Gender and Development 20 (3): 481–90.

3. The workshop was a two-day, closed event, where the members of the delegation presented and discussed their respective women's empowerment and gender equality initiatives.

4. This research project, Protection of Women's Rights in the Justice Systems of Ethiopia, was carried out by the ILPI in collaboration with six universities in Ethiopia and funded by the Royal Norwegian Embassy in Ethiopia.

5. See Minna Salami, "Awra Amba, an Ethiopian Village where Gender Equality is Real," https://www.msafropolitan.com/?s=Awra+Amba; and "Awra Amba: Where Gender Equality is Real," https://www.airbnb.com/rooms/21877650.

6. For the music video see Ahmed Teshome, "Awra Amba," https://www.youtube.com /watch?v=fk9eqAGam60.

7. In an earlier version of this manuscript, I used the term *simuloscene*, borrowed from Jeremy Trombley (2017). Since all simulations are models, but not all models are simulations, the term *modeloscene* is far more comprehensive, capturing the many forms and ways that models emerge and are put into use in our contemporary world. I am thankful to one of my former students, Laurin Baumgardt, for suggesting this as an alternative concept.

8. Gabriel Tarde (1843–1904) was a French sociologist, criminologist, and social psychologist known for his theory of imitation and innovation. Sampson (2012, 6–7) emphasizes that his book, *Virality: Contagion Theory in the Age of Networks*, is not a restoration or revival of Tarde's social epidemiology. Instead, he claims to offer "a resuscitation of his approach. This involves a carrying forward of an interpretation of Tardean ideas so that they can be linked, transversally, to contemporary notions, breathing life into social theory, and contagion theory, in particular."

9. See for example Lisa A. Boden and Iain J. McKendrick (2017), "Model-Based Policymaking: A Framework to Promote Ethical 'Good Practice' in Mathematical Modeling for Public Health Policymaking," Frontiers in Public Health 5 (68): 1–7; Robert Christley et al. (2013), "'Wrong, but Useful': Negotiating Uncertainty in Infectious Disease Modelling," *PLOS ONE* 8 (10): 1–13; Catherine Grant et al. (2016), "Moving Interdisciplinary Science Forward: Integrating Participatory Modelling with Mathematical Modelling of Zoonotic Disease in Africa," *Infectious Diseases of Poverty* 5 (1): 17.

10. With reference to parasitology, Serres (2007, 6) makes an important point in his work, emphasizing that the vocabulary used in natural sciences "bears several traces of anthropomorphism"; it is imported from "common customs and habits that the earliest monuments of our culture tell them [. . .]: hospitality, table manners, hostelry, general relations with strangers." In other words, if one assumes a historical perspective, the relationship between the social sciences and the natural sciences is not unidirectional. Just as the natural sciences may shape the ways we understand cultural and social dynamics, culture and society shape science. This is not surprising, since the natural sciences emerge from and are embedded in society and culture.

11. This is why certain mobile populations such as truck drivers and fishermen are more at risk of a pandemic than other less mobile populations. These mobile actors, in turn, may infect more sedentary populations when they go back to their villages and have contact with their wives/partners.

12. This differentiation—which may confuse the reader—is important. *A model* is a term we use about an unspecific, general phenomenon. When we give the model a name, such as *the Awra Amba model*, we acknowledge that the model is a unique, individual entity—an assemblage. Since all models are unique, historical entities that have been generated or have emerged in a particular context, all models are assemblages.

13. Sampson (2012, 6) also makes it clear that "Deleuze plays a central role in this resuscitation" of Tarde.

14. As DeLanda has argued, it is important to acknowledge that assemblage is both a process and a product.

15. I recognize that the feeling of hunger also is contingent on social and cultural factors. This does not mean that hunger is not biological. In fact, we can think of hunger as a state in which biological, emotional, and social processes are closely intertwined.

16. Zigon (2015, 502) defines a situation as "a nontotalizable assemblage widely diffused across different global scales that allows us to conceptualize how persons and

objects that are geographically, socioeconomically, and culturally distributed get caught up in shared conditions that significantly affect their possible ways of being-in-the world."

17. With his focus on following assemblic connections, Zigon hopes to move beyond a notion of globalization and the tracing of global connections. Nevertheless, it is difficult to see how assemblic ethnography is different from multisited ethnography. Apart from pairing the concept of assemblage with ethnography, Zigon's assemblic ethnography is not particularly original. His notion of assemblic ethnography could have been strengthened had he recognized that affect and emotions are key compositions of assemblages.

18. Headnotes is a term introduced by Simon Ottenberg (1990) to describe the unwritten form of fieldwork memories. Margery Wolf (1992) also discusses the relationship between field notes and headnotes in her book *A Thrice Told Tale*. Given the mobility and often chance and instantaneous encounters and events that go into making an object, image, model, or figure viral, headnotes are increasingly important in the traveling anthropologist's toolbox.

19. Developed in the late 1960s for the US Agency for International Development, LFA is a model that has been widely used by various multilateral organizations, including NORAD.

20. Othering is a term that is used in anthropology and other disciplines about representations and discourses that portray or label someone or something as essentially different and inferior.

Chapter 1: The Village

1. This information is taken from statistics displayed on posters on the wall in the Awra Amba welcoming center in 2015. From 2011 to 2015, the number of members remained relatively stable.

2. The *kebele*, also known as Peasant Association (PA), was introduced as the lowest administrative unit during the Marxist Derg regime (1974–91). The term *derg* means committee or council in Amharic.

3. While some of my informants gave me permission and even asked for their names to be included in this book, I have decided to use pseudonyms in most of the stories I tell. The exceptions are those figures whose engagement with Awra Amba is public in nature. This includes, but is not limited to, Zumra and Enaney, the Ethiopian American filmmaker Salem Mekuria, Lyfta CEOs Paulina Tervo and Serdar Ferit, and YouTube vlogger Evan Hadfield. As I introduce new actors in the story, I will indicate in a footnote when I use a pseudonym.

Chapter 2: Ethiopia—The Real Wakanda?

1. The year 1855 and the coronation of Emperor Tewodros II mark the beginning of what is considered to be modern Ethiopia.

2. See https://www.rollingstone.com/movies/movie-news/black-superheroes-matter-why-a-black-panther-movie-is-revolutionary-198678/.

3. See https://www.realclearpolitics.com/2018/02/10/the_revolutionary_power_of_039 black_panther039_433967.html.

4. Numerous commentators made this point during the first weeks after the movie's release. Tsedale Lemma, the editor in chief of *Addis Standard*, a monthly Ethiopian news magazine, concluded thus on Twitter: "I think what Lee [the writer-editor who created Black Panther] had in mind when creating the fictional enclave of #Wakanda, the E. African country that eluded colonialism, is #Ethiopia." "There is a Wakanda-like country in Africa. It is not fictional unless they want to plagiarize the facts and call it fictional, the story line and the characters in the movie do happen to copy an existing country in East Africa: Ethiopia," wrote *De Birhaner*, a news and analysis website that focuses on Ethiopia and East Africa. *The Washington Post* also ran a story titled, "Why Ethiopia is Africa's real Wakanda."

5. See https://www.theguardian.com/world/2013/dec/04/ethiopia-faster-rate-million aires-michael-buerk.

6. See https://www.nytimes.com/2015/03/04/world/africa/ethiopia-an-african-lion -aspires-to-middle-income-by-2025.html.

7. See https://www.gatesnotes.com/Development/Tenaw-Muluye-profile.

8. With reference to recent political reforms, the leading US Assistant Secretary for African Affairs, Tibor Nagy, in November 2018 hailed Ethiopia as a model for other African countries. See https://www.ena.et/en/2018/11/29/reform-in-ethiopia-model-for-other-afri can-countries-says-us-assistant-secretary/.

9. Levine described how conventional images of Ethiopia as a far-off place, a pious and just place, a magnificent kingdom, and a savage place have surfaced through history. He also discussed scholarly images of Ethiopia, which he categorized: an outpost of Semitic civilization, an ethnic museum, and an underdeveloped country.

10. According to Dessalegn Rhamato (2002), there were about sixty to seventy NGOs in Ethiopia in the late 1980s. A decade later, the number had increased to over 350.

11. See The Stories Behind the Data, https://datareport.goalkeepers.org/case-studies /maternal-mortality-ethiopia/, accessed December 19, 2018.

12. See https://reliefweb.int/report/ethiopia/ethiopia-tops-global-list-highest-internal -displacement-2018.

Chapter 3: The Emergence of a Traveling Model

1. The institute, ETH Zurich, is a highly ranked, prestigious Science, Technology, Engineering and Mathematics (STEM) University in Switzerland.

2. See "New Ethiopian Sustainable Town," http://www.nestown.org/, accessed February 18, 2020.

3. See *Spiegel Online*, "Ethiopia's Plans to Bridge the Urban-Rural Divide," http://www .spiegel.de/international/tomorrow/ethiopia-plans-to-build-8000-new-cities-in-country side-a-1197153.html.

4. This is a pseudonym.

5. The concept of the controlling model is in many ways similar to Clifford Geertz's (1957, 421, 424) worldview concept, which he terms "our assumed structure of reality" and which refers to the way we picture things, nature, society, and ourselves.

6. In his later works, Geertz (2007, 212) discusses the "ritual-as-a-model-system."

7. A critical journalistic account of the MVP can be found in Nina Munk's (2014) *The Idealist: Jeffrey Sachs and the Quest to End Poverty* (Norwell, MA: Anchor). For a critical scholarly overview and discussion see Japhy Wilson's (2015) "Paradoxical Utopia: The Millennium Villages Project in Theory and Practice," *Journal of Agrarian Change* 17 (1): 122–43, https://doi.org/10.1111/joac.12133.

8. By this, I do not mean to suggest that construction of the Awra Amba village was completely random. It would be naïve to think that the construction of the houses and the layout of the village were free from intentionality. The concentration of communal spaces (e.g., kindergarten, cooperative office, guesthouse, and shops) at the center of the village bears clear resemblance to Derg's village plans (see fig. 3.1), for example.

9. Moravia was located in what today is the Czech Republic.

10. I am thankful to Richard Rottenburg who made this point in response to a conference paper I presented at the 2016 American Anthropological Association annual meeting.

11. These models were by no means constant and static—they evolved. The NESTown architects describe the process of making the town in a very Latourian way— as a fuzzy process involving a wide range of actors. Still, it is interesting that they manage to convey a representation of their project as something relatively coherent and successful in terms of constructing an actual town.

12. See "Buranest Town Project: The Amhara Model Town," http://www.nestown .org/content/buranest-town-project-amhara-model-town.

13. See *Spiegel Online*, "Ethiopia's Plans"; and Tom Gardner, "Does a Struggling Ethiopian Model Town Offer Lessons for the Future?," https://www.reuters.com/article/ethio pia-landrights-towns/feature-does-a-struggling-ethiopian-model-town-offer-lessons-for -the-future-idUSL8N1NS3FE.

14. See Franz Oswald and Peter Schenker, "NESTown: The Making of the Amhara Model Town at Lake Tana," https://vimeo.com/15917534, accessed March 3, 2020; and Benjamin Stäli, "Buranest Model Town," https://vimeo.com/42607491.

15. See Arnon (2012) for a discussion of models as fiction.

Chapter 4: Alayhim—A Potential Disruption

1. The term *sect* that the author uses in his thesis is not a term that I would use myself; it is a highly problematic label that is often used in an exclusionary way to brand groups that are perceived to operate outside of what are considered to be legitimate religious and cultural practices.

2. This is a pseudonym.

3. This *salawat*, which is the act of sending blessings to the Prophet Muhammad, is

very particular to Alayhim. In the beginning of the *salawat,* they will use the term Alayhi, which means upon *him* and refers to the Prophet. After a few repetitions, there is a slight but important change from Alayhi to Alayhim. The latter translates to upon *them.* According to people in Alayhim, this is an act of sending blessings to the whole world. In conversations I had with Alayhim leaders, they emphasized that this reflects Sheik Saide's teaching, particularly his emphasis on interreligious peace and unity.

4. Mary S. Morgan is a professor of History of Economics at the London School of Economics. Her work on model theory also brought her into conversations with Clifford Geertz.

5. The visualization of the process of model making, as shown in these images, was developed by Arnold Merkies, in cooperation with the artist Koen Engelen who produced the drawings.

6. In recent years, there has been an increased focus on including religious leaders in women's rights-related initiatives. This is part of the turn to religion within the field of development. One should keep in mind, however, that this is, to a considerable degree, an instrumental recognition of religious leaders and not necessarily a recognition of religion per se. See Marit Tolo Østebø and Terje Østebø (2014), "Are Religious Leaders a Magic Bullet for Social/Societal Change? A Critical Look at Anti-FGM Interventions in Ethiopia," *Africa Today* 60 (3): 82–101, https://www.muse.jhu.edu/article/544388 for a discussion of the use of religious leaders in development interventions in Ethiopia.

Chapter 5: Modes of Transmission

1. This is a pseudonym.

2. The documentary can be found at https://www.youtube.com/watch?v=Out5aig b5Ls. It has been screened at numerous film festivals, including The Africa World Documentary Film Festival (https://www.africaworldfilmfestival.com/past-films.php?/2011/11); the Films from the South festival held annually in Oslo, Norway (http://www.film frasor.no/filmbase/2013/awra-amba); and the International Short Film Festival (Film Palace Fest, http://archive.inthepalace.com/en/2010/in_the_palace/film_program/by_film /films-go/byfilm/QQ==/1408.

3. This is a pseudonym.

4. See *Addis Journal: A Weblog on Arts & Culture, Life and Society,* https://arefe.word press.com/2010/06/13/ali-birra-receives-honorary-degree/.

5. PRI is a global nonprofit media company focused on creating "a more informed, empathetic and connected world by sharing powerful stories, encouraging exploration, connecting people and cultures, and creating opportunities to help people take informed action on stories that inspire them." See https://www.pri.org/about-pri, accessed June 6, 2019.

6. See https://www.pri.org/stories/2013-10-26/tiny-ethiopian-village-creates-greatest -place-earth-or-worst.

7. The documentary is titled "Awra Amba's Garden," https://vimeo.com/237589660, accessed February 21, 2020.

8. In a YouTube comment posted on one of the Awra Amba videos, one viewer jokingly suggested that the hat resembles a bathmat.

9. See note 7 above; Awra Amba's (E)utopia, https://vimeo.com/145472923, accessed June 15, 2019.

10. See https://www.youtube.com/watch?v=fk9eqAGam6o.

11. According to BookAuthority—the world's leading site for nonfiction book recommendations—Bradt's *Ethiopia* is "the most comprehensive, detailed and thorough guide available." It is also "the longest-serving English-language guidebook dedicated to the country, with a history of 25 years of research and expertise." See https://bookauthor ity.org/books/new-ethiopia-travel-guide-books, accessed May 28, 2009.

12. See for example http://mvmagazine.com/news/2018/07/01/finding-home; https://www.mvtimes.com/2017/07/19/island-rallies-ethiopian-village/; and http://www.andyex plores.com/blog-1/awra-amba.

13. Interview with Mandy Rose, an associate professor and director of the Digital Cultures Research Centre at University of the West of England; https://collabdocs.word press.com/interviews-resources/paulina-tervo-on-the-awra-amba-experience/, accessed June 13, 2019.

14. By October 2019, five months after it was published, the video had reached 142,000 views.

15. In addition to making videos about how to brush your teeth, make a sandwich, and sleep while in space, Chris Hadfield also became the first to produce a music video while floating aboard the International Space Station, singing and recording David Bowie's "Space Oddity." Thus far his video has more than forty-three million views on YouTube.

16. See https://www.forbes.com/sites/alexkantrowitz/2013/02/18/five-highlights-from -commander-chris-hadfields-reddit-ama-from-space/#23b4f1f41006.

Chapter 6: Going Viral

1. In Summer 2019, Paulina and Serdar moved from Helsinki to London to strengthen Lyfta's UK office. The company still has an office in Helsinki.

2. Interview with Serdar. See https://hundred.org/en/articles/meet-the-un-s-latest -education-and-learning-award-winner, accessed May 24, 2019.

3. From a personal reflection and review of Lyfta's history, written by Paulina on May 16, 2019, to celebrate the company's three-year anniversary. See https://www.linked in.com/pulse/lyfta-3-today-paulina-tervo/.

4. While acknowledging the existence of different rationalities and the role of translation in establishing what Rottenburg terms a meta-code, these processes are framed as rational processes. This is reflected in the use of words such as *decisions, reflexivity, understanding, agree,* etc.

5. Jane Bennett (2001) has challenged Weber's thesis that modernity is characterized by an inextricable process of disenchantment. I am here inspired by her work.

6. This is a pseudonym.

7. In fact, Tarde (Tarde and Toscano 2007, 630–31) argues that everything we consider being of value "is nothing, absolutely nothing, if it is not a combination of entirely subjective things, of beliefs and desires, of ideas and volitions. [. . .] Which is the man whose most cherished interest is not precisely that of avoiding any harm done against his faith and his pride, his heart and his worship? Will we say that the progress of reason, the supposed companion of the progress of civilization, takes responsibility for realizing little by little the abstraction imagined by economists, stripping the concrete man of all the motives for action besides the motive of personal interest? [. . .] Never, in any period of history, have a producer and a consumer, a seller and a buyer been in each other's presence without having first been united to one another by some entirely sentimental relation being neighbors, sharing citizenship or religious communion, enjoying a community of civilization and, second, without having been, respectively, escorted by an invisible cortege of associates, friends, and coreligionists whose thought has weighed on them in the discussion of prices or wages, and has finally won out, most often to the detriment of their strictly individual interest."

Chapter 7: Conditional Virality

1. The article was titled "A Healthy Cry on Father's Day." It has been removed from Lyfta's web page, which illustrates one of the points I make in this chapter: that virality is exclusive and limited.

2. See http://visitawraamba.com/, accessed March 5, 2020.

3. See *Lyfta is 3 Today*, https://www.linkedin.com/pulse/lyfta-3-today-paulina-tervo/.

4. See "Lyfta—Fostering Global Citizenship Skills and Empathy Through Immersive Storytelling," https://www.reimagine-education.com/26-lyfta/, accessed March 5, 2020.

5. Ibid., accessed October 28, 2019.

6. This is how Lyfta's producers often describe this feature.

7. See https://www.lyfta.com/videos, accessed February 22, 2020.

8. In fall 2019, I reached out to the University of Florida's library and asked them to explore the possibility of investing in a Lyfta subscription. After receiving the quote from Lyfta—which was almost three times the cost that Lyfta lists on its web page for a large school—the university concluded that the trial period was too short and the product too expensive to invest in.

9. This is a pseudonym.

Chapter 8: Being a Model

1. Whether this figure is correct is questionable. A representative from the district's Rural Land Administration and Utilization Office suggested that the community's total landholdings was closer to 50 hectares, and even Zumra admitted that he did not exactly

know how much land the community has. "I did not measure the land," he told me in one of our conversations. "I got this number from the government official who measured the land."

2. See http://heberasbl.wikeo.net/awra-amba.html, accessed March 26, 2019. Translated from French by Isabelle Walther-Duc.

3. "Secretary of State Clinton Praises Tostan as Model for Grassroots Development," https://www.tostan.org/secretary-state-clinton-praises-tostan-model-grassroots-development/.

4. It is, for example, not uncommon for religious colleges and universities to have policies that exclude and discipline students or faculty who fail to behave in accordance with institutional normative frameworks.

5. Following Durkheim, we can characterize Awra Amba as a moral community that is held together by a sacralization of Zumra's philosophy and mission, which transcends those of Muhammad and Jesus, as the quote demonstrates.

6. An herb which is common in Ethiopian cuisine.

7. This is a pseudonym.

8. Most of the weavers are men, something that can be explained by the fact that the weaving technique is physically challenging. Jumpei Itagaki (2003, 42), an anthropologist who has studied weaving in areas around Bahir Dar, including in Awra Amba, has described the technique as follows: "Weaving requires that one leg be outstretched, and weavers work in the same posture for at least three to four hours. Although I had experience weaving in my country, when I began working in the Bahir Dar area, I was not able to sit in this position for even 30 minutes, as this posture seems to place a burden on the waist. However, maintaining the same position over several hours allows the weaver to minimize surface irregularity and maintain consistent texture."

Conclusion: Infected

1. The term "flipped classroom" refers to a type of blended learning that reverses the traditional learning environment by delivering instructional content *outside* of the classroom and moving problem-solving activities aimed at deepening students' understanding and critical thinking through discussion with peers *into* the classroom.

References

Aalen, Lovise. 2014. "Ethiopia After Meles: Stability for How Long?" *Current History* 113 (763): 192–96.

Aalen, Lovise, and Kjetil Tronvoll. 2009. "The End of Democracy? Curtailing Political and Civil Rights in Ethiopia." *Review of African Political Economy* 36 (120): 193–207. https://doi.org/10.1080/03056240903065067.

Abbink, Jon. 1998. "An Historical-Anthropological Approach to Islam in Ethiopia: Issues of Identity and Politics." *Journal of African Cultural Studies* 11 (2): 109–24. https://doi .org/10.1080/13696819808717830.

Abebe Endale Assefa. 2013. "The Place of Children Through the Lens of Generational and Gender Relationships in Awra Amba Community, Northern Ethiopia." Master's thesis, Norwegian University of Science and Technology.

Abeje Berhanu, and Ezana Amdework. 2011. *Peasant Entrepreneurship and Rural Poverty Reduction: The Case of Model Farmers in Bure Woreda, West Gojjam Zone.* Addis Ababa: Forum for Social Studies.

Abu-Lughod, Lila. 1993. *Writing Women's Worlds. Bedouin Stories.* Berkeley: University of California Press.

Abu-Lughod, Lila. 2002. "Do Muslim Women Really Need Saving? Anthropological Reflections on Cultural Relativism and Its Others." *American Anthropologist* 104 (3): 783–90. https://doi.org/10.1525/aa.2002.104.3.783.

Abu-Lughod, Lila. 2009. "Dialects of Women's Empowerment: The International Circuitry of the Arab Human Development Report 2005." *International Journal of Middle East Studies* 41 (01): 83–103. https://doi.org/10.1017/S0020743808090132.

Adey, Peter. 2008. "Aeromobilities: Geographies, Subjects and Vision." *Geography Compass* 2 (5): 1318–36. https://doi.org/10.1111/j.1749-8198.2008.00149.x.

Ahmed Teshome. 2006. "Awera Amba." *Eyorika. Ethiopian Contemporary Music.* Nahom Records.

Ahmed, Sara. 2004a. "Affective Economies." *Social Text* 22 (2): 117–39.

Ahmed, Sara. 2004b. *The Cultural Politics of Emotions.* Edinburgh: Edinburgh University Press.

Althusser, Louis. 1971. "Ideology and Ideological State Apparatuses (Notes Towards an Investigation)." In *Lenin and Philosophy and Other Essays*, 142–76. New York: Monthly Review Press.

Angélil, Marc, Zegeye Cherenet, Sascha Delz, Fasil Giorghis, Sarah Graham, Dirk Hebel, Franz Oswald, Cary Siress, and Benjamin Stähli. 2013. *The School, the Book, the Town: Logbook. Ethiopia in a Timeline*. Berlin: Ruby Press.

Anteneh Tesfahun. 2012. "The Contribution of Conflict Resolution Mechanisms in Fostering Sustainable Peace: The Case of Awramba Community." Master's thesis, Institute for Peace and Security Studies, Addis Ababa University.

Arnon, Levy. 2012. "Models, Fictions, and Realism: Two Packages." *Philosophy of Science* 79 (5): 738–48.

Arriola, Leonardo R., and Terrence Lyons. 2016. "The 100% Election." *Journal of Democracy* 27 (1): 76–88.

Aston, Judith, and Sandra Gaudenzi. 2012. "Interactive Documentary: Setting the Field." *Studies in Documentary Film* 6 (2): 125–39. https://doi.org/10.1386/sdf.6.2.125_1.

Aune, Jens B. 2000. "Logical Framework Approach and PRA: Mutually Exclusive or Complementary Tools for Project Planning?" *Development in Practice* 10 (5): 687–690. https://doi.org/10.1080/09614520020008850.

Awra Amba Community, The. 2012. "Journey for Peace."

Bach, Jean-Nicolas. 2011. "Abyotawi Democracy: Neither Revolutionary Nor Democratic; A Critical Review of EPRDF's Conception of Revolutionary Democracy in Post-1991 Ethiopia."*Journal of Eastern African Studies* 5 (4): 641–63. https://doi.org/10.1080/1753 1055.2011.642522.

Bahru Zewde. 2002. *A History of Modern Ethiopia. 1855–1991*. Addis Ababa: Addis Ababa University Press.

Bailer-Jones, Daniela M. 2003. "When Scientific Models Represent." *International Studies in the Philosophy of Science* 17 (1): 59–74. https://doi.org/10.1080/02698590305238.

Baker, Tom, Ian R. Cook, Eugene McCann, Cristina Temenos, and Kevin Ward. 2016. "Policies on the Move: The Transatlantic Travels of Tax Increment Financing." *Annals of the American Association of Geographers* 106 (2): 459–69. https://doi.org/10.1080/0004 5608.2015.1113111.

Baker, Tom, and Pauline McGuirk. 2019. "'He Came Back a Changed Man': The Popularity and Influence of Policy Tourism." *Area* 51 (3): 561–69. https://doi.org/10.1111/area .12505.

Barry, Andrew, and Nigel Thrift. 2007. "Gabriel Tarde: Imitation, Invention And Economy." *Economy and Society* 36 (4): 509–25. https://doi.org/10.1080/03085140701589497.

Behrends, Andrea, Sung-Joon Park, and Richard Rottenburg, eds. 2014a. *Travelling Models in African Conflict Management: Translating Technologies of Social Ordering*. Leiden, The Netherlands: Brill.

Behrends, Andrea, Sung-Joon Park, and Richard Rottenburg. 2014b. "Travelling Models: Introducing an Analytical Concept to Globalisation Studies." In *Travelling Models in African Conflict Management: Translating Technologies of Social Ordering*, edited by Andrea Behrends, Sung-Joon Park, and Richard Rottenburg, 1–40. Leiden, The Netherlands: Brill.

Bellucci, Stefano. 2016. "The 1974 Ethiopian Revolution at 40: Social, Economic, and Political Legacies." *Northeast African Studies* 16 (1): 1–14. https://doi.org/10.14321/nortafristud.16.1.0001.

Bennett, Jane. 2001. *The Enchantment of Modern Life: Attachments, Crossings, and Ethics.* Princeton: Princeton University Press.

Bernal, Victoria, and Inderpal Grewal. 2014. "Introduction: The NGO Form; Feminist Struggles, States, and Neoliberalism." In *Theorizing NGOs: States, Feminisms, and Neoliberalism*, edited by Victoria Bernal and Inderpal Grewal, 1–18. Durham, NC: Duke University Press.

Bernhard, H. Russell. 2006. *Research Methods in Anthropology: Qualitative and Quantative Approaches.* Lanham, MD: AltaMira Press.

Bester, Angela. 2012. "Results-Based Management in the United Nations Development System: Progress and Challenges." A report prepared for the United Nations Department of Economic and Social Affairs, for the Quadrennial Comprehensive Policy Review. https://www.un.org/en/ecosoc/qcpr/pdf/sgr2016-studies-rbm-8jan2016.pdf.

Biehl, João. 2017. "Ethnography Prosecuted: Facing the Fabulation of Power." In *If Truth Be Told: The Politics of Public Ethnography*, edited by Didier Fassin, 261–86. Durham, NC: Duke University Press.

Biehl, João, and Peter Locke. 2017. "Introduction: Ethnographic Sensorium." In *Unfinished: Anthropology of Becoming*, edited by João Biehl and Peter Locke, 1–33. Durham, NC: Duke University Press.

Biehl, João, and Adriana Petryna. 2013. "Critical Global Health." In *When People Come First: Critical Studies in Global Health*, edited by João Biel and Adriana Petryna, 1–19. Princeton: Princeton University Press.

Biseswar, Indrawatie. 2008. "Problems of Feminist Leadership Among Educated Women in Ethiopia: Taking Stock in the Third Millennium." *Journal of Developing Societies* 24 (2): 125–58. https://doi.org/10.1177/0169796x0802400203.

Boden, Lisa A., and Iain J. McKendrick. 2017. "Model-Based Policymaking: A Framework to Promote Ethical 'Good Practice' in Mathematical Modeling for Public Health Policymaking." *Frontiers in Public Health* 5 (68): 1–7.

Borchgrevink, Axel. 2008. "Limits to Donor Influence: Ethiopia, Aid and Conditionality." *Forum for Development Studies* 35 (2): 195–220. https://doi.org/10.1080/08039410.2008.9666409.

Bourdieu, Pierre. 1977. *Outline of a Theory of Practice.* Cambridge: Cambridge University Press.

Box, George E. P. 1976. "Science and Statistics." *Journal of the American Statistical Association* 71 (356): 791–99. https://doi.org/10.1080/01621459.1976.10480949.

Box, George E. P. 1979. "Robustness in the Strategy of Scientific Model Building." In *Robustness in Statistics*, edited by Robert L. Launer and Graham N. Wilkinson, 201–36. New York: Academic Press.

Boylston, Tom. 2015. "'And Unto Dust Shalt Thou Return': Death and the Semiotics of

Remembrance in an Ethiopian Orthodox Christian Village." *Material Religion* 11 (3): 281–302. https://doi.org/10.1080/17432200.2015.1082745.

Brown, Steven D. 2002. "Michel Serres: Science, Translation and the Logic of the Parasite." *Theory, Culture & Society* 19 (3): 1–27.

Bruzzi, Silvia, and Meron Zeleke. 2015. "Contested Religious Authority: Sufi Women in Ethiopia and Eritrea." 45 (1): 37. https://doi.org/10.1163/15700666-12340028.

Büscher, Bram. 2014. "Selling Success: Constructing Value in Conservation and Development." *World Development* 57:79–90. https://doi.org/10.1016/j.worlddev.2013.11.014.

Butler, Judith, Jurgen Habermas, Charles Taylor, and Cornel West. 2011. *The Power of Religion in the Public Sphere*. New York: Columbia University Press.

Chambers, Robert. 1994. "The Origins and Practice of Participatory Rural Appraisal." *World Development* 22 (7): 953–69. https://doi.org/10.1016/0305-750X(94)90141-4.

Chambers, Robert. 2013. *Rural Development: Putting the Last First*. Oxon, UK: Routledge.

Chapman, William. 1991. "Slave Villages in the Danish West Indies: Changes of the Late Eighteenth and Early Nineteenth Centuries." *Perspectives in Vernacular Architecture* 4:108–20. https://doi.org/10.2307/3514226.

Christley, Robert, Maggie Mort, Brian Wynne, Jonathan M. Wastling, A. Louise Heathwaite, Roger Pickup, Zoë Austin, and Sophia M. Latham. 2013. "'Wrong, but Useful': Negotiating Uncertainty in Infectious Disease Modelling." *PLOS ONE* 8 (10): 1–13.

Clapham, Christopher. 1988. *Transformation and Continuity in Revolutionary Ethiopia*. Cambridge: Cambridge University Press.

Clapham, Christopher. 2006. "Ethiopian Development: The Politics of Emulation." *Commonwealth and Comparative Politics* 44 (1): 137–50. https://doi.org/10.1080/14662040600624536.

Clapham, Christopher. 2015. "The Era of Haile Selassie." In *Understanding Contemporary Ethiopia: Monarchy, Revolution and the Legacy of Meles Zenawi*, edited by G. Prunier and E. Ficquet, 183–207. London: Hurst and Company.

Clarke, David L. 1972. *Models and Paradigms in Contemporary Archaeology*. London: Methuen.

Claverie, Jean-Michel, and Chantal Abergel. 2012. "The Concept of Virus in the Post-Megavirus Era." In *Viruses: Essential Agents of Life*, edited by Günther Witzany, 187–202. Dordrecht, The Netherlands: Springer.

Closser, Svea. 2012. "'We Can't Give Up Now': Global Health Optimism and Polio Eradication in Pakistan." *Medical Anthropology* 31 (5): 385–403. https://doi.org/10.1080/01459740.2011.645927.

Cohen, John M., and Nils Ivar Isakson. 1987. "Villagisation in Ethiopia's Arsi Region." *Journal of Modern African Studies* 25 (3): 435–64.

Colebrook, Claire. 2001. *Gilles Deleuze*. New York: Routledge.

Collier, Stephen J., and Aihwa Ong. 2005. "Global Assemblages, Anthropological Problems." In *Global Assemblages: Technology, Politics, and Ethics as Anthropological Problems*, edited by A. Ong and S. J. Collier. Malden, MA: Blackwell Publishing.

Comaroff, John L., and Jean Comaroff. 2009. *Ethnicity, Inc.* Chicago: University of Chicago Press.

Costas, Jana. 2013. "Problematizing Mobility: A Metaphor of Stickiness, Non-Places and the Kinetic Elite." *Organization Studies* 34 (10): 1467–85. https://doi.org/10.1177/01708 40613495324.

Dalmedico, Amy, D. 2007. "Models and Simulations in Climate Change: Historical, Epistemological, Anthropological and Political Aspects." In *Science Without Laws: Model Systems, Cases, Exemplary Narratives*, edited by Angela N. H. Creager, Elizabeth Lunbeck, and M. Norton Wise, 125–56. Durham, NC: Duke University Press.

Darley, Gillian. 2007. *Villages of Vision: A Study of Strange Utopias.* Nottingham, UK: Five Leaves Publications.

Davis, Kimberley Chalbot. 2014. *Beyond the White Negro: Empathy and Anti-Racist Readings.* Champaign: University of Illinois Press.

DeLanda, Manuel. 2006. *A New Philosophy of Society: Assemblage Theory and Social Complexity.* London: Continuum.

DeLanda, Manuel. 2016. *Assemblage Theory.* Edinburgh: Edinburgh University Press.

Deleuze, Gilles, and Félix Guattari. 1987. *A Thousand Plateaus: Capitalism and Schizophrenia.* London: Continuum.

Deleuze, Gilles, and Claire Parnet. 2002. *Dialogues II.* New York: Columbia University Press.

Dereje Feyissa. 2011. "Aid Negotiation: The Uneasy 'Partnership' Between EPRDF and the Donors." *Journal of Eastern African Studies* 5 (4): 788–817. https://doi.org/10.1080/1753 1055.2011.642541.

Dereje Feyissa, and Bruce B. Lawrence. 2014. "Muslims Renegotiating Marginality in Contemporary Ethiopia." *The Muslim World* 104 (3): 281–305. https://doi.org/10.1111/muwo .12056.

Desplat, Patrick, and Terje Østebø. 2013. "Muslims in Ethiopia: The Christian Legacy, Identity Politics, and Islamic Reformism." In *Muslim Ethiopia: The Christian Legacy, Identity Politics, and Islamic Reformism*, edited by P. Desplat and T. Østebø, 1–24. New York: Palgrave Macmillan.

Dessalegn Rahmato. 2002. "Civil Society Organizations in Ethiopia." In *Ethiopia: The Challenge of Democracy from Below*, edited by B. Zewde and S. Pausewant, 103–119. Uppsala, Norway: Nordiska Afrikainstitutet and Forum for Social Studies.

De Vries, Pieter. 2007. "Don't Compromise Your Desire for Development! A Lacanian/Deleuzian Rethinking of the Anti-Politics Machine." *Third World Quarterly* 28 (1): 25–43. https://doi.org/10.1080/01436590601081765.

De Waal, Alex. 1991. *Evil Days: Thirty Years of War and Famine in Ethiopia.* New York: Human Rights Watch.

Di Nunzio, Marco. 2015. "What is the Alternative? Youth, Entrepreneurship and the Developmental State in Urban Ethiopia." *Development and Change* 46 (5): 1179–1200. https://doi.org/10.1111/dech.12187.

Dolowitz, David P., and David Marsh. 2000. "Learning from Abroad: The Role of Policy Transfer in Contemporary Policy-Making." *Governance* 13 (1): 5–23. https://doi.org/10 .1111/0952-1895.00121.

Donham, Donald L. 1999. *Marxist Modern: An Ethnographic History of the Ethiopian Revolution.* Berkeley: University of California Press.

Dynes, Michelle, Sandra T. Buffington, Mary Carpenter, Anna Handley, Maureen Kelley, Lelisse Tadesse, Hanna Tesemma Beyene, and Lynn Sibley. 2012. "Strengthening Maternal and Newborn Health in Rural Ethiopia: Early Results from Frontline Health Worker Community Maternal and Newborn Health Training." *Midwifery* 29 (3): 251– 59. https://doi.org/10.1016/j.midw.2012.01.006.

Emebet Mulumebet. 2010. "Trajectories of Women/Gender Issues and the Current Status of Gender Mainstreaming in Ethiopia." In *Gender Mainstreaming Experiences from Eastern and Southern Africa*, edited by M. Tadesse and A. Daniel, 71–77.

Emmenegger, Rony. 2016. "Decentralization and the Local Developmental State: Peasant Mobilization in Oromiya, Ethiopia." *Africa* 86 (2): 263–87.

Eskinder Teferi. 2012. "The Role of Gender Equality in Promoting Peace and Development: The Case of Awra Amba Community in Fogera Wereda of Amhara National Regional State, Ethiopia." Master's thesis, Peace and Security Studies, School of Graduate Studies, Addis Ababa University.

Eyben, Rosalind. 2010. "Subversively Accommodating: Feminist Bureaucrats and Gender Mainstreaming." *IDS Bulletin, Institute of Development Studies* 41 (2): 54–61.

Fantini, Emanuele. 2013. Developmental State, Economic Transformation and Social Diversification in Ethiopia. *ISPI Analysis* 163 (March 2013): 1–7.

Fassin, Didier. 2017. "Introduction: When Ethnography Goes Public." In *If Truth Be Told: The Politics of Public Ethnography*, edited by Didier Fassin, 1–16. Durham, NC: Duke University Press.

Federal Democratic Republic of Ethiopia, The. 2010. Growth and Transformation Plan (GTP) 2010–2011 to 2014–2015, edited by Ministry of Finance and Economic Development (MoFED), Addis Ababa.

Foucault, Michel. 1982. "The Subject and Power." *Critical Inquiry* 8 (4): 777–95. https://doi .org/10.2307/1343197.

Fourie, Elsje. 2014. "Model Students: Policy Emulation, Modernization, and Kenya's Vision 2030." *African Affairs* 113 (453): 540–62. https://doi.org/10.1093/afraf/adu058.

Gagliardone, Iginio. 2014. "New Media and the Developmental State in Ethiopia." *African Affairs* 113 (451): 279–99. https://doi.org/10.1093/afraf/adu017.

Gardner, Katy, and David Lewis. 2015. *Anthropology and Development: Challenges for the Twenty-First Century.* London: Pluto Press.

Gebeyehu Yihenew, Haileeyesus Adamu, and Beyene Petros. 2014. "The Impact of Cooperative Social Organization on Reducing the Prevalence of Malaria and Intestinal Parasite Infections in Awramba, a Rural Community in South Gondar, Ethiopia." *Interdisciplinary Perspectives on Infectious Diseases* 2014. http://dx.doi.org/10.1155/2014 /378780.

Geertz, Clifford. 1957. "Ethos, World-View and the Analysis of Sacred Symbols." *The Antioch Review* 17 (4): 421–37. https://doi.org/10.2307/4609997.

Geertz, Clifford. 1973. *The Interpretation of Cultures*. New York: Basic Books.

Geertz, Clifford. 2007. "'To Exist Is to Have Confidence in One's Way of Being': Rituals as Model Systems." In *Science Without Laws: Model Systems, Cases, Exemplary Narratives*, edited by Angela N. H. Creager, Elizabeth Lunbeck and M. Norton Wise, 213–24. Durham, NC: Duke University Press.

Geschiere, Peter, and Birgit Meyer. 1998. "Globalization and Identity: Dialectics of Flow and Closure; Introduction." *Development and Change* 29 (4): 601–15. https://doi.org/10.1111/1467-7660.00092.

Getu Demeke Alene. 2011. "Community Self-Help Development, Spaces for Scaling Up: A Case Study of Awura Amba Rural Self-Help Community in Northern Ethiopia." Master's thesis, Master of Philosophy (Mphil) in Development Studies, Department of Geography, Faculty of Social Sciences and Technology Management, Norwegian University of Science and Technology (NTNU). https://ntnuopen.ntnu.no/ntnu-xmlui/handle/11250/265417.

Gillespie, Kelly. 2017. "Before the Commision: Ethnography as Public Testimony." In *If Truth Be Told: The Politics of Public Ethnography*, edited by Didier Fassin, 69–95. Durham, NC: Duke University Press.

Ginnis, Paul. 2002. *The Teacher's Toolkit: Raise Classroom Achievement with Strategies for Every Learner*. Carmarthen, Wales, UK: Crown House Publishing.

Godin, Benoit. 2017. *Models of Innovation: The History of an Idea*. Cambridge, MA: MIT Press.

Gonzalez, Sara. 2010. "Bilbao and Barcelona 'in Motion': How Urban Regeneration 'Models' Travel and Mutate in the Global Flows of Policy Tourism." *Urban Studies* 48 (7): 1397–1418. https://doi.org/10.1177/0042098010374510.

Grant, Catherine, Giovanni Lo Iacono, Vupenyu Dzingirai, Bernard Bett, Thomas R. A. Winnebah, and Peter M. Atkinson. 2016. "Moving Interdisciplinary Science Forward: Integrating Participatory Modelling with Mathematical Modelling of Zoonotic Disease in Africa." *Infectious Diseases of Poverty* 5 (1): 17.

Grosz, Elizabeth A. 1994. *Volatile Bodies: Toward a Corporeal Feminism*. Bloomington: Indiana University Press.

Hadfield, Evan. 2019. "One Good Cult." https://www.youtube.com/watch?v=feYv2wZFbbo.

Hagmann, Tobias, and Jon Abbink. 2011. "Twenty Years of Revolutionary Democratic Ethiopia, 1991 to 2011." *Journal of Eastern African Studies* 5 (4): 579–95. https://doi.org/10.1080/17531055.2011.642515.

Halldin Norberg, Viveca. 1977. *Swedes in Haile Selassie's Ethiopia 1924–1952*. Uppsala, Sweden: Scandinavian Institute of African Studies.

Handelman, Don. 1998. *Models and Mirrors: Towards an Anthropology of Public Events*. New York: Berghahn Books.

Hannig, Anita. 2017. *Beyond Surgery: Injury, Healing, and Religion at an Ethiopian Hosptial*. Chicago: University of Chicago Press.

Haustein, Jörg, and Terje Østebø. 2011. "EPRDF's Revolutionary Democracy and Religious Plurality: Islam and Christianity in Post-Derg Ethiopia." *Journal of Eastern African Studies* 5 (4): 755–72. https://doi.org/10.1080/17531055.2011.642539.

Headland, Thomas N., Kenneth L. Pike, and Marvin Harris. 1990. *Emics and Etics. The Insider/Outsider Debate.* Thousand Oaks, CA: SAGE Publications.

Hirschkind, Charles, and Saba Mahmood. 2002. "Feminism, the Taliban, and Politics of Counter-Insurgency." *Anthropological Quarterly* 75 (2): 339–54.

Huggan, Graham. 2001. *The Postcolonial Exotic: Marketing the Margins.* Oxon, UK: Routledge.

Hutten, E. H. 1954. "The Role of Models in Physics." *The British Journal for the Philosophy of Science* 4 (16): 284–301.

Ibrahima, Aissetu B. 2017. "Asset Based Community Development (ABCD): An Alternative Path for Community Development." In *Transforming Society: Strategies for Social Development from Singapore, Asia and Around the World (Routledge Contemporary Southeast Asia Series)*, edited by N. T. Tan, 229–40. Oxon, UK: Routledge.

Ingold, Tim. 2008. "Anthropology is not Ethnography." In *Proceedings of the British Academy, Volume 154, 2007 Lectures*, edited by Ron Johnson, 69–92. Oxford: Oxford University Press.

Itagaki, Jumpei. 2003. "Gender-Based Textile-Weaving Techniques of the Amhara in Northern Ethiopia." Supplement, *African Study Monographs* 46:27–52.

Jarvis, Helen. 2017. "Christiania's Place in the World of Travelling Ideas: Sharing Informal Liveability." *Nordic Journal of Architectural Research* 29 (2): 113–36.

Jensen, Jeppe Sinding. 2011. "Revisiting the Insider-Outsider Debate: Dismantling a Pseudo-Problem in the Study of Religion." Method and Theory in the Study of Religion 23 (1): 29. https://doi.org/10.1163/157006811X549689.

Joumard, Robert. 2012. "Awra Amba, A Current Experiment of Utopian Socialism." https://local.attac.org/rhone/spip.php?article1681.

Kapoor, Ilan. 2014. "Psychoanalysis and Development: Contributions, Examples, Limits." *Third World Quarterly* 35 (7): 1120–43. https://doi.org/10.1080/01436597.2014.926101.

Kenyon, Susan M. 1995. "Zar as Modernization in Contemporary Sudan." *Anthropological Quarterly* 68 (2): 107–20. https://doi.org/10.2307/3318050.

Khan, Azizur R. 1979. "The Comilla Model and the Integrated Rural Development Programme of Bangladesh: An Experiment in 'Cooperative Capitalism'." *World Development* 7 (4): 397–422.

Kleinman, Arthur. 2012. "Caregiving as Moral Experience." *The Lancet* 380 (9853): 1550–51. https://doi.org/10.1016/S0140-6736(12)61870-4.

Kobishanov, Y. M. 1981. "Aksum: Political System, Economics and Culture, First to Fourth Century." In *General History of Africa II. Ancient Civilizations of Africa*, edited by G. Mokhtar, 381–400. Paris: UNESCO.

Koblinsky, Marge. 2014. "Reducing Maternal and Perinatal Mortality Through a Community Collaborative Approach: Introduction to a Special Issue on the Maternal and

Newborn Health in Ethiopia Partnership (MaNHEP)." Supplement, *J Midwifery Womens Health* 59 (1): S1–5. https://doi.org/10.1111/jmwh.12174.

Kristof, Nicholas D., and Sheryl WuDunn. 2010. *Half the Sky: Turning Oppression into Opportunity for Women Worldwide*. New York: Vintage.

Kulbaga, Theresa A. 2008. "Pleasurable Pedagogies: 'Reading Lolita in Tehran' and the Rhetoric of Empathy." *College English* 70 (5): 506–21. https://doi.org/10.2307/25472286.

Lane, Christel. 1981. *The Rites of Rulers: Ritual in Industrial Society; the Soviet Case*. Cambridge: Cambridge University Press.

Latour, Bruno. 2004. "Why Has Critique Run out of Steam? From Matters of Fact to Matters of Concern." *Critical Inquiry* 30 (2): 225–48. https://doi.org/10.1086/421123.

Lefort, René. 2012. "Free Market Economy, 'Developmental State' and Party-State Hegemony in Ethiopia: The Case of the 'Model Farmers'." *Journal of Modern African Studies* 50 (04): 681–706. https://doi.org/10.1017/s0022278x12000389.

Legg, Stephen. 2011. "Assemblage/Apparatus: Using Deleuze and Foucault." *Area* 43 (2): 128–33. https://doi.org/10.1111/j.1475-4762.2011.01010.x.

Le Roux, Hannah. 2017. "Bunna without Borders: Coffee/Making as a Relational Space." *Architecture and Culture* 5 (3): 463–74. https://doi.org/10.1080/20507828.2017.1379291.

Levine, Donald N. 1974. *Greater Ethiopia. The Evolution of a Multiethnic Society*. Chicago: University of Chicago Press.

Lombardo, Emanuela, Petra Meier, and Mieke Verloo. 2009. "Stretching and Bending Gender Equality: A Discursive Approach." In *The Discursive Politics of Gender Equality: Stretching, Bending and Policy-Making*, edited by Emanuela Lombardo, Petra Meier, and Mieke Verloo. London: Routledge.

Lund, Jens Friis, Eliezeri Sungusia, Mathew Bukhi Mabele, and Andreas Scheba. 2017. "Promising Change, Delivering Continuity: REDD+ as Conservation Fad." *World Development* 89:124–39. https://doi.org/10.1016/j.worlddev.2016.08.005.

Lyons, Diane. 2014. "Perceptions of Consumption: Constituting Potters, Farmers and Blacksmiths in the Culinary Continuum in Eastern Tigray, Northern Highland Ethiopia." *African Archaeological Review* 31 (2): 169–201. https://doi.org/10.1007/s10437-014-9149-4.

Maes, Kenneth, Svea Closser, Ethan Vorel, and Yihenew Tesfaye. 2015. "A Women's Development Army: Narratives of Community Health Worker Investment and Empowerment in Rural Ethiopia." *Studies in Comparative International Development* 50 (4): 455–78. https://doi.org/10.1007/s12116-015-9197-z.

Mahmood, Saba. 2005. *Politics of Piety. The Islamic Revival and the Feminist Subject*. Princeton: Princeton University Press.

Malkki, Liisa H. 2015. *The Need to Help*. Durham, NC: Duke University Press.

McCann, Eugene. 2011. "Urban Policy Mobilities and Global Circuits of Knowledge: Toward a Research Agenda." *Annals of the Association of American Geographers* 101 (1): 107–30. https://doi.org/10.1080/00045608.2010.520219.

McCann, Eugene, and Kevin Ward. 2012. "Policy Assemblages, Mobilities and Mutations:

Toward a Multidisciplinary Conversation." *Political Studies Review* 10 (3): 325–32. https://doi.org/10.1111/j.1478-9302.2012.00276.x.

McFarlane, Colin. 2009. "Translocal Assemblages: Space, Power and Social Movements." *Geoforum* 40 (4): 561–67. https://doi.org/10.1016/j.geoforum.2009.05.003.

Meles Zenawi. 2012. "States and Markets: Neoliberal Limitations and the Case for a Developmental State." In *Good Growth and Governance in Africa: Rethinking Development Strategies*, edited by A. Norman, K. Botchwey and H. Stein, 140–73. Oxford: Oxford University Press.

Merry, Sally Engle. 2003. "Human Rights Law and the Demonization of Culture (And Anthropology Along the Way)." *PoLAR: Political and Legal Anthropology Review* 26 (1): 55–76. https://doi.org/10.1525/pol.2003.26.1.55.

Merry, Sally Engle, and Peggy Levitt. 2019. "Remaking Women's Human Rights in the Vernacular: The Resonance Dilemma." In *Rethinking Gender Equality in Global Governance*, edited by L. Engberg-Pedersen, A. Fejerskov, and S. Cold-Ravnkilde. London: Palgrave Macmillan.

Mitchell, Shira, Andrew Gelman, Rebecca Ross, Joyce Chen, Sehrish Bari, Uyen Kim Huynh, Matthew W. Harris, Sonia Ehrlich Sachs, Elizabeth A. Stuart, Avi Feller, Susanna Makela, Alan M. Zaslavsky, Lucy McClellan, Seth Ohemeng-Dapaah, Patricia Namakula, Cheryl A. Palm, and Jeffrey D. Sachs. 2018. "The Millennium Villages Project: a Retrospective, Observational, Endline Evaluation." *Lancet Global Health* 6 (5): e500–e513. https://doi.org/10.1016/S2214-109X(18)30065-2.

Morgan, Mary S. 2012. *The World in the Model: How Economists Work And Think*. New York: Cambridge University Press.

Morgan, Mary S., and Margaret C. Morrison, eds. 1999. *Models as Mediators*. Cambridge: Cambridge University Press.

Mosse, David. 2003. "The Making and Marketing of Participatory Development." In *A Moral Critique of Development: In Search of Global Responsbilities*, edited by Philip Quarles von Ufford and Ananta Kumar Giri, 43–75. London: Routledge.

Mosse, David. 2004. "Is Good Policy Unimplementable? Reflections on the Ethnography of Aid Policy and Practice." *Development and Change* 35 (4): 639–71.

Mosse, David. 2005. *Cultivating Development: An Ethnography of Aid Policy and Practice*. London: Pluto Press.

Mosse, David. 2011. "Politics & Ethics: Ethnographies of Expert Knowledge and Professional Identities." In *Policy Worlds: Anthropology and the Analysis of Contemporary Power*, edited by Cris Shore, Susan Wright, and Davide Però, 50–67. New York: Berghahn Books.

Mosse, David, and David Lewis. 2006. "Theoretical Approaches to Brokerage and Translation in Development." In *Brokers and Translators: The Ethnography of Aid and Agencies*, edited by David Mosse and David Lewis, 1–26. Bloomfield, CT: Kumarian Press.

Müller, Martin, and Carolin Schurr. 2016. "Assemblage Thinking and Actor-Network Theory: Conjunctions, Disjunctions, Cross-Fertilisations." *Transactions of the Institute of British Geographers* 41 (3): 217–29. https://doi.org/10.1111/tran.12117.

Munk, Nina. 2014. *The Idealist: Jeffrey Sachs and the Quest to End Poverty*. Norwell, MA: Anchor.

Murphy, Michelle. 2017. *The Economization of Life*. Durham, NC: Duke University Press.

Murtagh, William J. 1967. *Moravian Architecture and Town Planning: Bethlehem, Pennsylvania and Other Eigtheenth-Century American Settlements*. Philadelphia: University of Pennsylvania Press.

Olivier de Sardan, Jean-Pierre. 2005. *Anthropology and Development: Understanding Contemporary Social Change*. New York: Zed Books.

Olivier de Sardan, Jean-Pierre, Aïssa Diarra, and Mahaman Moha. 2017. "Travelling Models and the Challenge of Pragmatic Contexts and Practical Norms: The Case of Maternal Health." *Health Research Policy and Systems* 15 (1): 60. https://doi.org/10.1186/s12961-017-0213-9.

Olson, Gary. 2013. *Empathy Imperiled: Capitalism, Culture and the Brain*. New York: Springer.

Orenstein, Mitchell. 2003. "Mapping the Diffusion of Pension Innovation." In *Pension Reform in Europe: Process and Progress*, edited by R. Holzmann, M. Orenstein and M. Rutkowski, 171–93. Washington, DC: The World Bank.

Østebø, Marit Tolo. 2013. "Translations of Gender Equality in International Aid: Perspectives from Norway and Ethiopia." PhD diss., University of Bergen.

Østebø, Marit Tolo. 2015. "Translations of Gender Equality Among Rural Arsi Oromo in Ethiopia." *Development and Change* 46 (3): 442–63. https://doi.org/10.1111/dech.12159.

Østebø, Marit Tolo. 2018. "Can Respect be Key to Gender Justice?" *Journal of the Royal Anthropological Institute* 24 (1): 71–89. https://doi.org/10.1111/1467-9655.12752.

Østebø, Marit Tolo, Megan D. Cogburn, and Anjum Shams Mandani. 2017. "The Silencing of Political Context in Health Research in Ethiopia: Why it Should Be a Concern." *Health Policy and Planning* 33 (2): 258–70. https://doi.org/10.1093/heapol/czx150.

Østebø, Marit Tolo, Haldis Haukanes, and Astrid Blystad. 2012. "Strong State Policies on Gender and Aid: Threats and Opportunities for Norwegian Faith-Based Organisations." *Forum for Development Studies* 40 (2): 193–216.

Østebø, Marit Tolo, and Terje Østebø. 2014. "Are Religious Leaders a Magic Bullet for Social/Societal Change? A Critical Look at Anti-FGM Interventions in Ethiopia." *Africa Today* 60 (3): 82–101. https://www.muse.jhu.edu/article/544388.

Østebø, Terje. 2013. "Islam and State Relations in Ethiopia: From Containment to the Production of a 'Governmental Islam'." *Journal of the American Acacdemy of Religion* 81 (4): 1029–60.

Ottenberg, Simon. 1990. "Thirty Years of Fieldnotes: Changing Relationships to the Text." In *Fieldnotes: The Makings of Anthropology*, edited by Roger Sanjek, 139–60. Ithaca, NY: Cornell University Press.

Pankhurst, Helen. 1992. *Gender, Development and Identity*. London & New Jersey: Zed Books.

Paulos Milkias. 1980. "Zemecha: Assessing the Political and Social Foundations Of of Mass Education in Ethiopia." *Studies In Comparative International Development* 15 (3): 54–69. https://doi.org/10.1007/bf02686466.

Pausewang, Siegfried. 2009. "Ethiopia: A Political View From Below." *South African Journal of International Affairs* 16 (1): 69–85. https://doi.org/10.1080/10220460902986164.

Peck, Jamie, and Nik Theodore. 2010. "Mobilizing Policy: Models, Methods, and Mutations." *Geoforum* 41 (2): 169–74. https://doi.org/10.1016/j.geoforum.2010.01.002.

Pedwell, Carolyn. 2014. *Affective Relations The Transnational Politics of Empathy.* New York: Palgrave Macmillan.

Planel, Sabine, and Marie Bridonneau. 2015. "Glocal Ethiopia: Scales and Power Shifts. Introduction." *EchoGéo* 31:1–20.

Ramundo, Kelly. 2012. The Female "Army" Leading Ethiopia's Health Revolution. *Frontlines: Child Survival and Ethiopia Edition.* https://2012-2017.usaid.gov/news-information/frontlines/child-survival-ethiopia-edition/female-army-leading-ethiopias-health-revolution.

Redfield, Peter. 2016. "Fluid Technologies: The Bush Pump, the LifeStraw® and Microworlds of Humanitarian Design." *Social Studies of Science* 46 (2): 159–83. https://doi.org/10.1177/0306312715620061.

Reese, Ashanté M. 2019. "Dear Graduate Student . . . ." *Anthropology News* 60 (6): 131–36. https://doi.org/10.1111/AN.1303.

Reyna, Stephen P. 2007. "The Traveling Model That Would Not Travel: Oil, Empire, and Patrimonialism in Contemporary Chad." *Social Analysis* 51 (3): 78–102. https://doi.org/10.3167/sa.2007.510304.

Ringrose, Jessica. 2011. "Beyond Discourse? Using Deleuze and Guattari's Schizoanalysis to Explore Affective Assemblages, Heterosexually Striated Space, and Lines of Flight Online and at School." *Educational Philosophy and Theory* 43 (6): 598–618. https://doi.org/10.1111/j.1469-5812.2009.00601.x.

Roe, Emery M. 1991. "Development Narratives, Or Making the Best of Blueprint Development." *World Development* 19 (4): 287–300.

Roossinck, Marilyn J. 2011. "The Good Viruses: Viral Mutualistic Symbioses." *Nature Reviews Microbiology* 9:99. https://doi.org/10.1038/nrmicro2491.

Rottenburg, Richard. 2009. *Far-Fetched Facts: A Parable of Development Aid.* Cambridge, MA: MIT Press.

Ruttan, Vernon W. 1984. "Integrated Rural Development Programmes: A Historical Perspective." *World Development* 12 (4): 393–401. https://doi.org/10.1016/0305-750X(84)90017-2.

Sackley, Nicole. 2011. "The Village as Cold War Site: Experts, Development, and the History of Rural Reconstruction." *Journal of Global History* 6 (3): 481–504. https://doi.org/10.1017/S1740022811000428.

Salami, Minna. "Awra Amba, an Ethiopian Village where Gender Equality is Real." https://www.msafropolitan.com/?s=Awra+Amba.

Salem Mekuria. 2017. "PHOTO ESSAY: Awra Amba; A Model 'Utopian' Community in Ethiopia." In *Global Africa: Into the Twenty-First Century*, edited by Dorothy L. Hodgson and Judith A. Byfield, 376–82. Oakland: University of California Press.

Sampson, Tony D. 2011. "Contagion Theory Beyond the Microbe." *CTHEORY Journal of Theory, Technology and Culture* 1 (Special Issue: In the Name of Security): 1–26.

Sampson, Tony D. 2012. *Virality: Contagion Theory in the Age of Networks*. Minneapolis: University of Minnesota Press.

Schmitz, Sigrid, and Sara Ahmed. 2014. "Affect/Emotion: Orientation Matters; A Conversation between Sigrid Schmitz and Sara Ahmed." *Budrich Journals* 20 (2): 97–108.

Scott, James C. 1985. *Weapons of the Weak: Everyday Forms of Peasant Resistance*. New Haven: Yale University Press.

Scott, James C. 1990. *Domination and the Arts of Resistance: Hidden Transcripts*. New Haven: Yale University Press.

Scott, James C. 1998. *Seeing Like a State*. New Haven: Yale University Press.

Seid Mohammed Yassin. 2008. "The Working Traditions and Their Contribution to Rural Development, in Awra Amba Community, Northern Amhara Region–Ethiopia." Master's thesis, Faculty of DryLand Agriculture and Natural Resources, Mekele University.

Selbervik, Hilde, and Marit Tolo Østebø. 2013. "Gender Equality in International Aid: What has Norwegian Gender Politics Got to Do With It?" *Gender, Technology and Development* 17 (2): 205–28.

Semalegne Kendie Mengesha, Jacquelyn C. A. Meshelemiah, and Kasaw Adane Chuffa. 2015. "Asset-Based Community Development Practice in Awramba, Northwest Ethiopia." *Community Development* 46 (2): 164–79. https://doi.org/10.1080/15575330.2015.1009923.

Serres, Michel. 2007. *The Parasite*. Minneapolis: University of Minnesota Press.

Shore, Cris. 2008. "Audit culture and Illiberal governance: Universities and the politics of accountability." *Anthropological Theory* 8 (3): 278–98. https://doi.org/10.1177/1463499608093815.

Shore, Cris, and Susan Wright. 1997. "Policy: A New Field of Anthropology." In *Anthropology of Policy: Perspectives on Governance and Power*, edited by Cris Shore and Susan Wright, 3–33. London: Routledge.

Shore, Cris, and Susan Wright. 2011. "Conceptualising Policy: Technologies of Governance and the Politics of Visibility." In *Policy Worlds: Anthropology and the Analysis of Contemporary Power*, edited by Cris Shore, Susan Wright, and Davide Però, 1–25. New York: Berghahn Books.

Skorupski, John. 1976. *Symbol and Theory. A Philosophical Study of Theories of Religion in Social Anthropology*. Cambridge: Cambridge University Press.

Sosena Demessie, and Tsahai Yitbark. 2008. "A Review of National Policy on Ethiopian Women." In *Digest of Ethiopia's National Policies, Strategies & Programs*, edited by Taye Assefa, 93–120. Addis Ababa: Forum for Social Studies.

Ståhl, Michael. 1989. "Capturing the Peasants through Cooperatives: The Case of Ethiopia." *Review of African Political Economy* 44:27–46.

Stone, Diane. 1999. "Learning Lessons and Transferring Policy Across Time, Space and Disciplines." *Politics* 19 (1): 51–59. https://doi.org/10.1111/1467-9256.00086.

Stone, Diane. 2004. "Transfer Agents and Global Networks in the 'Transnationalization' of Policy." *Journal of European Public Policy* 11 (3): 545–66. https://doi.org/10.1080/13501760410001694291.

Storeng, Katerini T., and Dominique P. Behague. 2014. "'Playing the Numbers Game': Evidence-Based Advocacy and the Technocratic Narrowing of the Safe Motherhood Initiative." *Medical Anthropology Quarterly* 28 (2): 260–79. https://doi.org/10.1111/maq .12072.

Svarstad, Hanne, and Tor A. Benjaminsen. 2017. "Nothing Succeeds Like Success Narratives: A Case of Conservation and Development in the Time of REDD." *Journal of Eastern African Studies* 11 (3): 482–505. https://doi.org/10.1080/17531055.2017.1356622.

Tadesse Tamrat. 1972. *Church and State in Ethiopia 1270–1527*. London: Oxford University Press.

Tarde, Gabriel, and Alberto Toscano. 2007. "Economic Psychology." *Economy and Society* 36 (4): 614–43. https://doi.org/10.1080/03085140701615185.

Temenos, Cristina, and Eugene McCann. 2012. "The Local Politics of Policy Mobility: Learning, Persuasion, and the Production of a Municipal Sustainability Fix." *Environment and Planning A* 44 (6): 1389–1406. https://doi.org/10.1068/a44314.

Temenos, Cristina, and Eugene McCann. 2013. "Geographies of Policy Mobilities." *Geography Compass* 7 (5): 344–57. https://doi.org/10.1111/gec3.12063.

Tervo, Paulina. 2009. "Awra Amba—Utopia in Ethiopia." Write This Down Productions, UK. https://www.youtube.com/watch?v=Out5aigb5Ls.

Tesfayie Debela, and Atakilt Hagos. 2011. *The Design and Implementation of Business Process Reengineering in the Public Sector in Ethiopia*. Addis Ababa: Organization for Social Science Research in Eastern and Southern Africa (OSSREA).

Thrift, Nigel. 2008. "Pass it on: Towards a Political Economy of Propensity." *Emotion, Space and Society* 1 (2): 83–96. https://doi.org/10.1016/j.emospa.2009.02.004.

Tillmann, Hans L., Hans Heiken, Adriana Knapik-Botor, Stefan Heringlake, Johann Ockenga, Judith C. Wilber, Bernd Goergen, Jill Detmer, Martin McMorrow, Matthias Stoll, Reinhold E. Schmidt, and Michael P. Manns. 2001. "Infection with GB Virus C and Reduced Mortality among HIV-Infected Patients." *New England Journal of Medicine* 345 (10): 715–24. https://doi.org/10.1056/NEJMoa010398.

Toon, Adam. 2010. "The Ontology of Theoretical Modelling: Models as Make-Believe." *Synthese* 172:301–15.

Tsing, Anna L. 2015. *The Mushroom at the End of the World: On the Possbility of Life in Capitalist Ruins*. Princeton: Princeton University Press.

Vaughan, Sarah. 2015. "Federalism, Revolutionary Democracy and the Developmental State, 1991–2012." In *Understading Contemporary Ethiopia: Monarchy, Revolution and the Legacy of Meles Zenawi*, edited by G. Prunier and E. Ficquet, 283–311. London: Hurst.

Vaughan, Sarah, and Kjetil Tronvoll. 2003. "Ethiopia: Structures and Relations of Power." Stockholm: SIDA. https://www.sida.se/English/publications/123056/structures-and -relations-of-power-in-ethiopia/.

White, Luise. 2000. "Telling More: Lies, Secrets, and History." *History and Theory* 39 (4): 11–22. https://doi.org/10.1111/0018-2656.00143.

Wilson, Japhy. 2014. "Model Villages in the Neoliberal Era: The Millennium Development Goals and the Colonization of Everyday Life." *Journal of Peasant Studies* 41 (1): 107–25. https://doi.org/10.1080/03066150.2013.821651.

Wilson, Japhy. 2015. "Paradoxical Utopia: The Millennium Villages Project in Theory and Practice." *Journal of Agrarian Change* 17 (1): 122–43. https://doi.org/10.1111/joac.12133.

Wolf, Margery. 1992. *A Thrice Told Tale: Feminism, Postmodernism, and Ethnographic Responsibility.* Stanford, CA: Stanford University Press.

Wolff, Joshua R., and Heather L. Himes. 2010. "Purposeful Exclusion of Sexual Minority Youth in Christian Higher Education: The Implications of Discrimination." *Christian Higher Education* 9 (5): 439–60. https://doi.org/10.1080/15363759.2010.513630.

World Bank. 2006. *Gender Equality as Smart Economics: A World Bank Group Gender Action Plan; Fiscal Years 2007–10* (English). Washington, DC: World Bank.

Yeshi H. Mariam. 1994. "Ethiopian Women in the Period of Socialist Transformation." *Economic and Political Weekly* 29 (44): WS57–WS62.

Zachariassen, Heidi Holt. 2012. "From the Bottom Up: Lessons About Gender Mainstreaming in the Andes from Digni's Women Empowerment and Gender Equality (WEGE) Programme." *Gender and Development* 20 (3): 481–90. https://doi.org/10.1080/13552074.2012.731749.

Zenker, Olaf. 2015. "Failure By the Numbers? Settlement Statistics as Indicators of State Performance in South African Land Restitution." In *The World of Indicators. The Making of Governmental Knowledge Through Quantification*, edited by R. Rottenburg, S. E. Merry, S. J. Park and J. Mugler, 102–126. Cambridge: Cambridge University Press.

Zigon, Jarret. 2015. "What is a Situation?: An Assemblic Ethnography of the Drug War." *Cultural Anthropology* 30 (3): 501–24. https://doi.org/10.14506/ca30.3.07.

Zuckerman, Harriet. 1988. "The Role of the Role Model: The Other Side of a Sociological Coinage." In *Surveying Social Life: Papers in Honor of Herbert H. Hyman*, edited by Hubert J. O'Gorman, 119–144. Middletown, CT: Wesleyan University Press.

Index

Page references in *italics* refer to figures.

Anthropology of Policy

Cris Shore and Susan Wright, editors

Drugs, Thugs, and Diplomats: U.S. Policymaking in Colombia

Winifred Tate

2015